MISSISSIPPI
SWINDLE

MISSISSIPPI SWINDLE

Brett Favre and the Welfare
Scandal That Shocked America

SHAD WHITE

LEBANON, NEW HAMPSHIRE

ALL RIGHTS RESERVED

For information about permission to reproduce
selections from this book, write to:
Steerforth Press, 31 Hanover Street, Suite 1
Lebanon, New Hampshire 03766

Cataloging-in-Publication Data is available from the Library of Congress

ISBN 978-1-58642-386-5
Printed in the United States of America

To my children, and the Mississippi they deserve.

Contents

Author's Note

This book is based on my own memory of events. Memories are fallible. But my memory is pretty good and is well supported by documentation and evidence. There will be some who lie and say what happened did not. I suspect those people will be the ones most embarrassed about their role in the scheme I recount in the following pages.

The credit for everything written here goes to the 140 men and women of the Mississippi Office of the State Auditor. They were the ones who stared at endless PDFs of documents, extracted information from interviewees, and pieced together the puzzle of the DHS — Department of Human Services — scandal. I have the honor of telling you what they did.

MISSISSIPPI
SWINDLE

Introduction

My cell phone buzzed in the empty passenger seat next to me. My family — my wife, our infant daughter in her car seat, and I — were traveling in our bright-orange Jeep to Florida, where I was slated to give a speech to a group of accountants. It was June 2019. Glancing down at my phone, I could see that I had several missed messages. The most recent notification was a voicemail from my office saying the governor of Mississippi was looking for me. He'd been calling my desk phone. It was important.

I serve as the state auditor of Mississippi. It's an elected position atop a state agency of 140 people. Our mission is to ensure that Mississippi's public money is spent legally. We do this by conducting routine audits, and if there is an allegation that funds have been stolen, we investigate. When we find a thief, we work with prosecutors to convict them. It's similar to the FBI's role for the federal government, except our jurisdiction covers only theft of taxpayer money — none of the heart-racing excitement of antiterrorism or counterintelligence work for us. We employ lawyers, career law enforcement officers who specialize in white-collar crime, accountants, a network intrusion specialist (a fancy way of saying "hacker"), and support staff.

It wasn't unheard of for the governor to call me with a question. But it was unusual for his office to dial me repeatedly until he got an answer. There aren't many auditing emergencies. It was also unusual that he did not call directly from his cell phone to mine. Because he'd been trying to call my office line, my secretary was leaving me messages about his persistence. The fact that the governor was calling from his government desk phone to my government desk phone suggested that he wanted an official record of the call to exist.

I called Governor Bryant back. Phil Bryant was a colorful two-term governor known for his southern twang and for wearing cowboy boots with the state seal on them to even the most formal of events. He was popular in part due to his visceral connection with rural voters and in part because of the seriousness with which he took recruiting businesses to the state.

"I need to turn a matter over to your office," Bryant said. More formal than normal for him. But Governor Bryant had previously served as Mississippi's state auditor, so he understood the gravity of our work.

Over the next few minutes, Bryant described an encounter he had just had with an informant from the Mississippi Department of Human Services (DHS). DHS is the agency in Mississippi that disburses funds from federal programs like Temporary Assistance for Needy Families (TANF, commonly known as welfare). In a state like Mississippi, with our high poverty rate, tens of millions of dollars flowed through the agency every year. And in Mississippi, the governor selected the head of DHS.

Governor Bryant said the informant had approached his office demanding a meeting. The informant brought a short, one-page document he called an internal audit. As the governor described the contents of the document, I could tell the allegations were serious. They involved corruption by DHS's director.

The phone crackled when Governor Bryant reached the meat of the allegations. I looked up to see that our Jeep was passing through Alabama's George Wallace Tunnel — a thick, white ceramic tile passage taking cars under the Mobile River — and the cell phone connection dropped. The pressure change inside the tunnel turned the rumbling sound of the traffic into a quiet whoosh. As a kid, my parents and I would hold our breath when we were passing through, seeing if we could make it to the other side without exhaling. Now the air in my lungs felt bottled up against my will.

"Put the phone down while you're driving," my wife said.

"Sorry! This one is important," I replied.

I redialed Bryant once we emerged from under the river, the gray battleship USS *Alabama* greeting us from the harbor outside the tunnel's mouth.

Bryant picked up and finished the story. His informant claimed there was a kickback scheme involving DHS director John Davis.

"Looks like Davis is paying some vendor — Restore, LLC? — for some kind of contract. The checks for the company are going back to a P.O. box owned by Davis in his hometown," said Bryant. "Doesn't look good."

DHS had paid a few thousand dollars in 2019 to a company called Restore, LLC. It was alarming to see a contractor to an agency being paid at a post office box owned by the head of that agency. But if Davis wanted a kickback for giving Restore an agency contract, why set up a P.O. box in his own name to receive the checks? It seemed like a careless paper trail to leave. Why not be paid in cash? Cash payments make kickback schemes hard to detect.

"Why wouldn't Davis just steal the checks from the office?" I wondered aloud. "Save the trouble of mailing them." As DHS director, Davis would have access to every physical space in his agency and could have easily put his hands on the checks before they were mailed. "And why have physical checks sent to yourself if you can't deposit them? Sounds like the checks are made out to Restore, whoever that is."

Regardless of the questions, I agreed with the governor that the situation was suspicious. Bryant closed the call by expressing concern for Davis.

Davis was an odd man. As our Jeep zoomed over marshy tidelands, shoots of green springing from the water, I reflected on our first encounter just a few months earlier. At the time, DHS's financial records were unclear and scant. My staff was concerned about how DHS was handling welfare money. The staff suggested that I talk to Davis and recommend he hire an outside CPA firm to do a dollar-by-dollar audit of their TANF spending. My auditors thought we did not have the staff on hand to do this ourselves, but they assured me that Davis could pay for an outside audit from his ample budget.

I'd called Davis, set a time for the meeting, and driven to his office alone. The office's appearance surprised me. DHS had taken over a lease previously held by one of Mississippi's wealthier law firms. The wall paneling and advanced security system were unlike anything I'd seen in any other state government office. I would later find out that, back in Davis's private office, he'd purchased a couch for tens of thousands of dollars and worked at an Italian desk. Plans were in the works to install high-tech glass walls that frosted when you touched them. At one point they even intended to build a shower in Davis's office that could be entered from either his office or the office next door, which seemed beyond strange. It didn't fit, knowing that DHS's mission was to serve the poor.

Davis's demeanor also struck me. He was a career DHS employee who'd advanced from small-town social worker to the boss — now a paunchy, balding man with a penchant for flashy ties and decor. With his thick southern accent, he slathered on praise, flattering me to the point of making me uncomfortable.

Davis had a team ready to meet me when I entered his conference room. He did everything to signal he was eager to listen and take any recommendations I had. I walked him through why he should contract for a private audit of his books. He agreed on the spot. DHS would hire a CPA firm to take a look at how they'd spent their TANF dollars. They would ensure they were complying with all the relevant laws, he said.

That audit never happened. And now, a few months later, driving away from the Alabama sunset into Florida, I was told Davis might have stolen some of that money.

Governor Bryant was worried that if Davis had indeed stolen money and realized an informant squealed, he might "stick a pistol in his mouth" over the weekend. I shared that concern. During my time in office, another person accused of embezzling funds had confessed, scrawled a note on a pad, and then shot himself in the head before his trial date arrived.

I also wondered if Davis might start destroying important documents. The proof of a kickback might be doused in gasoline and burning in a five-gallon drum behind his house right now.

"I'll get right on it," I said.

I hung up and dialed Richie McCluskey, the man I trusted most on white-collar investigations. I'd hired Richie to run the investigations division of my office right after I'd taken my position. Richie was a square-jawed fireball of energy and red hair. He'd spent his career in law enforcement, starting as a beat cop, attending the FBI academy in Quantico, and then working as the lead consumer protection investigator in the Mississippi Office of the Attorney General. While there, he'd successfully investigated some of Mississippi's civil rights cold cases. When I started my search for a chief investigator, Richie was home on early retirement and going crazy. He'd sanded, sealed, and painted his back fence two times in three months. And I was ready to put that energy back to good use.

"What do you think?" I asked him after describing the call with the governor.

Richie said Davis might commit suicide, but Richie believed he could manage the situation the right way. Richie believed, based on the tone of the governor's call, that Davis probably already knew about the informant. The best approach was a direct one. Richie would call Davis and tell him there were questions about his interactions with one of his vendors, Restore. Richie would demand Davis be at DHS's offices at nine o'clock sharp on Monday morning with copies of his personal bank statements from the past year. He should also be prepared to produce any documents on Restore that DHS had.

"Will Davis destroy those documents if he knows we're coming?" I asked.

Richie thought for a moment. "Probably not," he said. Davis would be on notice that he was under investigation. Destroying documents now would be another felony. He would be cutting his own throat if the matter ever went to trial. Also, Richie pointed out that our accountants on staff at the auditor's office might already have copies of many of the relevant documents in their stored files from previous routine audits of DHS.

We wrapped up the call, and I finished the drive to our hotel. I could smell the salty seawater creeping through the cracked car door windows as we approached our destination, but my mind was far from the beach.

The next morning, I kissed my wife and baby good-bye in our room and walked to a windowless hotel ballroom to give a speech to the Mississippi Society of Certified Public Accountants.

Just before I walked on stage, I huddled with the CPAs from my own staff who were there. Their leader was Stephanie Palmer-tree. Stephanie was thirty-six years old and whip-smart — the most knowledgeable CPA I'd met when it came to accounting standards. She was also pugnacious and eager to look under the hood of any agency we suspected of fraud. I liked that her instinct was to go hard after someone if there was good reason to believe he was breaking the law, even if it ruffled feathers.

After hearing about the tip, Stephanie agreed with Richie that we had already captured most of DHS's core financial documents in a recent routine audit. Those audits didn't uncover a kickback scheme, because finding fraud in an audit could be like plucking a needle from a haystack. But now our search was that much easier.

We mapped out a strategy: Richie and his team of criminal investigators would start on Monday with an interview of Davis. They would also find the informant and obtain the "internal audit" that had been given to the governor. Stephanie's team of CPAs would take stock of the DHS documents they had on hand as soon as they were back in Mississippi. They would also begin an audit of the TANF funds spent by DHS. It would stretch their capacity, but it was now a priority, given what we knew.

After that, I bounded the stairs to the stage to speak. I didn't know it at the time, but Stephanie, Richie, and I had just laid the groundwork for investigating the largest public fraud case in state history. It would stretch from Mississippi to Malibu, California. It would involve some of the most famous athletes in the country and a few of television's more notable professional wrestlers. The case would test my mettle — I was the youngest statewide elected official in Mississippi and the first millennial statewide official in the Deep South — and my judgment. Ultimately, we would discover that millions of taxpayer dollars intended to help the poor had been squandered by a group of wealthy power brokers.

"It's one of the hardest, best jobs in state government"

Some people talk about poverty or welfare in a way that reveals they haven't seen much of it. Where I grew up, in rural South Mississippi, poverty lived next door. I went to church with it. At school, it sat in the desk next to me. I remember eating breakfast in the public school cafeteria and being alarmed at how quickly one of my classmates (I'll call him William) ate, almost as if the eggs would fly off the green plastic tray if he didn't get them in his mouth fast enough. I asked my mom after school why William ate so fast. Mom knew his family, and she knew he probably ate his only two meals of the day in that lunchroom. By morning, he was starving.

William wasn't the only one. Across the street from my grandparents' house, two miles from our home, my classmates like William lived in trailers that looked like they could barely stand. While our house was not luxurious — we shared one bathroom among four people and there were a few spots in our floor where you could see through to the ground below — I counted myself lucky that my parents were employed, stayed married, and provided my sister and me with a stable life.

School meals were also my first exposure to public assistance. It seemed like every other kid in the lunch line would tell the woman at the checkout counter their identification number and then — magic — their lunch was free. I had to pay $1. I'd later learn I was watching the free and reduced-price lunch program. Families would attest to their own low income and were then eligible. I remember a teacher handing out the sign-up forms for the program at the beginning of the school year once. She said no one checked to see how much money anybody made. I took the form home excitedly, grinning through my crooked teeth, and showed my dad, saying, "Dad, we can do this form and get free lunches!" My dad, a roughneck oil pumper, rebuked me with a hint of pride in his voice, saying we did not take from the government.

Of course, the truth was more complicated. My grandfather — also a pumper and one of the most fiercely independent and brilliant men I've ever known — lived briefly in public housing as a young man.

As a kid, seeing poverty was such a routine part of life that, like breathing, I didn't think about it. The neighborhood boys were all too busy playing backyard football (my favorite player was Dan Marino) or wandering the woods. The thought of how much money any of us had didn't cross our minds. As I grew older, though, I realized that the trailers, stray dogs, and mattresses in the yard next door didn't exist everywhere else in the country. In eighth grade, I won an essay competition and flew on a plane — my first time — to Washington, DC. Mingling among the other young essayists, I met kids who went to something called boarding schools. They told me about their lives as we toured the city, squinting at the immaculate bleached buildings.

It occurred to me after that trip that in other places with more money, there were fewer kids who suffered like William. I became angry at a world that could fail children like him. Angry at his parents for not finding a way to hold down a job, angry at government programs that seemed incapable of helping him.

I passed my teen years skipping most of the parties and mostly playing soccer and reading. When I graduated public high school, just a handful of the 122 in my senior class went straight to a four-year university. I was one of them. I majored in economics and political science at the University of Mississippi, fascinated by the question of whether our schools could break the cycle of poverty. The problem of poverty seemed so fundamental, it only made sense that the fix would have to come early in a person's life, in classrooms and the home.

Even among my friends at university — among those of us who emerged from poorer parts of the state and made it to college — I could tell they felt the aftershocks of growing up in need. One of my three roommates in college was raised by a single mother and had never met his father. His mother had only had one job in her adult life, at a mental health facility, and he told me she was fired for stealing pills. By the time we were in college, she lived with, and off of, his grandparents. They lived ten minutes from my hometown, which was four hours from campus. I'd drive my roommate home from college some weekends if we both wanted to see our families. Watching my roommate and his mother interact, I could tell he cared for her, despite wanting to escape the downward pull of her vortex.

That question of why poverty seemed so intractable pushed me to look beyond Mississippi. The summer between my sophomore and junior years of college, I traveled to El Salvador to live for two months on money I'd managed to save. I stayed in San Salvador, the homicide capital of North America, working in a Catholic orphanage where five nuns cared for fifty-two girls. I mostly spent my time painting weathered furniture and playing soccer with the girls after lunch while the nuns napped. At night, I pulled a bedsheet all the way over my head to hide from the mosquitoes buzzing and popping the fabric protecting me. Under the covers, I read the musings of philosophers like Robert Nozick, Peter Singer, and John Rawls on the question of justice for those who are worse off. Their arguments tumbled through my head while I observed life in a developing country stricken by the needs that also plagued my home. Life expectancy for men in some Mississippi counties was actually worse than the average life expectancy in El Salvador.

Back at school, I explored what happened when even the highest performers in the economy fell on hard times. Two friends and I put together a research project on the downfall of Enron. Enron was once one of America's most promising companies, filled with talented young MBAs looking to take the world by storm. We traveled to Houston and stayed at the DoubleTree hotel just blocks from the old, abandoned Enron skyscraper. It was shiny and modern by design, one of the most beautiful buildings I'd ever seen. On the inside, it was a hollow shell.

We interviewed former Enron employees about how their lives changed after their employer's collapse. One man we talked to had graduated from Northwestern's business school and moved to Texas to work there. "My future was limitless," he told us. "Then it was taken away." He, like so many others, was left with worthless stock and without a job. The top Enron executives had cashed in their shares long before the price plummeted, leaving this man and other employees with nothing.

"What are your goals now?" I asked.

He paused. "To be a good dad," he said. "My girl's soccer team needs a winning record this year, so I'm going to work on that." There was a silver lining in there somewhere.

When we weren't doing interviews, my friends and I wandered the area surrounding the Enron tower. The company's fall had turned the neighborhood into a ghost town. There was scarcely anywhere to eat, save a McDonald's where several homeless people lingered outside.

Unsure of what to do after college graduation, I moved to Washington, DC, and worked for a think tank, the Pew Center on the States. There I poured myself into complex issues regarding how public schools were funded.

In the evenings, I volunteered once a week at an after-school program in Anacostia on the outskirts of the city. Anacostia was a place that prosperous Washington had left behind. To reach the school, my fellow tutors and I moved in a pack, walking the desolate, evening streets with hurried steps between the Metro station and the brick schoolhouse.

The after-school program arranged for young professionals from the city to help low-income students do their homework and occupy them until about 8:00 PM. I wasn't sure how I felt about keeping kids away from their families, but I also understood what their home life might be like. Regardless of my hesitations, the program seemed to work. The average GPA of the students increased after enrolling.

That first year after college, I also applied for the Rhodes Scholarship and was selected as one of thirty-two Americans to win a full ride to the University of Oxford in England.

Oxford, with its ancient architecture and strange accents, was eye-opening. Conversations I had with peers challenged my assumptions about the world. In my classes (or tutorials, as they are called at Oxford), I studied economic history. I dove in to the economic development of the United States, working to understand its journey from a rough frontier on a "new" continent into the most prosperous nation in the world.

Toward the end of my first year in Oxford, I remained transfixed by the idea that schools were the key to breaking generational poverty. If we could just find the right curricula, with the right funding level, and the right focus, I reasoned, we could motivate a child to take ownership over their life and give them the skills to succeed. From across the pond, I was fascinated by Michelle Rhee, the head of the District of Columbia's public school system. At the time, she was radically clearing away the brush of the DC school bureaucracy and focusing on student outcomes.

And then her boss, the mayor of DC, lost his bid for reelection in part due to the controversial speed of Rhee's changes to the public schools. Rhee was forced out. Her ouster meant the end of her proposed reforms, and it underscored that even if you proposed the right witch's brew of policy, it didn't matter unless you also had the political power to put the policies into place. People resist change, and unless elected leaders are willing to meet that political pressure, we will never upset the applecart for the greater good.

So I returned home to Mississippi and started working on political campaigns. My first was a congressional race in North Mississippi. I cut my teeth by writing the email blasts, social media content, press releases, and other posts coming from the campaign. In our final act on the campaign trail that year, I was traveling on the campaign bus with my boss, Alan Nunnelee, and one of his friends. The friend was an ascendant lieutenant governor of Mississippi with rugged looks named Phil Bryant. As I typed into my laptop in the back of the bus, pausing between bumps along the craggy highways, Bryant asked Nunnelee who was writing all the emails coming from the campaign. He liked them.

Nunnelee yelled at me to come forward and introduced me to Bryant. "This is the kid," he said with a smile. The conversation Bryant and I had that day began the chain of events that led to our call in the George Wallace Tunnel.

By the fall of 2011, after about a year working in politics, I found myself at Harvard Law School. Still distracted by the policy problems that tortured my mind in my early twenties, I'd become disenchanted by the idea of government intervention. How could a government program, no matter how well designed, compensate for a lack of a family or a safe community? Raj Chetty, a professor at Harvard, spoke to this. Through a large longitudinal study, he'd concluded that the most important determinant of people moving up the income ladder was the strength of community institutions like schools and churches. The two-parent family was also critical.

One evening during law school, I grabbed dinner with a friend, Jisung Park. Jisung and I had been Rhodes Scholars together, and while I was in law school, he was at Harvard earning his PhD in economics. Jisung has a gifted mind — he'd go on to teach economics at UCLA — and he was, at the time, researching antipoverty policies to identify those that were the most effective.

Seated in a dimly lit corner of the basement of Russell House Tavern, he said, "Shad, I've read hundreds of social science studies in the last two years. The biggest takeaway is that money spent helping children is so much more useful for economic mobility than money spent on anyone else. I can't understand why politicians don't see this."

By this time, the optimism of my youth had turned to hardened cynicism. "Because, brother, kids don't vote," I replied. As we sipped the last of our beers, he made me promise that, if I ever ended up in a policymaking position, I would look out for the people who needed help but didn't have a voice, even if it was hard to do.

With the answers to the poverty problem unclear in my mind, I looked for something simpler to study. Soon my attention was drawn to criminal law. Violations of criminal statutes — corruption, fraud, theft — all seemed straightforward in that they were obviously wrong. They required intelligence and skill to unravel, but stopping them seemed unequivocally good. You needn't worry about the unintended consequences of convicting an embezzler in the way you would worry about the unintended consequences of creating a government program. Not only was it a morally clearer way to make a difference, it was also subject to less political pressure to compromise. Or so I naively thought at the time.

I took as many classes as I could to understand white-collar crime — criminal law, criminal procedure, accounting for lawyers, evidence, and corporations — to understand corporate fraud. I also interned for a semester at the US attorney's office in Boston.

The importance of the US attorney's work was put on full display April 15, 2013. That day, I was at the federal courthouse, holed up in the law library researching wiretaps for a senior prosecutor. My friend Jordan Downs, who worked in Washington, called my cell. He sounded alarmed.

"You all right? You watching the news?" he asked.

My eyes had been locked onto a computer screen full of case law. "No, what's happening?" I asked.

"Turn on the news and call me back," Jordan replied.

By then the office was buzzing. Across town, a bomb had gone off at street level in the middle of the Boston Marathon. I ran to the window and looked down several stories. Outside the courthouse, a team of federal marshals holding long guns was taking up defensive positions.

We would eventually learn that two terrorists had planted explosive pressure cookers on the street, killing three and injuring hundreds. The city ground to a halt. The other interns in the prosecutors' office and I made our way back to campus through a mix of walking and subway rides once the trains restarted.

Back at my dorm, my classmates and I huddled around the television for hours, following the manhunt. Law enforcement eventually announced a shelter-in-place order for our entire area, so there was little to do except watch the news coverage.

Hours turned into days. One morning during the search, police blitzed into the apartment building across the street from our dorm. Their blue lights flickered on our neighbor's red-brick facade. I watched from my window as police conducted a frantic floor-by-floor search, only to come out empty-handed.

The police would eventually get their man. On April 19,

law enforcement raced down Memorial Drive about a mile from campus and ended the matter in a shootout in nearby Watertown.

Experiences like these steeled my resolve. I would move back to Mississippi and pursue law enforcement. On the week during my third year of law school, when Wall Street and DC law firms descended on campus to offer employment to every warm body with a Harvard degree, I skipped town and headed home to look for work. By leaving, I guaranteed I'd receive no big East Coast firm job offers. I burned the ships behind me. I pledged myself to the South.

It turned out, however, that my law enforcement ambition would have to wait. After I graduated from law school, Governor Bryant asked me to run his second and final gubernatorial campaign. The opportunity seemed too important to pass up. I also thought it wouldn't hurt having the governor as a reference when I went to apply for a prosecutor gig.

Once Bryant secured his campaign victory in November 2015, I started looking for a local assistant prosecutor's position anywhere in the state. No luck. Federal jobs were even harder to come by. I settled on civil law at a good firm in town and waited for a shot at criminal law.

I continued to burnish my résumé for that day, though. I took courses and earned a certificate in forensic accounting, the use of accounting to uncover fraud. To scratch the itch of public service, I put in an application to join the Mississippi Air National Guard. I would serve as a military attorney in the Judge Advocate General's Corps, or JAG for short. In that capacity I'd have the chance to handle criminal violations by service members. Military service was a family tradition. My paternal grandfather served near the Iron Curtain during the Cold War. My maternal grandfather fought in North Africa in World War II and earned a Purple Heart after a Nazi grenade shot shrapnel into his neck. I was honored to keep that tradition, though a part of me wondered if my ancestors — army men — were rolling in their graves at their grandson being part of the air force.

Finally, in June 2018, the opportunity to use my training and do the kind of public service work I most desired arrived, but in an unexpected way.

Rumors began to circulate early on a Monday morning that State Auditor Stacey Pickering, who had been in office for ten years, planned to step down. While the state auditor's position is elected in Mississippi, if the current officeholder vacates the spot, the governor appoints a replacement to fill the balance of the four-year term.

I'd followed the work of the Office of the State Auditor for years and knew its potential. That office had the resources to tackle the corruption that routinely landed Mississippi near the top of the rankings of the most corrupt states.

Even given our relationship, it was a long shot that Governor Bryant would appoint me to the spot. If he did, at thirty-two, I would be the youngest statewide official in recent memory. I also looked several years younger than that. If appointed, I would have to mount a statewide campaign to keep the job in an election slated for the fall of 2019 — seventeen months from when I'd be sworn in. I had no campaign infrastructure, no campaign bank account, no website, and no experience as a candidate.

I did have, however, strong ideas about how to improve the auditor's office that I'd been developing over many years. I'd interviewed some of the office's auditors for my undergraduate thesis and even helped edit some of their reports while in law school. I also had confidence that I could do the job. I called Governor Bryant the day Pickering announced his impending resignation. I told him I wanted to be considered for the job and listed five things I would do to improve the office.

The governor was gracious, but I could sense skepticism on the other end of the phone. He was blunt and said "dozens" of "his best friends" were already asking about the job. But he promised to take my proposal seriously. He said that "one way or another" he would let me know his decision.

Then I waited. A few days later, the governor's chief of staff, Joey Songy, called and asked me to come over to his house that evening for a beer. He said I should park in his garage so no one would recognize my vehicle outside. Eyes were out to see who might be under consideration for state auditor. Maybe the precautions were overkill, but Joey knew how the chattering class worked better than I did.

In Joey's kitchen, he told me the governor was becoming convinced that I was the right choice. For one, the governor had served as state auditor himself for eleven years. "It's one of the hardest, best jobs in state government," the governor had said. He would only give it to someone he knew had the brains and energy to do it right. He also disliked the way some state-wide officials treated their jobs as part-time positions, working two or three days a week. The governor had seen my work ethic firsthand on his campaign.

The governor thought my lack of political connections would be beneficial, too. I would have no problem investigating the powerful, because it was unlikely that they had ever met me or my family. My dad was a blue-collar worker and my mother a public school teacher in a town of seven hundred people.

Despite the logic, some of the more important people in the state had other ideas. In the days when the governor was weighing the decision, he was asked to participate in a conference with President Trump and other governors from around the nation at the White House. Governor Bryant invited the head of a large Mississippi corporation as his plus one. In the back of their black-tinted SUV on the way from the airport to Pennsylvania Avenue, the corporate executive turned to the topic of the state auditor's position. He told the governor he "needed" to appoint the corporation's favorite — a local state senator — to the spot. He said the governor "needed" the senator's political clout.

Telling a sitting governor he needs someone else politically is not the cleverest way of arguing for a friend to be appointed to a post. The comment didn't sit well with Bryant. Bryant told him that the executive may know a good deal about his business, but Bryant was the one who understood politics. He could decide for himself what he needed without any help.

Shortly after, Governor Bryant invited me to the governor's mansion. We sat at his long wooden conference table alone. A mural of a Mississippi landscape covered the walls of the room. Outside, I could see blossoming crepe myrtles through the windows. Bryant, the son of a diesel mechanic, had come a long way from tiny Morehead, Mississippi, where he was born. He looked at me and said, "Governor Kirk Fordice and I were in this room, at the other end of this table, when he told me he was going to appoint me state auditor."

I looked down at the dark oak. "Should we move to the other end of the table?" I asked, and he chuckled.

We talked candidly about the job. Halfway through the conversation, I could tell he'd made up his mind to appoint me. I asked him what he thought about my chances to win an election next year and keep the job. I told him I thought I could be a good candidate, but I'd never done this before. He told me to work hard and not worry about the rest.

We shook hands and ended the meeting. Outside the mansion I pulled my cell phone from my pocket and called my wife. She picked up from thousands of miles away at London's Heathrow Airport, where she'd just landed for work.

"Well," I said. "I think I'm about to be state auditor."

"Sounds like I may need to book a flight home," she said, laughing.

A few days later, on July 6, 2018, Governor Bryant introduced me, my wife at my side, as Mississippi's new auditor. He announced the appointment in the same room of the governor's mansion — adorned with the same nineteenth-century furniture and painted the same antique pink — in which his appointment had been announced twenty years earlier.

Looking back on the video of my speech that day and the media coverage of it, you could hear the shock from professional prognosticators. No one had heard of me. I worried that, while a fresh face can be an advantage in politics, my face might be a little *too* fresh. Detractors joked this would go down as Shad's summer as state auditor.

I was determined to prove them wrong.

The Wrestlers

Eleven months after I was sworn in as auditor, Governor Bryant placed the call to me about John Davis. After I returned from Florida, my team met in our office on the eighth floor of the Woolfolk Building, a historic tower with magnolia flowers emblazoned on its sides. Woolfolk houses much of the state government's bureaucracy. We assembled in the sparsely furnished conference room connected to my office. A dry erase board hung on the wall next to a pile of law books and a television for connecting to a laptop was all that we needed in our line of work.

Deputy State Auditor Pat Dendy sat at the opposite head of the table from me at that first meeting. Pat is a big man and career employee of the office who'd worked as an auditor and investigator almost as long as I'd been alive. He had dozens of stories of reading financial documents in the un-air-conditioned broom closets of small-town city halls or confronting deranged witnesses from his years of service. If I had the final say over office strategy, Pat was the CPA with the final say over technical auditing matters. His experience commanded respect, and he was a force in every meeting he attended.

I briefed Pat on the weekend's activities. "Well, no one jump to conclusions," he told the room. "I've seen too many whistleblower tips amount to nothing. We don't know anything yet, really." His levelheaded approach was helpful. We would see where the facts took us, and nothing more.

Across town that morning, Richie and his team started their work at DHS headquarters. They began by looking at Davis's bank statements, but nothing stood out as a kickback. Occasionally, in a kickback scheme, money will show up in a government employee's account around the time of a payment to the contractor. There was no trail that obvious here. And Davis, of course, denied being on the take from Restore.

But he did not deny that Restore's payments were coming to a post office box he owned. His explanation was strange. Davis said he was close friends with Restore's owner, Brett DiBiase. Brett was in a bad relationship, Davis claimed, and if Brett's checks were sent to his home, his wife or girlfriend (whomever he was with at the time) would steal the money. Davis had graciously offered to accept the checks for Brett so they never reached the house.

That story didn't hold water with me. Why didn't Brett set up a bank account that only he could access? Davis was adamant that everything at DHS was aboveboard, though, so Richie invited Davis and Brett to take a polygraph. They agreed. A few days later they presented themselves at a facility run by the Mississippi Bureau of Investigation. Hooked to the machine, with wires running from his arm to the table, Davis looked haggard, his face drooping.

At the end of the polygraph sessions, we knew two things: We still had no proof of a kickback from Brett to Davis, and the two men had failed the lie detector test on multiple questions.

Richie confronted Brett afterward with the results. "I don't know what's going on here," Richie said, "but I know you're not being totally honest with us." Brett didn't give ground. The men were anxious in their post-polygraph interviews, but they didn't divulge useful information. We had more work to do.

A few days later, Davis abruptly resigned as head of DHS. Governor Bryant then announced that Chris Freeze — a retired FBI agent — would take DHS's helm. To the outside world, it must have seemed an odd choice. Chris was a federal criminal investigator and former Tennessee Auditor's Office employee with few Mississippi connections. He was about to run a large, important agency dedicated to disbursing entitlement funds. Nothing in Freeze's background spoke to any experience with poverty interventions. But I saw Freeze's appointment as a signal that the governor wanted someone who would get to the bottom of any criminal activity. Freeze also didn't have loyalty to any of the existing DHS employees or their vendors, which was a plus.

Over the course of the next few weeks, Richie's investigators probed at DHS and the now-retired Davis. They interviewed DHS employees, analyzed financials, and gathered documents.

By early fall 2019, there was no way to deny it: There were signs of serious fraud. Richie had been briefing me on DHS about once a week for a while, but now he told me it was time to sit down and review everything they'd found so far.

Richie, Pat, and I met in the main conference room of the auditor's office to be briefed by Bo Howard, the deputy director of investigations. Bo had a boyish look, offset in that meeting by darkness around piercing eyes that looked like they'd spent considerable time slicing through financial paperwork.

Bo and Richie were different in almost every way. Where Richie was extroverted, Bo was quiet and brainy, a lawyer by training. If Richie had been a football player (he was, in high school), he was what you would call a good locker room guy — someone well liked by everyone and who drew people to follow his lead by force of personality. You'd want Bo on the coaching staff as offensive coordinator. He had a focused mind and could draw up the investigation plan we'd need to prove our case. He also understood what would fly in court and what would not. When I first met Bo, I thought, *He seems a little young for this job*. It was an ironic reaction, given my own age. But Bo proved to me what I was trying to prove to the state's voters: That youth, and the energy and willingness to take on the hardest challenges that came with it, could be a benefit.

Bo launched into his presentation. The wrongdoing likely went far beyond the simple kickback scheme we'd first suspected in the summer. It involved multiple players, some of whom had extensive political connections. And almost all of it was fueled by TANF dollars.

𝒥𝑅

Temporary Assistance for Needy Families is the name of a program with roots dating from 1935. In the midst of the Great Depression, the federal government started something called Aid to Dependent Children, later renamed Aid to Families of

Dependent Children (AFDC). It provided cash assistance to families — primarily single-parent households — according to the Congressional Research Service.

By the late twentieth century, AFDC was mired in allegations of ineffectiveness. Its harshest critics said it encouraged men to avoid marriage to the mothers of their children. The dissolution of Black families in America — after a big increase in AFDC funding in the 1960s — was particularly troubling. In the 1950s, Black women were equally as likely to be married as White women. Then that number started falling. The Brookings Institution noted that, in 1965, just 24 percent of Black children were born into single-parent households. By 1990, the number had ballooned to 64 percent.

So in 1996, President Bill Clinton and Republicans in Congress abolished AFDC and re-formed it as TANF. The Congressional Research Service stated that TANF was designed to be a "broad-purpose block grant to the states that helps fund a wide range of benefits, services, and activities to address the effects of, and root causes of, child poverty and economic disadvantage." Put simply, state governments would now have broader leeway to spend big pools of welfare money. The logic was that states — the laboratories of democracy — would know better how to attack the problem of chronic poverty in their own backyards than the federal government.

States were allowed to spend TANF dollars for four purposes: to (1) provide assistance to needy families so that children could be cared for in their own homes, (2) end the dependence of needy parents on government benefits, (3) reduce out-of-wedlock pregnancies, or (4) promote the formation and maintenance of two-parent families.

If a state spent TANF money outside those four purposes, the spending would violate federal law. The US Department of Health and Human Services, which administered TANF, could then demand that the state put its own cash up to make amends. For example, if a state used $5 million in TANF funds illegally to build a sports stadium, the feds could demand that the state take $5 million from state coffers and put it into TANF spending. The federal government could also levy a penalty on the state.

This block grant framework allowed states to do much more than just send checks to poor people, which is what most people thought of when they heard "TANF" or "welfare." States could now send money to a nonprofit, for instance. The nonprofit could then use the money to run a program for the poor, as long as it fulfilled one of TANF's four purposes.

✴

In Bo's fall 2019 briefing, we learned that DHS had indeed given a large amount of TANF funding to nonprofits under John Davis. Several of those nonprofits were controlled by Brett DiBiase or other members of his family.

The DiBiase family was a cast of characters. Brett's father, Ted DiBiase, was famous for performing as the Million Dollar Man, a television wrestler. "Everybody's got a price!" was his catchphrase. Portraying the villain, DiBiase wore a tuxedo jacket with dollar signs on the lapels over his spandex wrestler shorts. He enjoyed teasing audience members with $100 bills just out of their reach.

Ted DiBiase used his fame from that career to branch in to inspirational speaking to church groups, moviemaking, and other pursuits. He became a darling of southern evangelical leaders, like Governor Mike Huckabee in Arkansas, for his personal story about overcoming greed and addiction. His sons, Ted Jr. and Brett, joined the family business of wrestling. Ted Jr. became a B-movie actor as well. Both maintained a connection to their hometown, Clinton, Mississippi.

When Brett DiBiase was introduced to Davis, Brett was a Toshiba copier salesman pitching equipment to DHS. Davis immediately took a shine to Brett, who had young, chiseled good looks. The DiBiases sensed a much bigger opportunity than just a quick copier contract. Through a series of LLCs and nonprofits with names like Restore, Heart of David Ministries, and Priceless Ventures, the DiBiases pitched Davis on work they could perform for the state with TANF dollars. Restore, Brett's LLC, was hired to teach classes on drug addiction.

Millions flowed to those DiBiase entities within a short time. The more our investigators looked, the more they grew concerned that funding the DiBiase projects was not a legal use of TANF dollars. It wasn't clear how many low-income people were served or how some of the programs even helped the poor at all. For example, DHS staff told my team that Heart of David, a DiBiase entity, used TANF money to put on revival-style meetings — church services — and wrestling events for an unclear number of participants. It's unclear what taking off your shirt, greasing up, and jumping from the top rope had to do with helping the poor, but the DiBiases were able to translate their skills into big payments to their nonprofits and to themselves.

We continued to wonder if Davis was receiving anything in exchange for these contracts. While the lead about the mailbox didn't yield anything clear, investigators also found that the DiBiases left a personal credit card with Davis's administrative assistant. Was Davis spending money on the DiBiases' card in exchange for the TANF contracts he'd given them?

The answer was murky. It looked like the card was used to book trips for Davis, sometimes in high-end hotels. But Davis could make the argument that these trips were for official purposes. On one such trip, the DiBiases bought rooms at the Trump Hotel in Washington, DC, for Davis and other DHS staffers who had traveled to Capitol Hill to testify before a federal committee. Davis was staying at a nicer hotel than he would have otherwise thanks to the DiBiases. One might even consider this a bribe. On the other hand, a good defense lawyer could argue that the DiBiases had made a donation to state government and saved the taxpayers from having to pay for Davis's hotel at all.

Facts like these came up, were explored, and over time we focused on what mattered most: the relationship between Davis and Brett.

Bo described how Davis lavished Brett with attention and found creative ways to pay him despite Brett's lack of expertise in helping the needy. In addition to the contract with Restore, Davis hired Brett onto the DHS staff as the "Director of Transformational Change," a nebulous title that led to confusion among DHS employees about what Brett was there to do. He made around $95,000 per year — more than Mississippi's secretary of state, treasurer, and lieutenant governor.

As odd as these arrangements seemed, Bo said we couldn't see or understand the complete picture until we started looking at a mother-and-son team from a different family. Their names were Nancy and Zach New. They were connected political donors with the ear of both Governor Bryant and the governor-in-waiting, Lieutenant Governor Tate Reeves. And they were the final piece needed to understand how the TANF fraud was operating.

CHAPTER THREE

The News

Mustering a serious look and surrounded by a carefully cura-
ted group of children — boys and girls, Black and white —
gubernatorial candidate Tate Reeves looked straight into the
camera. When it came to teachers, he said, "We've got to pay
them more." In the background behind him stood full book-
shelves and the colorful charts of names and gold stars typical
of any classroom. The campaign commercial Reeves was film-
ing was about his plan for public schools. The classroom he
filmed in was at a private school owned by Nancy New.

When the commercial aired, Reeves's opponent, Attorney
General Jim Hood, a Democrat, pounced. Hood assembled the
media at his campaign office. Standing in front of a JIM HOOD
FOR GOVERNOR sign the size of a refrigerator — a swoop of gray
hair, a little shorter in the front than the back, hair-sprayed solid
in place on his head — Hood called the commercial "fraudulent" and a "con."

"[Reeves has] done nothing for public education," Hood
said. The fact that Reeves shot an ad about public schools while
standing in a private school, along with the fact that Reeves had
taken thousands of dollars in campaign donations from New,
was proof of Reeves's hypocrisy, according to Hood. Reporters
gently pointed out that Hood, too, had taken thousands from
New.

The first time I heard Nancy New's name was from someone
who described her as a mega-donor, or a person who bankrolls
political campaigns. Campaign finance reports confirm there
was some truth to this.

New's biography didn't shed any light on where all that
money came from. In the early 1970s, a young Nancy New,

with big hair and a Cheshire cat grin, started her freshman year of college at the University of Southern Mississippi, where she struggled. She had trouble remembering the right word to say at the right time. Math gave her fits. Eventually, with the help of a professor, she discovered something important about herself: She was dyslexic.

Pushing through that challenge, New graduated and later earned a doctorate. She then went to work as a teacher and school administrator. By the time Hood and Reeves were locked in their election battle, her claim to fame was that she'd founded a school for children with disabilities like her own.

But running a school was hardly the stereotypical profile for big campaign donors, who tended to be owners of lucrative private businesses or lobbyists.

One large source of income for Nancy was TANF, as we later found out. Nancy acquired that money through a nonprofit she created called the Mississippi Community Education Center (MCEC). Founded in 1992, MCEC didn't make waves for its first few decades. It was housed in a nondescript office building — white walls, brown roof, few windows — on the frontage road of an interstate. Its purpose was the "promotion, improvement and expansion of community education."

But by 2017, Zach New, Nancy's younger son, was involved. Even though he was by this time in his thirties, he still looked like a Southern Miss frat boy. He had a permanent five o'clock shadow and wore some beer weight around his face. Once he set his hands to MCEC's business, the place took on a more entrepreneurial feel, if you can call it that. MCEC started to draw millions in TANF funds from Davis and DHS. In the fall of 2019, the numbers were so big that Attorney General Hood accused Reeves of taking campaign dollars from the News in exchange for the grants that went to MCEC. Hood waved away concerns about New's donation to his own coffers.

A few days after the Reeves ad aired, on October 31, 2019, the Mississippi Economic Council held its annual event called Hobnob, which was attended by every major business leader in the state. Politicians spoke and shared their thoughts about where the state was headed. I was invited and took the stage midmorning, using the opportunity to announce the arrest of a corrupt mayor we'd been investigating.

As I walked off the stage and headed for the exits, I saw a woman making a beeline for me. By the time she was a few feet away, I recognized her.

"Shad, I'm Nancy New," she said, pushing her hand out. She was sporting a bright-green top and beaming a smile behind thick makeup. Shiny bangles hung from her wrists. She gave me a triple dose of eye contact.

"Hi, Nancy," I said.

"Someone told me I should meet you," she said. She was warm in the way of a distant, older aunt who was eager to connect at a family reunion. Her voice was firm, though — a woman who punches the air with her fingers to make a heartfelt point.

"Well, it's nice to meet you, Nancy," I replied. There was a pause, so I politely walked away. It was the first and only time I ever spoke to her. As I was told once by a mentor, sometimes the people who want to impress the state auditor are the people the state auditor finds himself investigating.

Nancy wasn't just working the room at Hobnob, though. Around this time, she was working new DHS director Chris Freeze for money, just as she had Davis.

Shortly after Freeze was appointed DHS director, he cut off funds for MCEC and instead instituted a formalized procurement process. Now Nancy's MCEC would have to compete with every other nonprofit in the state to obtain welfare grants. But Nancy wasn't a woman who took no for an answer. She requested a meeting with Freeze at Governor Bryant's office.

At the meeting in front of the governor, Freeze walked through his new process. If Nancy wanted a grant, she could submit a proposal along with everyone else. It would then be scored by a team of experts from the agency. The meeting concluded, and Nancy and Freeze left the governor's presence. Outside the door, Nancy asked when they could meet to get the ball rolling on the grant.

Freeze laughed. It was as if she hadn't heard a word that was said in the meeting. Or, more troubling, Nancy was accustomed to a song and dance in front of the elected officials, and then the real business would be done without the constraints of the rules that had been discussed in the company of the governor. Either way, Freeze said there would be no next meeting.

Just as the News seemed to materialize everywhere at political events and government offices, mentions of the News appeared in document after document at DHS. The next step for understanding those documents was confronting the woman who knew Nancy's books better than anyone: her accountant, Anne McGrew.

Anne was a heavyset CPA in her midsixties, with hair that stopped just short of her shoulders. She technically worked at MCEC, but she was in a position to explain whether TANF money had been misspent across all Nancy's businesses, including Nancy's school. Richie assigned a seasoned investigator, Jerry Spell, to learn as much about MCEC's money movements as possible and to try to interview Anne. Jerry was one of the new investigators we'd hired after I took office, but he brought with him years of experience at the attorney general's office.

After weeks of preparing, Jerry made his move. Driving his unmarked cruiser, he followed Anne home from work one day. Once she exited her car, Jerry approached her, introduced himself, and asked to chat. Jerry could be spotted as a law enforcement officer a mile away with his close-cropped hair and a seriousness that he carried with him after some time spent in Afghanistan. In situations like these, though, he had a wit that put interviewees at ease. He could get them to talk, and Anne was willing.

The two of them sat down at Anne's kitchen table. Within minutes, Anne understood what Jerry was after. She'd been the accountant moving money for an entity that had purposefully misled the state for the benefit of its owners. Someday soon that would be public knowledge. When that happened, Anne's bosses, the News, would blame her. And unless she wanted to be the one held responsible for the ordeal, Anne would need to tell us what happened.

A few hours later Jerry knew everything he needed to know. We had a fraud case. Jerry closed his interview with Anne by telling her there was now a chance we would raid MCEC's offices. If we did, she should act surprised when the investigators walked in.

Jerry's interview meant Bo and Richie needed to take another trip into my office.

"We're at a decision point," Bo said the next day across the desk from me. Based on everything we knew, Bo and Richie believed MCEC had in its possession documents that would connect the dots of a fraud scheme involving Davis, the News, and potentially the DiBiases. "We need to get a search warrant to put our hands on the MCEC documents and everything else in their possession."

"Guys, if we do this, the cat will be out of the bag," I said. Thus far we'd kept our inquiry quiet. But search warrants meant armed investigators in windbreakers walking in unannounced and scooping up folders and laptops in the middle of the workday. The public would take notice.

"The News will clam up, too. And lawyer up," I said. I knew the News would retain some expensive law firm.

I didn't mention it at the time, but I also knew that the wealthiest families in the capital, Jackson — many of whom were friends with the News — would start to whisper about an overreaching young state auditor. After all, Nancy was, as I was told by someone in her circle, a wonderful woman. She couldn't have possibly stolen any money.

Richie and Bo convinced me the time was now, though. Anne's interview sealed it. We needed to know if MCEC's documents backed up Anne's story. "Let's go," I said.

Not long after, a team of agents walked into MCEC's offices with a warrant and grabbed computers, documents, and other evidence. Anne played the part of "stunned accountant" well. All that was left was to pore through the grant paperwork, emails, contracts, and endless reams of invoices.

What we found in those documents confirmed our suspicions. MCEC had been used to illegally funnel money to Brett DiBiase. The financial papers showed that, beneath the facade of the TV wrestler, Brett had a drug problem. And Davis, for whatever reason, decided Brett needed rehab, and he needed it at a resort location.

Davis then arranged for Brett to be sent to Rise in Malibu, a luxury drug treatment center in California. From the pictures, Rise in Malibu looked like an opulent celebrity getaway. Addicts could sit on leather furniture, rub their toes through the fur of zebra-print rugs, and enjoy panoramic views of palm trees and the ocean while detoxing. The facility promised "holistic, traditional and modern treatment methods that treat your mind, body, and spirit" with "luxurious accommodations." Such accommodations were expensive, so Davis had MCEC use some of its TANF money to pay for Brett's stay.

Once Brett was there, Davis made trips to see him. They'd traveled extensively together during DiBiase's time at DHS, making trips as far away as Las Vegas and Washington, DC.

With the Malibu fraud proven, we had our first clear criminal case. Brett and Davis had converted TANF funds to personal use, intentionally and illegally, with the help of the News and MCEC.

In some criminal cases, it's helpful to confront the targets of investigations with the facts and ask for an explanation. The more suspicious their story, the greater the likelihood of fraud. When we asked Davis and the News why TANF money was used to pay for Brett's Malibu stay, they told us lies. They claimed the payments to Malibu were to train Brett to teach drug addiction classes. They were not; the money was actually used to *treat* Brett. We had proof in the form of documents and the recorded audio of a phone call involving Davis, Brett, and the Malibu clinic. Fortunately, Rise in Malibu kept diligent records of the calls placed to them by patients.

While Brett was in Malibu, an aide to Davis named Latimer Smith sat down at a computer. Latimer was callow, still sporting his college haircut, and eager to please his DHS boss, Davis. Latimer typed up fictitious invoices for Restore, Brett's company, for the phantom opioid addiction classes Brett should have been teaching.

Latimer presented the phony invoices to DHS contracting staff. They cut a check for Restore. Latimer then took a jaunt down the street to the bank and deposited the funds in Restore's bank account. On the black-and-white footage captured by the bank's security cameras, you could see Latimer saunter into the branch and dutifully hand over the payments.

Apparently no one — neither Davis nor Latimer — stopped to think how strange it was for DHS employees to be doing the work of drafting invoices and depositing payments on behalf of a vendor. They also didn't consider what it would look like if someone found out they were writing invoices for work that was never done.

A part of me felt sympathy for Latimer. He might have been cowed by Davis into believing these maneuvers were normal. Or maybe Latimer felt he would be fired if he didn't do as Davis said. Still, Latimer had time to consider his actions. He wrote multiple fake invoices for Restore from late 2018 to early 2019. So he became a target of our investigation, too. If your boss asks you to do something illegal, just say no or leave.

Each time Bo or Richie updated me, I could see the charges stacking up. The News and Davis treated TANF like their own piggy bank, spending as they saw fit. A jury would balk at welfare money paying for luxury drug treatment for a close friend of the agency head.

It also appeared that the News had moved TANF money to a bank account for their private business, New Learning Resources. Welfare money was being used to pay expenses for the business, and there was no evidence that those expenses were TANF-eligible. At least one transfer of funds to New Learning Resources looked like it was accomplished by forging the signature of a New Learning employee, a principal at Nancy's school.

After all the documents obtained in the MCEC raid had been analyzed, Bo, Richie, Jerry, and I sat in the conference room and walked through everything. "There's one final scheme we think we've got," Bo said. "It's weirder than the rest."

"Look at this," Jerry said. He opened a video on his laptop showing a local news story. It featured Dr. Jacob Vanlandingham, a bespectacled Florida State professor with a hard part in his hair down the middle. He was standing on a football field, but he looked like he'd never laced up a pair of cleats in his life. Next to him was Brett Favre, the legendary football player and Mississippi native. The report was about a new concussion treatment Dr. Vanlandingham had invented. Vanlandingham described how a short straw, with one end inserted in the mouth and one end in a nostril, could be used to deliver a drug. The drug could allegedly reduce brain inflammation after a hit to the head. Favre demonstrated the straw and concussion treatment by blowing air out of his mouth, cheeks puffed out, and into his nose.

"What does this have to do with TANF?" I asked.

"Exactly," said Bo.

Jerry and Bo recounted how Nancy and Zach used TANF money to buy shares in Dr. Vanlandingham's companies. I was in disbelief.

"How in the world?" I asked. Jerry stated that Nancy had some connection to Favre, maybe through her role on the board of the University of Southern Mississippi's Athletic Foundation. Favre had played at the university and was next to godlike for fans of the school. Nancy was a graduate of USM herself, though I still could not understand how the founder of a school for children with disabilities landed on a board populated by the uber-rich. One of her fellow board members was the richest man in Mississippi. Favre was an honorary member.

Richie's team guessed that, at some point, Favre pitched the News on investing in the concussion company. The News then pulled from the large pool of free money they had access to: TANF funds.

"We need more time with this concussion thing to prove everything," Bo said, wrapping up. Bo explained they would need to contact Dr. Vanlandingham, learn more about Prevacus (Dr. Vanlandingham's company), and review more documents. "Give us a little more rope, and then we'll be ready to discuss taking this to a prosecutor," he concluded.

"How much money are we talking here, guys?" I asked. "How much TANF money was misspent?"

"Millions," Bo said.

The team left the room. My curiosity about these TANF schemes turned to anger. I rubbed my eyes with my palms and thought about the chutzpah one would need to misspend welfare money, especially for their own benefit. This was Missis-

sippi, with the highest poverty rate of any US state. Staring
out the office window above our coffeepot on the eighth floor
of Woolfolk, I could see blighted homes, caved-in roofs, and
impassable streets.

My eyes locked on the city, I reflected on all that I'd read
about welfare in the past few years. My mind tracked back to
a few articles by a young investigative reporter named Anna
Wolfe. Wolfe was a fish out of water in Mississippi. She'd moved
here from Washington State wearing big, horn-rimmed glasses
and hair that occasionally changed colors.

For years, Anna wrote about something strange happening at
DHS: Few poor people were being served despite DHS spending millions. In 2017, Anna noted while working at the *Clarion-
Ledger* newspaper in Jackson that just 1.5 percent of people who
were applying for TANF funds were deemed eligible. She also
noted that the state spent $90 million in TANF funds that year,
but only $10 million went directly to recipients. The rest was
going to something else.

Anna also wrote that MCEC, the News' nonprofit, had
received $30 million in TANF grants by around 2018. The
nonprofit could only point to ninety-four people they had
helped write a résumé and seventy-two people they had helped
complete a job application from 2017 to 2019 to show for it.
Those articles made more sense in light of what I'd just heard.

Late in 2019, the investigators returned to my office with
another update. We had just moved Jennifer Morrow, a data
analytics wiz, to the investigations division from our finance
audit division. Jennifer "scheduled" out payments (tracked and
recorded money movements) from DHS to the News' nonprofit
and company. She could now tell the News were using public
money to pay for things like a new home for Nancy.

In fact, Jennifer and the other investigators showed Nancy had
received a grant and then quickly moved the public money —
taxpayer dollars — through a series of accounts over forty-eight
hours in early June 2019. When the money stopped moving,
it landed in a $255,495 check Nancy made out to "Cash." The

check had the number "1800" in the memo line. That same day, Nancy purchased a new home at 1800 Sheffield Drive in Jackson. Again, we had identified intentionally misspent money, concealed through rapid transfers of the funds, that personally benefited New.

The question now was simply when to approach a prosecutor, not if.

While our criminal investigators finalized the proof we'd need for court, Stephanie Palmertree's auditors were scouring DHS's finances. Richie's investigators focused on proving criminal cases with the intensity of heat-seeking missiles. Stephanie's team, by contrast, needed to do a broad, exhaustive review of how DHS spent money. They had to spotlight expenditures in contravention of federal law even if there were no criminal penalties for the violations.

That fall, to no one's surprise, Stephanie's auditors found that DHS's books were riddled with misspending. DHS had given tens of millions of dollars to MCEC and another similar nonprofit in North Mississippi called the Family Resource Center (FRC). The accounts of those two nonprofits showed bizarre spending choice after bizarre spending choice.

DHS also had a duty to monitor the spending of the nonprofits after sending them money. DHS staffers — whether through incompetence or due to instruction from their superiors — failed to adequately watch the nonprofits. Some staff would later admit that John Davis told them not to monitor MCEC.

On the night of November 5, 2019, dressed in a business suit with my necktie loosened around my collar, I drove my truck home from an election-night party. Several hours earlier, the media had announced I'd been elected to my first full term as state auditor. Now the radio commentators were discussing a much more hotly contested affair: the race for governor.

"That's it. The Associated Press has called the race for Lieutenant Governor Tate Reeves, who has defeated Attorney General Jim Hood," the broadcaster announced.

I had a mild cold at the time, and my foggy brain felt like it'd shut off. The truck was driving itself. I had no room to feel excited about my election. The only thought I could hold was that the current director of DHS, former FBI agent Chris Freeze, would likely begin a campaign to keep his current job. Governor-Elect Reeves had the right to appoint whomever he wanted at DHS. Freeze had only been on the job a few months, and I wondered what he might do to audition for the role.

⚞⚟

In December, Stephanie walked into my office and said, "Chris Freeze is planning to give MCEC another grant." Despite public awareness that we were investigating MCEC, DHS published an "Intent to Award" document describing plans to give MCEC millions more.

We faced the ethical question of whether we could sit on our knowledge about the misspending we'd discovered and allow more money to be pilfered from taxpayers and the poor.

Stephanie and I walked to Pat's office. Leaning over the back of a chair, I shared the news with him and asked him what he thought.

"Auditors aren't supposed to tell anyone how to spend their money before they spend it," said Pat, chopping the air with his hands as if to draw an invisible line we should not cross. He was right. Our role was to look backward, after spending happened, to reflect on whether the numbers added up and whether laws or policies were shunted aside.

"But there's something else to think about," he added. "Sometimes we have a responsibility to tell our clients, mid-audit, if we see problems." I knew what he meant. This was a call only I could make.

My judgment was that we had an obligation to point out to the client, DHS and the State of Mississippi, that MCEC might not be trustworthy. I thought I could explain to Freeze the potential consequences of giving MCEC more money without dictating to him how the money should be spent.

By Christmas, we'd reached D-Day. DHS was going to give a multimillion-dollar grant to MCEC if I didn't step in. I requested a meeting with Freeze and Governor Bryant, who was in the final days of his time in office. We met in the governor's mansion, along with Bobby Waites, the governor's most senior attorney.

Sitting at the same table where the governor had interviewed me for state auditor, I explained to the three men that, while I could not go into detail about what an audit would reveal before it was finished, I could guarantee MCEC had misspent TANF money. The total losses would be staggering. And I warned them that, if the state continued to pour money into MCEC, the federal government might levy heavy penalties, perhaps even treble damages, on Mississippi.

Bobby was an old pro who looked like a quintessential senior partner in a law firm — weathered, balding, and with eyes that told you to cut to the chase. He, along with Bryant, seemed to understand. Freeze was less sympathetic. Freeze asked if I was telling him to cut off all aid to the poor who were benefiting from MCEC's programs. The question was ridiculous, given how few low-income Mississippians were actually being helped by the money going to MCEC. I wondered if Freeze felt political pressure to keep sending MCEC grant money.

Freeze's comments forced my hand. I would have to reveal some examples of the misspending.

"There is serious misappropriation here," I said. "We're talking TANF dollars being used to advertise at college football bowl games. Big payouts to celebrities. No clear evidence of programs helping the poor. This is going to be a disaster when it comes out, and everyone will be held accountable for what you do now that we know all this."

The governor's eyes were pained. "I've also had a complaint from the community college board," he said. This was news to me. The community college board was a small state agency that doled out a variety of grants. "The college board tells me they've given money to some of the same nonprofits that got TANF money from DHS. They've noticed strange spending habits. Strange travel expenses being paid with their funds. They just turned their grants to the nonprofits off." Two different agencies, led by people Governor Bryant trusted, were now suspicious of the same nonprofits.

The governor sighed. He had a thick head of perfectly coiffed gray hair, and he looked like he wanted to pull it out. His wife, First Lady Deborah Bryant, was friends with Nancy. They'd even loaned each other clothes on occasion. "I told Deborah," he said quietly, "she's not your friend because she likes you. She's your friend because she likes that you're the First Lady."

Bobby ended the meeting by asking me to put my concerns in writing. On December 27, 2019, I sent Governor Bryant and Director Freeze a letter warning them about MCEC. That meeting and the letter put a stop, for the moment, to a big new grant flowing down the MCEC drain. Freeze didn't recover, though. By January, he'd been informed by Governor-Elect Reeves's team that he would not be invited back to DHS.

The Prosecutors

One of the most difficult decisions for a state auditor is choosing the prosecutor to handle each case in which a criminal violation is suspected. A case usually begins with a whistleblower tip to the auditor's office. A manager in my office then assigns the case to an agent. The agent conducts interviews and reviews documents to determine if a criminal statute was violated. If the agent concludes there was a violation, they wrap their evidence into a tidy package and send it to the directors of investigations, Richie and Bo. The directors then examine the applicable statutes to determine if they concur with the investigator's conclusion.

Many times, we find that both federal and state laws have been violated. White-collar crime often involves the electronic transfer of money, for instance, which means the federal wire fraud statute might have been violated even if the crux of the case is embezzlement under state law.

My office then has to pick a prosecutor. We have no authority to take a case to court on our own. Most cases coming from the auditor's office can be sent to either a local district attorney or the attorney general for violations of state law or to the United States attorney — the federal prosecutor appointed for our area — for violations of federal law.

There are benefits and drawbacks to each option. Federal prosecutors are excellent, but the federal investigative system is slow. Before I was named state auditor, the auditor's office built a full investigation on a kickback scheme at the Mississippi Department of Education. The office decided to take the case to the US attorney. The prosecutors then, out of an abundance of caution, turned the case over to the FBI to look over what the state auditor's office had found.

After a long wait — six years — federal prosecutors finally obtained guilty pleas on several individuals, including a former director at the Department of Education. While those six years slowly ticked by, my investigators were incensed. In their eyes, the federal indictments simply restated the work our auditors had already completed. No new suspects had been arrested. No bigger fish had been landed. Years had been wasted. Moreover, my team was frustrated that the feds kept them in the dark during the wait.

Behind closed doors, federal investigators blamed their prosecutors for the lack of speed. They said the prosecutors would take a month to write a subpoena. That was something my office could do in an afternoon. Federal prosecutors blamed federal investigators, saying they moved too slowly gathering documents and interviewing witnesses. The reason for the delays was immaterial to my team and me. We just knew the result took too long and the feds were too secretive about *their* prosecution of *our* investigation.

Early in my tenure, a new leader, Special Agent in Charge Michelle Sutphin, was assigned to run the FBI's local office. One morning, I climbed into Richie's F-150 pickup with its black-tinted windows, and we went to see her about the strain in our relationship caused by the Department of Education case. The local FBI office is a compound on the outskirts of Jackson. It's surrounded by a military-grade black metal fence and a guard shack with retractable concrete barriers in the ground. Richie and I navigated our way through that security and sat on the couch in Michelle's office. It was adorned with memorabilia from her career, which included stints investigating Ferguson, Missouri, after the death of Michael Brown and leading a team that looked into the crash of Flight 93 on 9/11 in Shanksville, Pennsylvania.

"Michelle, some of our folks are not happy with how the education case has played out," I said. She was receptive to the criticism. Michelle knew that building and keeping relationships in law enforcement was a surefire way to expand the FBI's capabilities. "My people know there's a need for operational security," I added. "You can't let information out that might jeopardize a case. But we also feel like we deserve better updates when we spend Mississippi taxpayer resources on a case."

"I get it," she replied. Michelle was a straight shooter, and she pledged to eliminate some of the needless firewalls around intelligence. It was a pledge she kept for the duration of her time as the special agent in charge.

Back in Richie's truck, on the drive returning to our office, Richie and I discussed the constraints Michelle was under. "The feds are slow, man," he said. "I love them, but they're slow. They're big. Big operations mean more rules. More middlemen."

I viewed the inherent federal slowness as an opportunity for state agencies. In Louisiana, for example, a local pharmacist had earned national fame when he joined forces with state regulators to shut down a pill mill poisoning his neighborhood. The pharmacist, Dan Schneider, was obsessed with a local doctor who handed out opioids like candy. When he complained to the Drug Enforcement Agency, a federal body, they worked the case but never seemed to make progress.

Schneider grew impatient and approached a state regulatory body, the Louisiana Board of Medical Examiners. The pill mill doctor was finally stopped when the state agency revoked her license. Law enforcement followed right behind, raiding the doctor's offices for documents and then prosecuting her. The bust made national news and inspired a documentary called *The Pharmacist*.

Much like the Louisiana board, my agency couldn't handle every detail of large cases. But we could prove part of a complex case faster than the feds and put a stop to illegal activity. Think Al Capone being scooped up for tax evasion, even if they couldn't yet prove he was a murderer.

When it came time to make the decision about which prosecutor to approach with the DHS case, my agents didn't want to take the case to the feds because of their experience with the Department of Education. At least, not the first arrests. But there was a problem with taking the case to the local DA, too. The problem's name was Robert Shuler Smith.

Robert Shuler Smith was the elected district attorney for Hinds County, the county that is home to the state capital,

Jackson. It would have been a euphemism in the extreme to describe the relationship between his office and the state auditor's as strained. Before my time in office, Smith accused two agents in the auditor's office of interfering with a prosecution. He indicted the agents. Those two agents would later leave the auditor's office, and Smith would drop his charges, but the well was poisoned. All my current agents wanted to avoid contact with DA Smith at all costs.

Thankfully, the November 2019 election changed our calculus. Smith had left his DA post to run for the Democratic nomination for governor against Attorney General Jim Hood. With the DA seat vacated, there was an open-seat election. The winner was a young attorney named Jody Owens.

Jody sports a short haircut and has a sturdy frame that fills out a blue suit in a way that looks fit for public office. On paper, he and I had nothing in common. Jody is a Democrat; I'm a Republican. Before becoming DA, Jody was the director of Mississippi's office of the Southern Poverty Law Center; as an attorney at a different nonprofit, I represented charter school parents and fought Jody in court when his center challenged the funding mechanism for our schools.

But Jody and I had a good relationship. We'd both trained at the same law firm, so we had many friends and former colleagues in common. Jody and I also converted to Catholicism at the same time and in the same church. Conversion is not a quick process. It involves months of meetings, once a week for several hours at a time, to discuss theology with the other soon-to-be Catholics. We'd attended those classes together. We also both served in the military (Jody was a reservist, I was in the National Guard).

Shortly after Jody was elected, I asked him to lunch at Steve's Deli in downtown Jackson. We sat in a booth munching white sauce barbecue sandwiches. The smell of baked cookies and the sounds of hushed lunch chatter filled the room. Jody updated me on his transition into office. At some stage, I came to the point.

"Jody, I can't give you any details, but we have a large white-collar crime case that took place here in Jackson. It would be in your jurisdiction. In the past, we would never have taken this case to DA Smith, but I want to consider bringing the case to you," I said.

Jody knew about the challenges with the former DA. He was eager to turn the page himself. "Absolutely," he shot out. "We can handle it." Jody tended to talk faster than most people can listen. His words came out in an eager blur.

We spent the next few minutes discussing the capacity of his office. We talked about his assistant district attorneys, their skill level, and the docket in Hinds County and whether it was too crowded.

"I'll be honest," I said, "and tell you my biggest concern is the quality of the team of prosecutors you're inheriting." Jody said the team he was building could handle a financial crimes case. We discussed the idea of recruiting one of our friends at a law firm to serve as a pro bono assistant district attorney if we presented the case to Jody's office and they found it too complex. A litigator at a top firm might jump at the chance to help try a high-profile case just for the experience, even if there was no pay involved.

We ended the lunch and left the restaurant, parting ways on the sidewalk in front of the white Greek columns of the antebellum governor's mansion. At that moment I felt, at minimum, we had another viable option for prosecuting the DHS case if we chose not to take it to the feds.

Back at the office, Bo, Richie, Jerry, and I met in Richie's office. We debated the pros and cons of each prosecution team. Bo, stretched out on Richie's brown couch, made the most convincing argument for taking the case to Jody.

"Look," he said, propping one foot on top of the other and crossing his arms. "This is how it will probably go. We can indict the people we have a case on in state court with Jody. The money to Nancy gets cut off. The case will immediately get attention. The feds will want in. The FBI will investigate, and they will probably indict the same defendants, too. They may even add to the pile of defendants. The defense attorneys will then come to their senses and see they need to get all this resolved. They'll ask for a meeting with both state and federal prosecutors. The defendants will then probably plead guilty in a global resolution to all the criminal charges."

I thought about the possibility as he paused. "If I were those defendants, I would want to negotiate to spend my time in a federal facility, not state prison," I added. State prisons in Mississippi were not a fun place to be.

"Exactly," said Bo, "I don't think this thing will ever see trial." The strength of Jody's team to litigate might be a moot point.

There was another reason to take the case to Jody rather than the federal prosecutors. The current US attorney — the lead federal prosecutor who would handle the case — was Mike Hurst. Hurst and I had known each other for a few years. He was also a Republican. I feared someone might allege that the Republican state auditor and the Republican US attorney went soft on New, an influential Republican donor. I knew the media scrutiny on the case would be intense. Having a Democrat like Jody on the team making the final decisions on charging and sentencing recommendations would be a good thing. No one would accuse Jody of doing any favors for wealthy Republicans who stole from poor people.

Putting all this aside, the most important factor in the decision was speed. I knew if we handed the case to the feds, it would be at least a year before anyone was indicted. The FBI would want to check our work, if not redo all of what we'd spent the past few months doing.

On top of that, DHS was actively trying to hand Nancy more money. While my meeting with Governor Bryant and DHS director Freeze put a stop to more grants for Nancy for the moment, a new sheriff would be in town soon. The new DHS director could easily turn the spigot back on. Nancy had cranked political pressure toward that end. Legislators and other politicians were calling my office asking why money for MCEC was being withheld "by the auditor's office." One influential Jacksonian called me and said, "You know that woman didn't do anything wrong. Why are you bothering her?"

The day he called I was at my wit's end, tired of hearing those complaints. I lost my cool and said, "Are you prepared to say that on the stand?" There was stunned silence on the other end of the line.

The truth is that political pressure had a way of focusing our minds. Richie's team barricaded themselves in one of our conference rooms. You could see the evidence of long hours. Laptops. Stacks of documents. Skoal cans and empty Red Bulls in the corner garbage. The musty smell of people cooped up too long in a closed space. They weren't going to let the case drag on.

I pitched in where I could be helpful. When the team realized they would need to confront Dr. Vanlandingham in Florida to obtain the final pieces of evidence in the concussion scheme, the investigators called me in.

"We're worried Dr. Vanlandingham may have gotten wind we are investigating. He might start destroying documents," said Richie. "We need to get our hands on the contract between Vanlandingham and the News and the text messages between them. We also need to know what Florida laws may have been broken here, in case Dr. Vanlandingham may himself become a defendant. And we need to do all this fast."

I had an idea and asked them to give me a couple of hours. Richie agreed and put Michael Guynes, one of our DHS investigators, in the car on the way to Tallahassee.

I fast-walked back to my office, pulled out my cell phone, and dialed a friend from law school who was now an attorney for Florida governor Ron DeSantis.

"Colleen, I've got a problem," I said. I described our issue. If there were other criminal violations — for instance, if Vanlandingham's device was a fake cure or if he'd committed securities fraud — I wanted Florida investigators to be in on the ground floor. Colleen immediately connected me to the head of the Tallahassee office of the Florida Department of Law Enforcement and an investigator at the Florida Office of Financial Regulation in Miami.

Among the three of us, we made a plan for how to execute our encounter with Dr. Vanlandingham and share anything important across the three offices. By the time Michael reached Tallahassee, we had the pieces in place. Michael confronted Dr. Vanlandingham and gathered the needed evidence, sharing copies with Florida investigators.

The sense of urgency was healthy. We knew that, if my office was receiving calls about why grant money to MCEC had stopped, DHS was probably hearing from the same people. And if the money started flowing again, millions of dollars intended for the poor would line the pockets of people who shouldn't be receiving it. So we pushed, setting our sights on January for taking the case to a prosecutor. That prosecutor would be Jody Owens and his team in state court.

To prepare for the presentation of the case to Jody, we asked two senior attorneys — a former assistant DA in Hinds County and a prosecutor at the Office of the Attorney General — to come and hear about our case first. We wanted them to punch holes in it, both the substance and the form of our presentation, if they could.

Jerry Spell and Michael Guynes were our presenters. They stood at the front of our conference room and flipped through slide after slide in a PowerPoint deck, each one showing account numbers, how money trickled from the federal government into the pockets of the perpetrators, and what the penalties were for taking welfare money. By the end of the presentation, the attorneys confirmed the case was strong.

We were ready to show it to the Hinds County DA.

I called Jody and asked him to bring over his best assistant DA in the next few days. The investigators and I spent the intervening time cleaning up the presentation.

Investigators are, by nature, detailed people. Their presentation was heavy on the story of how the interviews went and how the investigation started. I helped them speak the language of lawyers: show the elements of the statute, how the law had been broken, and how we could make a jury care.

On the day of the presentation, Jody brought over Assistant District Attorney Jamie McBride, and we got down to business. Michael was particularly persuasive and clear in the meeting. He had the build of an athlete and was the best shot with a Glock among our law enforcement officers, and if he was ever forced to play a prosecutor on TV, he would do just fine. When Michael showed Jody the check of government money for Nancy's home at 1800 Sheffield, Jody said, "Dear Lord." My eyes cut to Richie, and he smiled. Jody understood what had happened here. The News had alchemized welfare money into a fraud scheme.

"This is incredible, guys," Jody said. He pointed to one of the dollar figures on a slide and laughed. "You've got this theft down to the penny. Only the state auditor's office would do that."

After the presentation, I pulled Jody aside and asked him what he thought.

"It's solid," he said, straightening his tie. "If you're comfortable with it, I'm comfortable moving forward." His eyes darted out the window. I could tell he was already considering how to present the case. Jody asked me to let them look at the evidence and come back with questions. I agreed.

By late January, I knew I would have to break the news about my agreement with Jody to federal prosecutor Mike Hurst. I thought Mike would be disappointed not to be given a big case, but I didn't think it would destroy our working relationship. My team was partnering with Mike's office on plenty of other cases, and Mike and I went back a long way. We'd met several years prior when Mike was on a failed run for attorney general. We hit it off. After Mike lost his bid for AG, he helped start a conservative legal advocacy organization called the Mississippi Justice Institute. Then, in 2017, when he was appointed US attorney, Mike recruited me to take his place as director of the institute.

In short, we had a bond prior to the DHS case. We sometimes met for breakfast at Primo's, an old-fashioned café in Flowood, Mississippi, and we decided to meet there again to catch up. I walked into Primo's the morning of our meeting. Mike was already posted up near the back in a blue chair, sipping black coffee and reading the paper.

Mike is tall and has short-cropped blond hair; I couldn't remember seeing him without a suit and tie on. He's what you'd get if you called central casting and asked for a politician. He was also deeply politically connected, particularly to Governor Reeves. They'd attended a small liberal arts college called Millsaps together.

I sat down, and we chatted about a couple of upcoming cases. Then Mike turned the conversation to DHS.

"Are you investigating John Davis and DHS?" he asked pointedly.

It was not a huge secret after we'd served the search warrant on MCEC and taken evidence from their offices. The News had a way of spreading stories around town, even if it wasn't clear why spreading those stories helped them.

"I ask because the News reached out to me for a meeting," Mike said. The News were trying to head off any potential charges by making their case directly to a prosecutor. That would be the only reason for going straight to Mike before the investigation was concluded. But more important, if you were a prosecutor, why would you even entertain a meeting like that? What good could come from putting yourself in a position to be influenced by a potential defendant without knowing what they might have done, turning yourself into a witness in any future trial?

Mike didn't discuss what the News had said to him, but now my guard was up. We would confirm later that Mike did have that meeting, which was foolish on his part, and the content of the meeting was never made available to us.

Nancy's text messages, which were made public two years later, told the tale. "I am going to work on getting appt. with some more people that will hopefully help [get us past the investigation]," Nancy said to her son. "It will obviously take a lot of money and time but we may need to go on and file once we find out what Mike Hurst says."

Back in the blue café chairs, I explained to Mike that we were investigating fraud at DHS and MCEC. Without going into detail, I told him we had a phased plan for the case, because it was massive. Phase one would be to take the case to state court and obtain indictments for the fraud schemes we'd already proved. Phase two would be to hand over everything to federal authorities and work together, jointly, to uncover any remaining crimes. Phase three would be for prosecutors to file federal charges and to, ideally, bring every defendant to justice with full coordination among all law enforcement.

I could tell Mike was angry but was trying to mask it. "Are all these stolen funds federal funds?" he asked, going into cross-examination mode.

"Yes," I said. "So far, at least, all the stolen funds are TANF."

"Do you think it's appropriate that you cut out federal prosecutors if the funds are all federal funds?" he asked.

I explained that we were not cutting out federal prosecutors. We expected his team to be full partners. If he was asking whether state charges were appropriate, then yes, they were appropriate. The subjects in this case had violated multiple state laws, like fraudulently manufacturing state documents. They had done so through a state agency. State court was an appropriate first venue.

Mike made some half-baked argument about the statute of limitations in state court, which was incorrect, and I ignored it.

Finally, Mike made it clear that he wanted to be phase one. I told him I understood, but — speaking bluntly — I had concerns about the speed with which he could handle this case. I added that DHS wanted to continue paying MCEC money. My team did not want to watch the News take any more. If I handed the case to Mike and it took him years to prosecute while millions more were wasted, the public would (rightly) never forgive me for ignoring Jody as an option.

He refused to acknowledge that his office had been slow in the past. He instead blamed the FBI. I told him I understood but that, in our eyes, it did not matter who was at fault. The federal system was slower. We didn't have time to waste. We'd proved our case.

Mike wasn't satisfied, but I had given him my answer. Breakfast was over. I hopped into my gray pickup and returned to the office. On the drive, I replayed the conversation in my mind. Mike was not happy, but he did not seem irrationally angry. Perhaps he would sleep on it, realize he would ultimately get a piece of this case, and that justice would be better served by using state court to quickly put a stop to the fraudulent TANF spending.

Back at Woolfolk State Office Building, the state prosecutors fired questions our way via email. They wanted to narrow down their case to the fraud schemes with the strongest proof. Eventually they gave a thumbs-up. They were ready to go to a grand jury and seek indictments.

After one of our final meetings before the grand jury, Jody asked me to chat privately. Looking out at the dome of the capitol, he asked, "What do you think about trying this case? Are you interested?"

"Me?" I said. There was an argument to have me on Jody's trial team. I was an attorney with an active license, and I'd been a litigator at a firm for a couple of years and at the Mississippi Justice Institute.

I'd also served as a special prosecutor for two small matters while I was at the firm. The son of a popular local elected official was caught burglarizing a home in Brandon, Mississippi, with one of his friends. Every employee at the Rankin County DA's office knew the elected official. The DA believed those conflicts of interest precluded them from trying the case. The DA asked me — I'd interned for him in law school — if I would be interested in taking the case. While the thought of working for free on the case (on top of the billable hour requirement I had at the firm) seemed a little overwhelming, I agreed. I realized that if I didn't take the case I would be passing the buck to someone else. I also thought I could do a decent job, and I believed the young man should be held accountable regardless of who his daddy was.

The DHS case, however, was not a simple burglary. I talked the matter over with my team. Pat Dendy said I should consider taking the trial.

"One day, we'll have a strong case that we've investigated, and every prosecutor we approach will be unprepared to try it alone. When that day comes, you might want to be ready to jump in that case and help them," he said.

He was right that a day like that might come. But today wasn't that day. Even though I knew the facts of the case, if I took it, it would consume my life. The DHS trial would stand in the way of my doing the job the voters had elected me to do, which was to run the Office of the State Auditor.

I ultimately told Jody that I was not interested. I had faith in his team. If they needed help, I would help recruit a pro bono lawyer from the private sector or hire an attorney in my office who could help them.

"One more thing," Jody said. He told me how, in the past few days before the grand jury, Nancy and MCEC had invited Jody to join a task force on childhood poverty. Jody had never met the News. He chortled, "I guess they're trying to cozy up to me."

"Just came out of the blue, huh?" I laughed and said, "Can't blame them for trying."

"I told 'em no. Not that kind of prosecutor," Jody blurted, flashing a toothy smirk.

I was feeling better already. We were ready to go before a grand jury in Hinds County to seek the indictment of the DHS fraudsters.

⚜

Across town, Governor Phil Bryant was texting Dr. Jacob Vanlandingham. Bryant and Vanlandingham had kindled a relationship starting around Christmas 2018 when Vanlandingham, with the help of Brett Favre, booked a meeting with Bryant in Jackson. According to emails to Bryant, Vanlandingham used the meeting to pitch the idea of testing and manufacturing his concussion treatment in Mississippi. They met at Walker's Drive-In, one of the capital city's best restaurants, where you could choose to eat in renovated 1950s-style booths left over from the establishment's glory days, or you could opt for a private room and enjoy your Redfish Anna, their specialty, with more privacy.

Around the time of that 2018 meeting, Favre texted Vanlandingham, "Don't know if legal or not but we need [to] cut him [Bryant] in." Then later Favre said, "Also if legal I'll give some of my shares to the Governor."

Vanlandingham conveyed that idea to Bryant. "We want you to know we want you on the team and can offer stock. We don't know the rules but are willing to do what is needed to bring you on board."

The morning after the 2018 Christmastime meeting, Vanlandingham and Favre texted Bryant, thanking him for the chat and pressing for his intercession. Vanlandingham needed state help to get his business model off the ground. He suggested manufacturing his drug in Mississippi. Favre sent Bryant a message saying, "It's 3rd and long and we need you to make it happen!!"

Bryant pledged to assist. "I will open a hole."

Favre followed up by connecting Vanlandingham with Nancy New, who was handling millions of welfare dollars through her nonprofit. "She has strong connections and gave me 5 million . . . Offer her whatever you feel like."

Favre and Vanlandingham were operating in complete ignorance of, or disregard for, a basic principle in the law: Public officials and those handling public money cannot benefit personally from handing out that public money. "[If] this all works out we need to buy her [New] and John Davis surprise him with a vehicle I thought maybe John Davis we could get him a [F-150] raptor," texted Favre. The Raptor — Ford's most expensive F-150 package — could cost north of $100,000.

They also had no qualms about using John Davis's DHS money to enrich themselves. After texting about the Raptor they would potentially buy for John, Favre asked Vanlandingham, "Honestly give me your thoughts on what you think all this means . . . When we will make money." Favre's goal, according to his texts, was to "take home 20 million."

Vanlandingham was effusive to Favre after his call with Nancy New. "I'm going to venture out on a limb and say of all the times you've helped me the key contact that gets us over the top will end up being Nancy New. Thx brother she's great." Vanlandingham would go on to milk that connection for millions, and even try to use Bryant and New's alma mater as a source of capital.

The News, per Vanlandingham's request, immediately began funneling a windfall of TANF money to Prevacus — and arranged for the financial gain from the investment to go to a private LLC owned by Nancy, Zach, and Jess New (Nancy's other son).

When Bryant appointed Chris Freeze to replace John Davis, though, Vanlandingham's forward progress stalled. Vanlandingham texted Favre, "I heard John Davis retired. Shit!!!"

Favre replied by telling him the "new guy," Freeze, "ain't our type," according to Nancy.

"Fuck," said Vanlandingham. "Well we may need the governor to make him our type." Beneath Vanlandingham's nerdy exterior was a calculating operator who was willing to manipulate every political connection to supercharge his company with cash.

Two years after their 2018 meeting, after Prevacus received a war chest of welfare money, Bryant and Vanlandingham were communicating again.

"Now that you're unemployed I'd like to give you a company package for all your help," Vanlandingham texted Bryant on January 16, 2020, two days after Bryant left office. "Let me know when you come up for air but know we want and need you on our team!!!"

Eight minutes later, Bryant replied, "Sounds good. Where would be the best place to meet. I am now going to get on it hard . . ."

Bryant sent these controversial texts after my office took our findings to Jody Owens, so they were not central to the opening salvo of the case. They hadn't even been sent when we went to Jody. But the message would go on to be a focal point for every prosecutor who looked at the matter from then on. How federal and state prosecutors interpreted his messages — had Bryant agreed to accept something of value in exchange for an official act? — would determine Bryant's future.

The Proof

The fan blades turned round and round above my bed. *They're moving slowly enough. Maybe I should count the number of revolutions.* Anything to help me sleep.

In the days leading up to the grand jury, the pressure built. At night, I'd stare up at the ceiling fan above my bed, eyes wide open, replaying the details of the case over in my mind — what we had discovered, what we could not prove. I knew if we did not act, millions would have been misspent, and no one would be held accountable.

But if we indicted and arrested the people at the heart of the DHS case, my investigators and Jody's prosecutors would be involved in the biggest drama of our careers. It would make national news. If I lost a case this important, this early in my tenure, I might never recover. The News were influential. They would ensure that everyone in the state with money knew about my mistake. I was a Harvard-trained lawyer, so no one would believe it if I said I was relying on staff to make the right call. If I had concerns to take to Jody before the grand jury, I had to raise them myself.

The pressure was magnified by the fact that new governor Tate Reeves announced that Jacob Black, John Davis's top deputy, would be interim head of DHS. I wondered if Black would try to restart the flow of money to MCEC. We would learn more than a year later, during an audit, that he did.

What if DHS is burning more money right now? When can we be certain we're ready to move? Is there ever a sure thing in white-collar cases? At night I searched for answers. And I counted things — spinning fan blades, imperfections in the paint — until my mind soothed itself into submission, and I fell asleep.

Back in the office, I called Bo and Richie in for a few final meetings to review our evidence. Our focus was on intent. The heart of most criminal white-collar cases is proving that the defendant intended to defraud the victims. Plenty of people make mistakes with money. Accounting errors, paperwork mistakes, accidentally spending on a new office chair with grant money designed to pay for something else — these were the sorts of lapses in judgment that required money to be repaid. But they didn't typically result in criminal charges. Criminal charges require the defendant to *intentionally* violate the law.

Because we cannot enter the minds of criminal defendants to establish intent, we must look to the evidence surrounding the transactions. We look for facts that suggest the defendant knew that what they were doing was wrong. Did they say or write something they knew was false, for example. Did they attempt to cover their tracks in the process? Did they do so knowing they would financially benefit? These were markers of an intent to steal.

The challenges with proving intent could be seen in other high-profile white-collar cases. Elizabeth Holmes was at one time the world's youngest female self-made billionaire. She started the Silicon Valley healthcare company named Theranos. Theranos claimed they could test for a variety of illnesses with a single, small sample of blood from a patient. But that promise was a mirage. Prosecutors hauled Holmes into court, alleging she'd committed fraud. They claimed she knew that Theranos could not perform the tests it promised and that Holmes knowingly lied to investors about Theranos's technology in order to boost the value of the company and line her own pockets.

The central question at the Holmes trial was intent. Prosecutors could show that Theranos made claims that were not true. The company talked up its partnerships with big pharmaceutical companies and even put the big pharma logos on marketing documents. But those partnerships did not exist. Theranos claimed to be working with the military, but there were no military contracts in place.

Holmes was asked how the big pharma logos ended up on documents designed to persuade investors.

She took responsibility. "I wish I had done it differently," she said.

Was this enough to convict her? A jury thought so. At trial, Holmes was convicted of wire fraud.

Bo walked through my office door. "I've tried to put our thinking about mens rea proof all in one place," he said. *Mens rea* is literally "guilty mind"— the mental state needed to commit a crime.

"Take a look at this." He slid a memorandum across my desk. I put it side by side with some handwritten notes I'd been taking over the previous two weeks.

The more I looked at his summary, the stronger I felt about our intent case. First, MCEC's accountant, Anne McGrew, could establish that the News deliberately spent TANF money in ways that were not allowed, and they knew it. Anne wasn't accidentally making payments to a resort in Malibu, for instance. She was being instructed to do so by people who knew that was wrong.

Moreover, MCEC's bank statements showed it was impossible for the News to believe they were not spending TANF money. They were intentionally burning through welfare cash.

That deception had its roots years prior. Beginning in 2016, John Davis sat down with Nancy to discuss how they could work together. They struck a deal. They would begin with a simple $1 million agreement. In exchange for that money, MCEC committed to "improve the welfare of children and families" in the state. The prior year, MCEC had raised less than $2.5 million in contributions and grant revenue, so a $1 million grant from DHS was a big deal. By 2018, just two years later, they reported revenues nearly ten times what they had in 2015, thanks to Davis.

The News *knew* they'd received a massive haul of TANF funds beyond their normal MCEC budget. From 2016 to 2019, a full $58 million of MCEC's income was from grants; less than $900,000 came from private donations. They spent TANF funds with abandon, and Anne could describe all of this.

Anne could also testify about how the News' spending was not recorded properly, which showed an intent to conceal.

Plenty of MCEC's accounting entries were false and did not match bank statements. The original accounting entries for the money sent to Rise in Malibu, for example, were labeled "curriculum," as if they were paying for teaching materials rather than Brett DiBiase's drug treatment. The false accounting entries were evidence of an attempt to hide what the money was actually going for.

Finally, Anne could tell the world how MCEC sent incorrect descriptions of their TANF spending to DHS staff. The falsehoods on the ledgers were important because they hid the true beneficiaries of the spending, the News. For example, MCEC lied in the documents sent to DHS about how much they were sending to their private business, New Learning Resources. Omissions and inaccurate numbers on these official forms are not just bad bookkeeping: If they conveniently cloak someone obtaining a personal benefit, it is fraud.

"Bo, let's talk about this one again: Could Nancy or Zach say they believed all the money they were paid was an administrative fee for handling TANF grants?" I asked.

"Like I say" — *like I say* was Bo's verbal tic — "if the News think the money they had taken was owed to them as fees, they seemed to believe those fees should be pretty fat," he explained. The News were driving nice cars paid for with TANF funds. MCEC also paid the News' salaries and bought them gadgets like cell phones and tablets with TANF funds. The News had invested a great deal of TANF money in Dr. Vanlandingham's concussion venture. And that's to say nothing of the money moved to New Learning Resources. All told, they walked away with millions of dollars of value in about three years.

Bo added, "Then there's the laundering" — intentionally sending money to various accounts to conceal its original source. The money movements Nancy made — like quickly ferrying public money around bank accounts to pay for her Sheffield house — walked and talked a lot like money laundering.

And finally, there was a mountain of lies about spending for Brett DiBiase's treatment. Fraudulent sign-in sheets had even been created to try to show he taught fake classes. The Malibu embezzlement may have been small compared with the total amount of misspending in the case. But if the DHS Six (the original six people Jody wanted to indict) were willing to lie so blatantly about the Malibu money, the other circumstantial evidence of deceit started to look intentional. In the words of Enron prosecutor Sean Berkowitz, "When you lie about the little things people think you lie about the big things."

Brett, to his credit, would find an honest streak as the case went on, telling an agent he'd spent the proceeds he'd gotten from DHS's checks on a Cuban stripper from New Orleans.

I looked back at Bo and then rubbed my forehead with the tips of my fingers, calming my tired eyes. "In other words, what you're telling me is these people had no regard for the law," I said. "And they tried to hide what they'd done."

"Yes. Don't forget, their bank account got fatter in the process," he said. "Bank robbers can claim they didn't know they were stealing from a vault, but that's a hard sales pitch to make when they're found holding bags of cash that didn't belong to them."

Bo and I talked about how some spending by MCEC didn't rise to the level of criminal charges, but it still looked fishy. For example, Nancy and Zach were paying Nancy's other son, Jess, a massive consulting fee from TANF funds. It was possible Jess was performing some real "consulting" work for MCEC in exchange for the quarter million dollars he was paid, but we couldn't tell.

We also saw that the News had created a real estate company that bought property and then rented it to MCEC for offices. The rent, per usual, was paid with TANF money. The profits went to the News. One particularly suspicious feature of this spending was that the News' real estate company, Avalon Holdings, charged above-market rates. Avalon would charge MCEC — meaning the taxpayers — north of $20,000 monthly for a space when a similar space (say, a dentist's office next door) was going for less than half that.

And some of the property MCEC rented from Avalon was completely unused. The News had their nonprofit — again, meaning the taxpayers — pay their private real estate company for a useless office.

Whether prosecutors could make a criminal charge out of this was a different matter. A talented defense lawyer might say wasting money on an empty office was stupidity instead of theft. The prosecutors eventually decided to back away from a charge related to the rent.

To help Jody's prosecutors, I told Bo and the rest of the team to assemble a folder on the intent element — combing through every email for communications that might establish a criminal mind-set and saving the statements that showed a desire by the News to obtain a personal benefit.

At the end of a criminal case, the public often wants there to be a smoking gun. They want a text message where one conspirator says to another, "Let's steal that TANF money!" Real life is not the movies. Smoking guns usually don't exist. Instead, investigators need to piece together evidence, stacking the facts on top of one another to reach a conviction.

Those pieces of evidence can be small and independent but powerful in combination. WorldCom symbolized this. WorldCom was the crown jewel of Mississippi's economy in the late 1990s. It was a telecom company exploding in size, building palatial offices in Clinton, Mississippi, and attracting talented employees from around the Southeast to the state. At the heart of WorldCom was Mississippian Bernie Ebbers, a tall former hotel owner and basketball coach who sported a thick gray beard. He'd figured out how to grow a mom-and-pop long-distance phone company into a world beater by acquiring other mom-and-pop long-distance companies. By the time it became the second largest long-distance phone company in the world, WorldCom looked like Mississippi's ticket out of last place. Perhaps a booming telecom business could turn the state capital region into another Atlanta or Charlotte.

In 2002, the WorldCom house of cards came crashing down. At the time, the entire telecom industry was tanking. Markets were spooked over the idea that the industry had overbuilt and could not promise revenues to recoup the expenditures. And as famed investor Warren Buffett once said, "Only when the tide goes out do you discover who's been swimming naked."

Bernie had been swimming naked. As the market went

down, managers at WorldCom fraudulently classified some of their operating expenses as capital expenditures. They reported that some expenses, like leases, were actually capital assets. In doing so, the company misled investors about the strength of their finances. An internal auditor and certified fraud examiner (the same certification I held) named Cynthia Cooper discovered the misstatements.

Not long after, the Securities and Exchange Commission (SEC) made its case that WorldCom executives and Ebbers had engaged in fraud. Then authorities faced the perennial challenge: How do you prove that the misdeeds were intentional rather than a mistake? In particular, how do you prove Ebbers had knowledge of what was going on? He was benefiting from WorldCom's artificially inflated share price, but that alone wasn't enough. Ebbers maintained that he was clueless and, as a simple basketball coach, wasn't sophisticated enough to understand the financial machinations.

The proof of Ebbers's knowledge and intent — the evidence that contradicted his defense — came in the form of voicemails and interviews. For instance, SEC investigators captured a voicemail left by Scott Sullivan, WorldCom's CFO, for Ebbers. On the call, Sullivan told Ebbers that the "accounting fluff" they're doing is "disguising what is going on." Standing alone, one voicemail might not be enough to show intent. Combined with the riches Ebbers accrued off the stock price, the incentive Sullivan and Ebbers had to hide expenses, and all the other evidence, however, the message was enough to make charges against Ebbers stick. In 2005, Ebbers was convicted of fraud. WorldCom became the largest bankruptcy in US history at the time. Billions in value evaporated overnight.

Just like the Holmes and Ebbers cases, we saw no single piece of damning evidence at MCEC but instead puzzle pieces scattered all around. When we put the puzzle together, though, we could reach no other conclusion than that Nancy and Zach had intentionally misspent government money.

Stepping back from the puzzle, the case fit with some of the foundational academic research Dr. Donald Cressey had conducted on fraud. Born in 1919, Cressey weathered the Great

Depression as a boy and a world war as a young man. After serving in what was then called the Army Air Forces in World War II and seeing action in the Pacific, Cressey returned home to work as a professor. He was a man with a serious face, and even after leaving the service, he kept his hair closely shorn on the sides and a bit longer than a "high and tight" on top. In less than ten years, Cressey's PhD dissertation made him one of the country's leading thinkers on white-collar crime.

Cressey created a framework called the Fraud Triangle. According to the triangle, white-collar criminals typically have a "financial problem which is non-shareable," "are aware this problem can be secretly resolved by violation of the position of financial trust," and "are able to apply to their own conduct in that situation verbalizations" (justifications) for stealing.

First, fraudsters usually have an opportunity to steal. Their jobs put them in a position to be able to take someone else's cash or property. I always think of a cashier handling money and counting inventory at a small store when no one else is watching.

Second, fraudsters often have pressure on them. A fraudster might be living a lifestyle beyond what they can afford on their salary. Enron's CFO Andy Fastow comes to mind. He lived a lavish lifestyle and had to turn a simple gas pipeline company into a much more profitable energy finance company to maintain it. He achieved that goal by committing accounting fraud.

Third, fraudsters justify the theft to themselves. As state auditor, I'd heard all sorts of "verbalizations," as Cressey called them: "I deserve more than I make," "I was going to pay the money that I took back," "everyone does this," et cetera. The rationalizations allow the perpetrators to sleep at night and not face the idea that they have created victims.

I could see the Fraud Triangle at work when I looked at the DHS perpetrators. First, all the DHS culprits had the opportunity to steal. They had access to a mountain of cash in their

TANF bank account. The money was given to them up front — not on a reimbursement basis — so no one outside MCEC checked individual expenses before checks were cut. Because they were working together, Davis and the News could control the flow of money from beginning to end. John Davis could arrange for large grants to be given out. The News could spend the grants on anything as long as they also did whatever Davis wanted them to do, like spend it on Brett DiBiase. Davis also maintained an environment of fear at DHS for the staff who might consider crossing him, so no DHS employee dared ask questions.

The News had a need, too. Several members of their family were living off MCEC or New Learning Resources, and they wanted to maintain a certain level of luxury.

As for the "verbalizations" to justify the theft, I heard from enough people close to Nancy to know she satisfied this point. They parroted her when they said things like "She's really helped the state" and she "does so much good." In Nancy and Zach's minds, I imagined, their private school for dyslexic children was doing so much good that they deserved something beyond what is normally allowed. Once a rationalization that insidious plants itself in your brain, you can make and live with all sorts of immoral decisions.

In fact, Harvard professor Eugene Soltes, a modern successor to Cressey's white-collar research, observed this pattern. Soltes tracked down white-collar criminals after their prison sentences and interviewed them. His 2016 book, *Why They Do It*, describes how the criminals, even after admitting guilt in court, often still believed they'd done nothing wrong. Sure, they sounded contrite when they were being sentenced, but that was to obtain a shorter prison term. In reality, once someone intellectually justifies a theft, they will often go to their grave believing they should not have been punished.

And so, with all this swirling through my mind, I pondered the decision to arrest the DHS Six. I knew in my bones that if prosecutors presented the case to a grand jury, the grand jury would indict. But could the News hire a fantastic defense lawyer, probably using their TANF cash reserves, for trial? Yes. Once you have such an attorney, a guilty verdict is never guaranteed.

Lying in bed one night in January, I ran through the facts of the case with my wife once more. My wife, Rina, is a brilliant woman. She has degrees from the Wharton School at the University of Pennsylvania and Harvard Law School, made a perfect score on the law school admissions exam without much effort, and has advised the governor of Louisiana, her home state. She's also my closest confidante.

I told Rina that I could see a world where every Nancy connection — every donor she knew from the small circle that ran Mississippi; every famous athlete she'd befriended; every connection at every media company who'd been paid to run an MCEC advertisement; every attorney at every law firm she'd hired; every lobbyist she'd employed — all trained their fire on me. But I couldn't imagine a world where we let Nancy walk free after she'd misspent so much money intended to assist poor people. We had to arrest them and then trust the jury to understand the case, if it went to trial.

My mind wandered as we drifted off to sleep. I thought of the scene at the end of Martin Scorsese's film *The Departed*. In the movie, Leonardo DiCaprio plays an undercover cop inside the mob. He discovers that Matt Damon's character is a mob mole inside the Massachusetts State Police. DiCaprio confronts Damon on top of a building and puts him in handcuffs. Damon laughs at DiCaprio, saying that DiCaprio will never be able to explain a situation this complicated to a Suffolk County jury. To go undercover with the mob, DiCaprio forfeited his badge and even went to prison. Now he was arresting a decorated member of the state police because Damon was a plant. "I could give a [insert your favorite four-letter word] if the charges don't stick. I'm still [insert another four-letter word] arresting you," said DiCaprio.

My eyes closed knowing we were about to do the right thing, regardless of what it would do to my career. I had to stop speculating about whether every charge would stick. Jody was ready, so I should be ready. The DHS fraudsters needed to be arrested for what they had done.

"A nice woman"

During the frozen week of February 3, 2020, investigators from my office presented their case against John Davis, his aide Latimer Smith, Nancy New, Zach New, their accountant Anne McGrew, and Brett DiBiase to Jody's grand jury in Hinds County. The grand jury indicted all six.

When an indictment is handed down, the machinery of government goes into action. Paperwork goes to a court clerk. The clerk issues a capias — the document giving investigators the right to arrest the defendant. Investigators then take the capias and find the defendant.

On the morning of February 5, agents from my office executed their arrest plan. Later that morning, I walked down the street through crisp air to the governor's mansion. The new governor — Tate Reeves — and I were slated to have lunch, but unbeknown to him, I was also bearing the news of the arrests.

This was just my second substantive conversation ever with Governor Reeves. He was rosy-cheeked with a full head of blond hair as we sat facing each other across a table. His glasses and well-tailored suit gave the impression he might be more comfortable in his previous role as a financial adviser than as a politician.

"Governor, I can't provide a ton of details, but today my office is arresting several people," I said. "It's in connection with what we think may be the largest public fraud case in Mississippi history."

What did I get myself into? he must've thought. In the first few weeks of Reeves's time in office, a hundred-year flood soaked the capital city. Mississippi's prison system was in newspapers nearly every day for a series of tragic inmate deaths. He'd soon be handed a pandemic, too, though we had no sense in that moment what COVID-19 would mean for Mississippi, and the world, in a few short weeks. I told the governor that our case would rival the prison issue in terms of its need for his attention. He did not pry beyond what I told him, stating that he knew everyone in the Office of the State Auditor would do their jobs.

Not long after lunch, all of the DHS Six had been taken into custody. When Zach New was arrested, he dropped onto the ground, heaving. Jess New screamed obscenities at the agents who took his mother. Nancy moved slowly. She'd allegedly suffered a stroke a few weeks earlier, though the purported stroke hadn't robbed her of her fire. "Don't touch me!" she said to Jerry as he helped her into a cruiser. Davis turned himself in to the state prison in Raymond, Mississippi, without incident after he found out we were looking for him.

Reporter Anna Wolfe happened to be at one of Nancy's MCEC centers that day. It was open but uninhabited save for a janitor. A toy stuffed dog sat in the middle of a vacant room. Shelves for food giveaways for the hungry were barren except for a few cans of vegetables. On social media, Anna's pictures of the empty, worthless facility — a Potemkin village of services for the poor — were starkly juxtaposed against the mugshots of the defendants.

When Logan Reeves, my communications guru, posted the press release announcing the arrests, it hit Mississippi hard. Well-to-do Jacksonians who knew Nancy or Davis had suspected something was up for months, but the arrests still came as a surprise. The headlines screamed across the pages of the *New York Times* and other national publications. So much welfare money — more than $4 million at the time of the arrests — being misspent by residents of a state with such a high poverty rate was big news.

Some of the investigators became a little famous. The day after the arrest, Jerry and Michael walked into a soul food restaurant in Jackson. They were wearing polo shirts with the Office of the State Auditor logo on the front. When they entered the main dining area, patrons of the restaurant stood and gave them an ovation. It was probably the first and last time an auditor would get such a warm welcome.

By the day after the arrests, people in the media were clamoring for a press conference. I thought our press release told the story well, and my first plan was to issue the release without additional information. Reporters were asking more detailed questions, though. I came to realize that they, and the public, deserved to know more about what had happened. So, midmorning on February 6, I called Jody to propose a joint press conference. His staff was also fielding questions for which the public deserved answers. We called the press together outside his office in the February cold, flanked by his staff that same afternoon.

Just before heading over to the press conference, Mike Hurst, the US attorney, called. I could tell he was not pleased. He told me he was planning to put out a statement of his own.

"Why?" I asked.

"People are asking me about the case," he replied. I told Mike that people asked me all the time about other agencies' cases, including his cases. I didn't comment because they weren't my cases. I also didn't ever want to jeopardize their work by questioning it publicly.

Mike didn't care. "I'm going to issue a statement," he said again, and he ended the call.

Just before 1:00 PM, Mike sent me a draft of what he was going to say. It was asinine and unnecessary. He complained that his office had not been "contacted by the State Auditor or the Hinds County District Attorney about this investigation." This was not true. I'd told Mike a few days earlier about our plan: indict the DHS Six to quickly stanch the flood of TANF money to them, then work with the FBI and Mike's office to get to the bottom of everything else. He even acknowledged he had been told this later in his statement, contradicting himself.

But more damaging than that, Mike's statement implied that my team and Jody's prosecutors were incompetent. He accentuated how Jody and I were "new" at our jobs — saying it twice. Never mind that I'd been state auditor just nine months less than Mike had been US attorney. And never mind that my investigators had decades of experience.

I couldn't imagine a world in which I'd issue a press statement after Mike announced a case of his own. I also wouldn't publicly call into question his abilities. If I had, I'd have federal prosecutors and investigators at my door within minutes telling me I'd set them up for an acquittal of their defendant.

After reading his statement draft, I called Mike immediately. He wouldn't take the call. I told Mike as nicely as I could via text that his statement was defensive and would create problems. He didn't reply. Minutes later, Mike's statement went public. I hopped in Richie's F-150 and rode with him to Jody's office for the press conference, fuming.

On the way, I debated how to handle press questions about Mike. The public discussion should have been focused entirely on the theft of millions of TANF dollars in a poor state by a rich political donor, but I knew I would be asked about my reaction to what Mike had just said. Reporters love a good intra-party fight, and Mike had given them what they wanted.

Richie and Pat Dendy advised me not to spit fire back at Mike. That might draw attention to the content of what he said. It might even hurt our case. The public, and judges, were watching.

I knew they were right. When Jody and I took the podium in the middle of the gray, breezy afternoon, I bragged on the agents, told the world why the case mattered, and explained why I'd chosen to take the case to Jody. I knew if I took the case to Mike, federal authorities might do what they did to our education case from 2017: reinvestigate the matter themselves and take years to come to the same conclusions. All the while, money would be streaming to the News and not helping the poor.

One Mississippi reporter later wrote that maybe I'd just thought Jody would do a better job than Mike. That was true in the sense that I knew Jody's office would move faster than Mike could.

When I returned to my office, a senior member of the FBI in Jackson called me. She was livid with Mike. She didn't like that he had mentioned the FBI in his statement without telling the FBI beforehand. She was also angry that he had roped the FBI into his corner without her permission. She said she had called Mike and told him that. She apologized on behalf of the FBI. I told her she had nothing to apologize for, as it wasn't her statement.

After that, the bond between my office and the FBI became stronger. We would go on to work well together on a host of cases, some high-profile. Unfortunately, Mike's words exacerbated some long-standing tensions between him and the bureau. The rumors were that Mike had been directing FBI agents as if they worked for him, creating animosity with FBI bosses. To my understanding, those issues chilled the relationship between Mike and the FBI until the end of Mike's time as US attorney.

As for the DHS Six, they landed in jail and posted bail to go home. The following days were crucial. We would need to prepare as if trial could happen soon. We needed to organize our files (all twenty-nine thousand pages of them), turn them over to federal authorities, and start to work with them to see what other fraud schemes we could prove.

I also knew we'd have to weather some criticism. Nancy was popular among the moneyed community in Jackson. It's normal for folks in a community to doubt the validity of charges against someone they know, no matter how airtight the proof. The skepticism of her powerful friends posed its own set of risks for my office.

Not long after the arrests, a friend of mine who'd grown up in Jackson, had attended one of the elite private schools in town, and ran with the money crowd called me. He said he'd heard more than once that the auditor's office was just wrong about Nancy. The people in his circle cited no proof, of course. They'd just seen Nancy at PTA meetings and church and elsewhere her whole life, so she couldn't be a crook.

"What are you telling these people?" I asked.

"I'm telling them I've known Shad White since college," my friend replied. "If he and his office say something happened, you better believe they can back it up." I thanked him for defending us. But I knew he wouldn't be present for every conversation among the upper echelon of Mississippi society where my integrity would be questioned. We would have to counter all the influential naysayers in the next few months.

And most important, Stephanie Palmertree's team needed to finish their full audit of TANF money. This was the audit looking at all the ways DHS misspent or misallocated TANF funds under Davis, not just those schemes and transactions we could prove were criminal.

As her results came in, I called Stephanie into my office and asked her what I could expect.

Dressed in black attire befitting a funeral, she fixed me with a look of certitude and said, "It's beyond ugly."

The Welfare Game

The general welfare is a phrase that appears twice in the United States Constitution. It's in the Preamble, which states that promotion of the general welfare is one of the reasons the Constitution was written. It also surfaces in the section that gives Congress the right to tax and spend.

From the earliest days of the republic, there was debate about the extent of the grant of power conferred on Congress by that language. Some, like Alexander Hamilton, argued that the grant of power was wide. Congress should have the power to spend on any number of things, they argued, and this power should not be limited to items specifically mentioned in the Constitution. This is one reason lawmakers used the term *welfare* when they created expansive new government programs like AFDC, which later became TANF.

Some people today call a whole host of programs — from Social Security disability payments and food stamps to public housing and childcare assistance — welfare programs. The language has been stretched to justify programs the Framers of the Constitution could not have imagined.

My view of that language is different from those who have used it to justify new programs. One of the fundamental divides inside a democratic republic is the tension between a narrow, special interest and the general public. Well-organized, small groups of people — think about the association of professional engineers in a state, for example — will often try to bend public policy in ways that suit them. This is their right in our form of government. And it's not always a bad thing. The association of engineers might help non-engineer lawmakers write legislation that improves safety standards for engineering work.

But many times, the special interest contorts policy to its benefit in a way that hurts the public. A case I had when I practiced
law at the Mississippi Justice Institute comes to mind. My client
was an aspiring small businessman (weirdly, his name was also
Shad) who wanted to start a taxi company in Jackson. He didn't
have much money, but he saved enough to buy a single car.

The problem was that the existing cab companies in Jackson
had strong allies on the city council. The council wrote a series
of ordinances that made it nearly impossible for my client to
start his company. The ordinances required him to have at least
eight cabs in order to start a taxi service. He also had to have a
dispatcher on duty twenty-four hours a day and have an office
inside the city limits, among several other restrictions. The ordinances did nothing to advance the safety of taxis. They were
there to protect entrenched cab companies from competition.
In doing so, the general public had access to fewer cabs. They
also paid higher prices when they found one.

The shortage of cabs became so acute that Jackson's airport
could not find a cab company to accommodate customers in
a wheelchair. The airport feared that the federal government,
through the FAA, would withhold airport grants because there
weren't adequate transportation options for those customers.

Normal people don't have time to pay attention to these
sorts of regulations. They are busy raising children, going to
work, and paying bills. Doing away with the regs would benefit
them in small ways, like lower taxi fares, but their daily lives
are filled with matters more urgent than forcing the city council to change policies. So the Mississippi Justice Institute sued
the City of Jackson for our client. We ultimately lost the case.
Sometimes the only consolation when we fought battles like
this was that press coverage informed the public that city policy
was to blame for their long wait in the cab line or the high price
of that ride to the airport. Then those voters might hold the
elected officials accountable.

When I read the "general welfare" language in the Constitution, I think of this tension — the struggle between the small
group of influential power players and the larger group of people
disadvantaged by special treatment given to special interests.

Perhaps some of the Framers shared my view. In the essay Federalist No. 10, James Madison wrote about the dangers of powerful special interests. He called them factions, referring to those "who are united and actuated by some common impulse of passion, or of interest, adversed to the rights of other citizens." In the final analysis, Madison worried more about what happens when a faction becomes the majority in Congress and uses their control of a democracy to terrorize others. That is always a concern. But his analysis was incomplete. Factions can also be smaller groups. And those small groups can be dangerous, especially if they exercise deleterious power and cloak it from public view.

In light of this potential for small groups to capture large institutions, economists have tried to understand whether government is, on the whole, making the rich even richer or redistributing wealth downward. The government takes in money from its citizens, by and large in the form of taxes, and then gives it to the poor via various programs. Theoretically, our tax code, with income taxes at its heart, is designed to tax people according to how much they make. But government has simultaneously created countless loopholes for those taxes and imposed myriad regulations on businesses. The biggest corporations with the best lawyers and accountants to navigate and take advantage of all this are the ones that benefit the most from the growth of government.

So where does the ledger come out? In their book, *The Captured Economy*, Brink Lindsey and Steven Teles of Johns Hopkins University argue that, in the end, government helps the powerful, mainly through regulations that protect existing businesses, subsidies for big banks, land-use restrictions, and other mechanisms.

I tend to think they're right. I also think this is why the Framers put language about the "general welfare" front and center in the Constitution. It's an in-your-face reminder that our government should guard against the predations of a powerful minority.

While the Lindsey/Teles research is compelling, I'll admit I agree with them in part because their conclusion was baked into my bones from an early age. Much of my personal political philosophy comes from my maternal grandfather, Papa.

My mom called Papa a "crusty old oil hand," but she meant it in the nicest of ways. He had rough skin all over, tanned from a life spent working in the sun, first in the army and then in the red clay of Mississippi's oil fields. Every day of the week he wore a blue uniform — literally a blue collar — and would "tangle" with an oil pump, as he said. As a boy, I spent every weekend with him. I still remember riding in his rusty pickup with a ROSS PEROT sticker on the front and listening to his concerns about the country. For Papa, politics was not to be understood as a battle of big-government advocates versus small-government advocates. Instead it was a struggle between the rich and connected versus the rest of us.

The words *general welfare* remind me of the responsibility of elected officials to work on behalf of the quiet masses — the rest of us. It's the reason I wanted to be state auditor. No other position, in my mind, could do more to lift the fortunes of the public against the strong. The auditor could find corrupt politicians who had rigged an office to benefit themselves personally. He could find wasted taxpayer dollars that did nothing to benefit the men and women who gave the government some of their paychecks each month. He could challenge large corporations that took public money in violation of a law. It was a small way to address my grandfather's concerns.

My first face-off with a powerful company came early in my time as auditor. The company was one of a few pharmacy benefit managers operating in the United States. Pharmacy benefit managers (PBMs) are businesses hired by health plans to manage the plans' prescription drug programs. PBMs are paid to send the payments from a health plan, like your insurance company, to a retail pharmacy when you fill a prescription. The idea is that the money pays the retail pharmacy for the cost of the pill, and the PBM takes a portion of the money given to it from the health plan. Their portion pays for the PBM's costs of handling the payment.

PBMs had amassed amazing wealth in that middleman role. Using complex contracts and hiding behind a wall of subsidiary companies, their profits spiked as Americans spent more and more on prescription drugs. Then came consolidation. The biggest PBMs bought their smaller competitors. By 2021, just three PBMs controlled more than 80 percent of the pharmacy benefit business in the United States.

One of the biggest companies in the PBM game was Centene, a Fortune 50 company. Centene had extensive political influence. They gave more than $200,000 to Governor Reeves's campaign and tens of thousands of dollars to Mississippi lawmakers like the Speaker of the Mississippi House and the lieutenant governor. They also gave hundreds of thousands to President Joe Biden — more than five times what they'd given to President Trump. Crossing Centene meant that your opponent in your campaign was going to have money in their coffers.

In Mississippi, Centene inked a lucrative contract with the state's Medicaid program. Centene, in turn, owned a PBM called Envolve, which they used to manage prescription drug payments for Mississippi Medicaid beneficiaries. To understand how their services worked, imagine that a Medicaid patient walks into a pharmacy to fill a prescription. The patient might pay $3 or so for the drug to the retail pharmacy. The rest of the cost of the pills has to be paid by Medicaid. In order to be paid, the retail pharmacy would tell Envolve (the PBM) that they needed to be reimbursed. The PBM would then bill its parent company, and the parent company would charge a per-patient fee to Medicaid — the taxpayers — for these costs.

In 2018, Ohio's state auditor investigated Centene and found they were bilking Ohio's Medicaid program. As soon as I read the Ohio report, I started looking for Medicaid experts I could hire. I wanted to see if Centene was doing something similar in Mississippi.

By April 2019, I landed a deal with the same data analysts who worked for Ohio's auditor. Many months and meetings later, they reached a conclusion: Centene's PBM was overcharging for drugs. The prices they were allowed to charge were limited by Centene's contract with Medicaid, and the PBM had exceeded those price ceilings. Unfortunately, because the overbilling was happening through payments made from Centene to its own PBM, no one was aware of the overpayments. Medicaid staffers could not see bills being paid from one arm of Centene to another. Centene could pass the cost of that overbilling on to Mississippi taxpayers by charging Medicaid higher per-person fees if they wanted.

In late 2020, I, along with Attorney General Lynn Fitch — whose team would have to litigate against Centene if Centene chose to fight our findings in court — told Governor Reeves and his Medicaid director what we'd found. Governor Reeves and Medicaid director Drew Snyder pledged to be helpful in getting to the bottom of the matter.

A group of attorneys hired by the state then began negotiating with Centene. By June 2021, they reached a breakthrough. Centene was ready to settle with Mississippi and Ohio. They were also willing to put into place transparency measures to ensure the overbilling never happened again. The negotiating attorneys accepted the deal, and Centene paid Mississippi more than $55 million. The agreement represented the largest civil settlement following an investigation by the Office of the State Auditor in Mississippi history.

The *Wall Street Journal* covered the breaking news about the Centene settlement. I told Mississippians that I didn't care how big or powerful a company was. Mississippi taxpayers deserved a square deal when the state spent money on prescription drugs.

Like the PBM investigation, the DHS case would become another example of stopping the powerful in their tracks. Nancy and her son, along with some influential friends, realized they could milk their connections to get rich at taxpayers' expense as well as at the expense of the people who should have been served by the program. The News could put their hands in the till because the general public had no way of knowing what was going on behind the high-security, closed doors at DHS. Just like the patrons waiting on a cab in Jackson or the elderly woman struggling to afford her prescription drugs, the public was getting hosed and didn't even know it.

The Peddlers

Over the weekend after the arrests, I heard rumblings about a second round of news stories that might be written. Some reporters were latching onto Mike Hurst's comments. I heard that one reporter might suggest I'd hidden the case from federal authorities on purpose.

The rumors angered me all over again. I could damn well send my case to any prosecutor I pleased, as long as they had jurisdiction. Allegedly, Mike was implying to others that I'd kept the feds in the dark to protect other, more important people, like Governor Bryant, from being investigated. I had no idea if Mike was actually saying this, but people would have to be dumber than a bucket of nails to believe it. If I wanted to engage in a cover-up to protect Bryant, why would I even make the case public at all? If I wanted a prosecutor who would go easy on Governor Bryant's allies and not ask questions about anyone higher up, why would I give the case to Jody Owens, a Democrat?

Tensions naturally occur between law enforcement offices in a big case. One of Mike's predecessors, a former US attorney for the Southern District of Mississippi, fought over who would litigate the WorldCom case with the US attorney from the Southern District of New York, for example, in the 2000s. But questioning the integrity of your colleagues — publicly and without basis — is going too far.

I decided to cut the head off the Bryant conspiracy theory in one fell swoop. On Sunday, February 9, I publicly announced we would take our case file on an external hard drive to the FBI that week. I would also brief Michelle Sutphin, the head of the FBI office in Jackson. The FBI could fully investigate the matter and reach their own conclusions. We would help in any way possible and give them access to everything we had.

That weekend I also publicly called on DHS to hire an outside CPA firm to do a comprehensive audit of all of John Davis's TANF spending. This was the same forensic audit I'd asked DHS directors to do since my first awkward meeting with Davis. All of them, from Davis to Freeze to Black, had refused.

Put differently, I was recommending that DHS hire a private CPA firm to check our work. That would be a third independent set of eyes — us, the FBI, and a CPA firm — to plumb the depths of the case. Interim DHS director Jacob Black would never do it, perhaps because he'd been there during the misspending. But I'd made my point. I wanted everyone who'd done anything illegal to be caught and sent to prison. I was not pulling any punches.

On Monday morning, Richie and our DHS investigation team loaded into SUVs and trucks and took the case file to the FBI's Jackson office. I went with them and presented to Michelle and her fellow agent Steve Chambers. They were impressed with our work and proposed a joint team composed of the FBI, the Office of the Inspector General (OIG, a federal entity that looked for abuse of government programs), and my office. I agreed. We left the files with them and went on our way.

After my announcement about taking the case to the FBI, Mike asked for a briefing, too. My agents were angry at Mike because of his comments. Some even suggested that we not brief him. They felt he had questioned their work unfairly. In their minds, we only needed to cooperate with the FBI, not Mike. The FBI could check our work, investigate other potential perpetrators if they wanted, and *then*, if *the FBI*, as federal investigators, wanted to take the case to Mike, the federal prosecutor, they could do so.

I vetoed my team. Despite my frustration with Mike, I wanted to show our case to anyone with appropriate authority. If we didn't brief him, it would give Mike another reason to complain and to inject himself into every press story about the case when the focus should be on what had happened to the money.

On a Monday afternoon, Richie, Bo, and I drove to the federal courthouse where Mike's offices were located for a prearranged meeting. We walked in to his lobby, filled with people in dark suits and ties who were there to represent the OIG; the Department of Health and Human Services in Washington, DC; the FBI; and the other US attorney's office in the state in North Mississippi. I was glad to see so many people. It would save us the trouble of presenting our findings to them separately and give everyone a chance to look at the case at once.

As we were waiting in the lobby for the meeting to begin, Mike's assistant asked me to step inside for a private meeting with Mike. I followed her to Mike's office to find Chad Lamar, the North Mississippi US attorney, also waiting with him.

Mike sat up tall behind his desk, a giant American flag pinned on the wall next to him. As I sat in the chair in front of him, I sank down in its upholstery to what felt like a foot below the height of Mike's desk chair.

"Yeah, sorry about the chair," he said.

Mike aired his grievances about the DHS matter. I told him I already understood that he'd wanted the case, and, for Chad's benefit, I explained my logic for taking the first findings to Jody. Mike started asking me yes-or-no questions about whether I'd taken the case to the FBI. He was obviously angry at both me and the FBI. I imagined the anger at the FBI was driven in part by the call where the senior FBI agent had admonished Mike for his press release. There were rumors that FBI agents made complaints directly to the Department of Justice higher-ups in DC about Mike, too.

Mike's yes-or-no questions were part of an old prosecutor tactic when cross-examining a witness. I'd crossed people myself, so it wasn't foreign to me. But it was not how you treat a colleague. When Mike was done with the little routine that I figured he'd practiced in the mirror that morning, he closed by saying he'd called this meeting because he wanted to handle all this face-to-face. "Like men," he said. I laughed, because a few days prior his manliness hadn't given him the courage to answer my phone call when he'd sent me his draft press statement.

Chad was uncomfortable the entire time. It must have felt

to him like he was the dinner guest at a home where the host couple started fighting in front of him.

Mike then accused me of ruining some of Chad's cases because we'd already interviewed and arrested the DHS Six. Mike said Chad had similar investigations going.

Now Mike was asking the dinner guest to take a side in the argument. If Chad had similar schemes his team was trying to uncover, this was news to me. I looked at Chad as if to ask if Mike's statements about his ongoing investigations were true. Chad's eyes darted down below his glasses, and he said, "Well, um, those are really just some civil matters we were looking at." Mike cut him off to avoid losing the point and then closed the meeting. For the rest of Chad's time as US attorney, he never filed any of those chimerical charges, or even a civil complaint, related to DHS or TANF. He never claimed we'd in any way impeded something he'd been working on. I think Mike just made it up.

At that point, I was hot. Mike's attempt at a good-cop-bad-cop routine was childish and ineffective because Chad hadn't played along. We walked into the larger meeting from Mike's office. On the way down the hall, Chad tried to smooth over what had happened with small talk, asking me where I was from. I didn't feel like discussing my family tree at the time and gave him a curt response.

We walked back into the larger conference room. The various law enforcement teams were spread out in the windowless space. At the center of the room, a horseshoe of gray tables was reserved for my team, Mike's prosecutors, and the FBI. The remaining agents or lawyers sat farther back, off the main table.

I sat beside Bo Howard, who could see anger in my eyes. I was ready to tell the room what a clown show the pre-meeting had been, but I kept my mouth shut out of respect for everyone's time. They came to hear about the case, not Mike's behavior.

Once we settled in, Bo set out the DHS case in broad strokes. Pens scribbled on legal pads around the room as he spoke. When Bo was done, I jumped in. I made it clear that one of the primary reasons I took the case to state court was that I knew the prosecutors could move faster, indict these individuals, and cut off the money. I meant no disrespect to the feds. But I could not, in good conscience, go on watching the fraud.

I also knew the public would not forgive me if I sat on clear criminal findings and waited for the feds to do something. I didn't mention it in that meeting, but a few years prior, the previous state auditor was criticized for doing just that, not just once, but twice. The former auditor learned of corruption at the Mississippi Department of Marine Resources. When a local newspaper realized the auditor was investigating, they filed a public records request and asked for the investigative file. The auditor's office then tried to turn the file over to the feds while simultaneously refusing the paper's request. The paper sued for the documents, took the case all the way to the Mississippi Supreme Court, and won.

As the court case about the records was litigated, the newspaper criticized the auditor. The public was left believing that, at worst, the auditor was trying to cover for the politically influential head of the marine resources department. At best, they thought he was trying to pass the buck to federal authorities and not do his job.

A similar scenario also played out at the Mississippi Department of Corrections during my predecessor's tenure. The head of the department was caught in a kickback scandal. The feds prosecuted it, and the public said the feds were forced to come in to do the work the state auditor's office failed to do. I knew the team at the auditor's office back then, before I'd arrived, had helped on the case, so the criticism wasn't entirely fair. But helping the feds wasn't enough. Taxpayers expected the state auditor to lead, not just follow. I wasn't going to put myself in a position where I looked like I was asleep at the wheel.

At some point in the meeting, after our presentation, Mike leaned forward for his only real comment of the day. Elbows on the table, his head craned toward the middle of the room. "You mean to say we [federal authorities] could not have cut off the money, too?" he asked. Before I could reply, an HHS investigator from the back of the room, someone I'd never met, chimed in.

"We're terrible at cutting money off," the HHS rep said.

Everyone turned in their chairs to look at him. The HHS investigator gave an example of a case where he'd investigated someone and even indicted them but they still drew down taxpayer cash up to their trial date. He'd just proved my point. Mike stared at the investigator, shooting daggers with his eyes, and never brought it up again.

The big meeting ended. Mike shook hands around the room like he was running for mayor and left out of a side door. An assistant US attorney walked over to me and said, "Sorry about . . . all that," looking in Mike's direction. I told him not to sweat it, because I didn't. He congratulated my agents on their work, and we left.

🎙️

A week later, I stood up from the wooden pew at church and started gathering my daughter's things, fumbling to grab a burp cloth on the floor, a half-drunk bottle, and a stuffed goat. As the organ music faded, a woman in the pew in front of me caught sight of me.

"You're the state auditor," she said.

"Yes, ma'am."

"That Zach New arrest . . ." She paused, and her eyes narrowed. "He's a good boy. And you are wrong." I finished scooping up my one-year-old and headed for the aisle.

This was my first taste of the social and political pressure triggered by the DHS case.

After the arrests of the DHS Six, DHS was forced to cut off funds not only to Nancy's MCEC but also to a separate, similar nonprofit in North Mississippi, the Family Resource Center. MCEC and FRC had been the two biggest grantees of TANF money during Davis's tenure. And they had friends.

We knew FRC, run by a woman named Christi Webb, did some good work. They provided documents to us about actual, needy Mississippians helped by some of their services. Judges sometimes ordered FRC to provide resources for indigent children in cases that came before the court, for instance. But we also knew that any grant money handed out by John Davis could have come with some of his strings attached. Evidence we gathered at MCEC showed Davis had a penchant for demanding that money be spent to his liking, whether it was legal or not.

When DHS cut off money to FRC, FRC put its political connections to work. FRC must've told everyone I was standing in the way of their funding and asked their allies to call me. Those allies included a number of politicians, legislators, and the occasional congressional staffer asking for the money to be turned back on — even after the news about the DHS scandal was made public. I asked these callers, "You know we've made multiple arrests, right? You know it's all still under investigation? And FRC could be implicated? And you still want me to call for funding to be turned on for them?"

Plenty of those callers didn't seem to care about fraud allegations. They wanted money going to their friends. Perhaps they'd seen FRC do good work in the community and felt morally compelled to ask for the funding to be restored. Two things can be true at once, though: FRC could have been doing some good work, and some of the money could have also been wasted or stolen. We already knew at that point that FRC paid some questionable travel costs for the DiBiases, for example.

Others continued to claim that both the News and Webb were good people who couldn't have done anything wrong. It boggled my mind how people could trust so easily. Being cordial to others at a dinner party did not mean one was honest.

One day in the middle of the week, I stopped by my wife's workplace to take her on a lunch date. A receptionist out front stopped me and asked about the Nancy New case. When I finished giving her a quick update, the receptionist paused, as if she'd been waiting for the chance to tell me what was next. "Nancy is just a great Christian woman," she said.

The evidence I'd just taken the time to share with her didn't matter. "Well, Nancy's accused of stealing from the welfare fund," I said flatly.

"She's a great Christian woman," the receptionist insisted, confident. I turned and walked away.

And more calls came. Beyond the willful ignorance around the case, I sensed the real reason for some of the calls was a primal desire to wield influence. People just liked the idea of making a well-placed request and telling their friends they'd changed something. It was strange. If I'd made calls like that, I would wonder every time I looked in the mirror if I'd just asked someone to give money to fraudsters. The hubris it took for callers to assume they knew better than a criminal investigator, who had more facts at his fingertips, was incredible.

I just ignored these influence peddlers. I would do my job, even if they badmouthed me at the local Rotary Club. The truth was that I couldn't afford to care about what people said. In the words of my friend John Dougall, the state auditor of Utah, "Sometimes the state auditor has to be the skunk at the party."

Truth be told, I'd already been primed to ignore this yammering. In my first year at law school, as everyone was getting to know one another, a group of us were invited to a classmate's apartment in Cambridge to watch a baseball game. At the party, the host spent most of the game talking about how much he despised the United States. It was baffling to me. Coming from a rural community in the middle of nowhere, I felt lucky to be admitted to any law school, let alone Harvard. We must live in one of the greatest countries in the world if my admission to Harvard was possible.

After several innings, I was sick of the diatribe. When he took a breath, I said to the host, "Yeah, I agree with you. We'd be much better off living in North Korea or Iran. Things are looking up over there right now." He glared at me. I suppose I'd shot my chance at being popular in the room. But what the people there said about me afterward just didn't matter (though I wasn't invited back for any more baseball games).

During the DHS investigation, I started to take a strange pride in telling people no. I recoiled at being called and asked in good-ole-boy fashion to "handle that case quietly." Those requests flew in the face of the need for public transparency. Many of these people spent a lifetime assuming their relationships could trump the law or what was right. It was why Nancy cozied up to famous people and why Davis sought to please anyone with influence.

I often wondered if this internal drive to say no was generational. At thirty-four, I was considerably younger than most of the people pressuring me. Maybe, in a previous era, deals were done behind closed doors. By contrast, folks my age, in the social media generation — where people put videos from inside their homes online for strangers to see — expected a clearer look into how decisions were made. Transparency was my generation's watchword. And it didn't matter if the decision in question was a local government picking the vendor for the garbage collection contract or a giant tech company adjudicating which posts to allow on their platform. We wanted to know why powerful people made the choices they made.

Around this same time, my staff found out that Apple, the large tech company, was telling school districts around the state that Apple computer products were not subject to traditional procurement laws. The issue became heated at a conference of school district employees. An attorney in my office was speaking to the conference about purchasing regulations, and an Apple sales representative stood up to claim that my attorney was wrong. She said Apple's products were "sole source" and did not have to compete against other similar products when districts were buying.

My staff had never encountered a company so brazenly ignoring the law and telling others to do the same. I'd read stories about an Ohio school superintendent who was so fed up with Apple's bullying that he took them on. He complained that Apple would not let his district buy Apple products from a third party, like Best Buy, even though the products were cheaper at Best Buy. It seemed that the Apple strong-arm tactics had come to Mississippi, too.

I told my staff to arrange a meeting among my attorney who was presenting at the conference, my leading school auditors, Apple, and me. A corporate officer from Apple flew to my office several days later. I'd seen his type before. He had the affect of some of my more polished law school classmates who seemed destined for Palo Alto or Wall Street.

The Apple rep started by explaining that Apple was a sole source provider of technology, regardless of what we believed. My lawyer countered that *sole source* was defined in Mississippi law, and that, by law, a brand cannot be a sole source. Apple could not sidestep standard purchasing law just by saying the magical incantation "We're Apple." They needed to compete against other computer providers, just like a Ford dealer would have to compete against Chevy if a local government was buying a car.

I could tell the rep was used to getting his way. As the largest company in the world, and given all the campaign donations Apple handed out, who could blame him? He looked at me and asked if it would help if his lawyers sent a letter explaining why Apple was sole source — a subtle threat. I told him I didn't think his California lawyers knew Mississippi law better than my lawyers. It was the state auditor's job to understand laws like this, and we didn't need Apple to read the statutes for us. Apple needed to comply with purchasing law to make sure Mississippi taxpayers got the best bang for their buck. With that, and a little more small talk, the Apple folks left unhappy.

A few weeks later, a lobbyist called me and said Apple was attempting to hire him. He said their pitch to the lobbyist was that they needed help reining in the new state auditor. To his credit, the lobbyist told him that was a bad idea. If that was the task, he didn't want the work.

I would see echoes of this tactic over and over in my job. I saw how the fear of being removed from a job pushed other elected officials to cave to people with deep pockets or extensive political connections. My first thought, though, was not about keeping my job. It was about what my grandfather would think if I acquiesced. Papa would have told me that if I were willing to bend the knee to a person with power and ignore what was right, I didn't deserve to be in this role in the first place.

CHAPTER NINE

The Audit

The City of Jackson was carved out of the wilderness to be Mississippi's capital in the nineteenth century. Over its life, Jackson lived in a cycle of potential and optimism followed by destruction and disappointment. The early explorers, sent by state lawmakers to find a suitable site for the state capital, wrote of a place with clear water and plenty of timber. Men and saws went to work, slicing through the forest and building a town where no settlement existed before.

The enthusiasm of those early days ended with the Civil War. General Tecumseh Sherman and his Union army liberated enslaved people but blazed a path across the South, burning most of Jackson to the ground. When the fires were squelched, bystanders said the only things left standing were the chimneys. Jackson took on its permanent moniker: Chimneyville.

That rhythm of hope and decline would repeat itself. Reconstruction gave way to Jim Crow. Industrialization morphed into urban chaos. Brilliant writers and musicians produced world-renowned art, all while the common schools for the public collapsed.

Black Mississippians fought for and won key victories on the streets of Jackson during the civil rights movement. After some time, Mississippi had more Black elected officials than any other state in the country. Jackson elected its first Black mayor in 1997. The city gobbled up surrounding areas via annexation.

But then policy mistakes of the late twentieth and early twenty-first centuries pushed the city to the precipice. Jackson expanded too quickly, assuming responsibility for policing and providing services for too much geography. Between 1960 and 2020, the city tripled in size while only adding 6 percent in population. Its revenue increased from 2000 to 2020 — but not fast enough to service all the pipes and infrastructure needs it'd accumulated. Jackson's city government failed to collect water bills from all its dispersed customers. By 2022, the national media was reporting on unsafe drinking water and residents unable to flush their toilets for lack of water pressure.

Simultaneously, the consequences of years of societal collapse and the breakdown of families came to town. In 2021 and 2022, Jackson was the per-capita homicide capital of the United States among major metropolitan areas. Police were stretched to the limit, patrolling too much ground. The force was understaffed by nearly a hundred officers, according to the police chief. The future wasn't promising, either. Jackson's public schools were among the worst in the country and were filled with children coming from turbulent homes and dangerous neighborhoods.

In the city bearing the weight of this history, Stephanie Palmertree walked into my office looking sleep-deprived. She came to tell me what had happened to the welfare funds that should have been used to alleviate the pain of Jackson's, and Mississippi's, poor.

I knew that having a new small child at home was wearing on Stephanie, but the more likely reason for her fatigue was her DHS audit. For months, while the criminal investigators built their cases, she'd quarterbacked a more comprehensive look at DHS spending. Her team of auditors spent that time stuffed into cubicles and in front of their computer screens, deciphering expenditure after expenditure.

Early in the audit, Stephanie and her team realized that the documents they needed for the audit did not exist at DHS. The invoices, the contracts, and all the other paperwork necessary to review the massive amount of TANF spending mostly lived at the offices of the grantees who received the money, like MCEC. So they started gathering. They visited MCEC, FRC, and the other nonprofits to pull whatever documents the nonprofits were willing to give them. Those core documents would serve as the basis for what Stephanie's team discovered over the next few months.

Those months were grueling. The auditors rifled through transactions, half-baked contracts with insufficient details, emails, and everything in between to try to determine how TANF money was being handled.

With each passing week, Stephanie's conclusions mirrored those reached by Richie's criminal investigators: There'd been a disgusting amount of waste and theft.

Now Stephanie was bringing me a first look at her report. She dropped into the chair in front of me and handed me her summary. I put my nose between the papers, scanning quickly.

"This is insane," I said, thumbing through the findings.

"I've never seen anything like it," she said.

A term that recurred throughout the summary was *questioned costs*. Anytime Stephanie's team audited federal spending, the audit format they used — a format dictated by the federal government — required her team to identify such questioned costs, which were expenditures that at least *looked* to be illegal. Perhaps they were done without proper documentation, for example. If there were doubts about whether an expenditure was legal, our team flagged it as a questioned cost and moved on.

"People are going to be livid when they read this," I said. She agreed and said they'd need more time to conclude their work. "When will it be finished?" I asked.

"I'm thinking the end of April. That's our goal," she replied.

I told her to take whatever time her team needed. "Some of what you're seeing is probably going to come out before then, though," I said.

It was obvious from reading the newspaper every day that, after the arrests, reporters were turning over every rock to see what they could learn about DHS's spending habits. Journalist Anna Wolfe redoubled her efforts to cover what happened. Right on her heels was another young, intrepid reporter in town named Giacomo "Jack" Bologna.

We didn't have to wait long for reporters' efforts to bear fruit. In March 2020, they gave the public a sneak preview of what Stephanie's team was seeing in their work. That month, Jack won the lottery with one of his public records requests to DHS. DHS sent him — I think inadvertently — a spreadsheet showing how MCEC claimed they were spending money.

The spreadsheet was a gold mine. MCEC was spending

welfare money on items that didn't pass the smell test. Thousands were spent on salaries and travel for the DiBiases, including multiple trips to the Royal Sonesta, a hotel in the French Quarter of New Orleans with a rooftop pool. There were $400 visits to steak houses. Christian rock musician Jason Crabb earned $85,000 for playing concerts (along with the security and hotel stay that Crabb required) and for thousands of copies of his children's book. And there were also the "grants" to Nancy's private company, New Learning Resources, and the hundreds of thousands in rent paid in TANF dollars to the News.

Across town, Anna was not pleased. She called my office, seething.

"*Where did Jack get this?*" she asked.

Her first instinct was not happiness that the truth about TANF spending had finally found the light of day. Instead she was angry that the scoop hadn't been hers. Beneath the truth-teller veneer there was a competitive journalist muscling for clicks.

By May it was Stephanie and her team's turn to show their work. The topline fact was simple and crashed in like a spiked brick: DHS had likely misspent or wasted $98 million in the past three years. No one in my office could remember a previous audit finding that big.

The first and most galling finding from the audit was the waste that had landed in the News' pockets. Richie's team had already told the world about the News' investment in the concussion treatment company and their moving money to New Learning Resources, a private business that ran a private school. Stephanie's audit put new light on other rivulets flowing to the News. Taxpayers were now told that TANF had been used to buy three vehicles valued at more than $50,000 each for Nancy, Zach, and Jess New. Jess was the executive director of the Mississippi State Oil and Gas Board, a small but important state agency. Welfare funds even paid for a speeding ticket Nancy earned zipping around in her expensive ride.

Our audit went into greater detail, too, about how taxpayer money made its way from MCEC to New Learning Resources and then to the News' pockets. Money was constantly moving back and forth from the MCEC account that received government funds and the New Learning account. Those cash moves from MCEC to New Learning were coded with misleading labels like "Amex," even though the actual checks for the transfer would be to New Learning Resources. Once the money was washed through the New Learning account, the News apparently felt free to do what they wanted with it.

The most egregious example was the check for Nancy's 1800 Sheffield Drive home. Nestled between lush oaks and pines, the house sat just down the street from one of Jackson's most expensive private schools, where Nancy's grandchildren attended. The signs of a world isolated from the rest of Jackson's challenges were all around. Private security. A gated park. Nancy's son Jess around the corner, with his brick Georgian home and a child's swing hanging from an oak branch in the front.

In another instance of personal gain, Zach New and a New employee took out a loan against their retirement funds. The other employee had to repay the loan with money from his paycheck every month. But Zach pulled money from MCEC's TANF bank account to make his retirement fund whole. Zach treated the welfare account like it was his own.

Disguising transfers of money with false accounting entries was a theme. For instance, MCEC originally typed into their books that the source of money for the Prevacus concussion investment was TANF, which was accurate. When auditors asked for the documents for that payment, though, MCEC went frantic. They changed the source of money in their accounting software to "Bingo." We could tell the timing of entries based on keystroke information stored in the accounting software. "Bingo" was a reference to a charity bingo parlor in North Mississippi that occasionally sent money to MCEC. The change to the books to hide the source of money didn't change the truth of who paid for the investment, however. Taxpayers paid for it.

Then there were the salaries. Nancy, Zach, Jess, Zach's wife, and Jess's wife each drew a salary from MCEC, often paid out of taxpayer funds. MCEC also paid for an iPhone and data for each of them, along with an iPad with data for Nancy and two iPads with data for Zach.

How did we fail to see this as a state? I wondered. Nancy and her family were living borderline extravagant lives. She was sitting on boards with the wealthy, driving nice cars, living in nice houses, handing out donations to charities and politicians all around town, and allegedly even acquiring a private box at the University of Southern Mississippi's football stadium. No one — or at least no one who had bothered to approach the auditor's office — stopped to question how she could afford all this.

Nancy's case reminded me of another well-known fraudster, Rita Crundwell. Crundwell was famous because she'd orchestrated maybe the largest municipal fraud in US history. She was the comptroller of tiny Dixon, Illinois — population sixteen thousand — and stole $53 million from them. When Crundwell's theft was discovered in 2012, observers around the country wondered how a woman who should have been making less than $100,000 a year could embezzle and spend $53 million without drawing suspicion. Crundwell had purchased a massive ranch and expensive show horses all in plain sight.

Crundwell evaded questions about how she obtained her money by saying she'd once had a boyfriend who became sick and then left her the money. That was all it took. The public looked the other way.

In Nancy's case, the entire state — the political class, leaders around town, people who worked with her — looked the other way, too.

I saw Nancy's ability to get away with it all as an example of what is called the king's pass. This is a form of rationalization. A person like Nancy convinces herself that she is doing important work and the importance of this work justifies whatever minor indiscretions she may commit. Others around her may have come to similar conclusions. If Nancy is helping children with disabilities, who were you to question what she drove? The dark irony was that Nancy had done little good with the welfare money she'd spent.

Stephanie's audit also showed that the News spread money so widely around town that it was in plenty of folks' best interest to not question it. Charity after charity — from the American Heart Association to a local library — received donations from Nancy.

Local high school bands, education foundations, the Mississippi Military Relief Fund, the Junior League of Jackson, the National Guard Association, a cross-country booster club, beauty pageants, meals for the highway patrol, a group of cheerleaders — you name it, and Nancy donated to it with welfare money. If you were on the board of one of those cash-strapped philanthropies, why question how Nancy obtained the money? And Nancy made appearances at all sorts of events around town, and seemed to be trusted by plenty of good, influential people, so how could her wealth be stolen?

In a small way, this brought to mind the Sacklers, the family who fleeced America by pushing opioids through their company, Purdue Pharma. They used their riches to put their names on buildings throughout the United States and around the world, from the University of Oxford in England to the Louvre in Paris. Their over-the-top donations bought praise, access, and a chance to legacy build. It was all paid for with the lives of addicted Americans. Nancy's largesse was paid for with tax dollars and forgone services to the poor.

In addition to their donations, another reason the News were so influential was that they spent money on direct political persuasion. MCEC paid hundreds of thousands of welfare dollars to high-priced lobbyists in town. Many had deep connections to state legislators. One *was* a former legislator. The lobbyists did what they were paid to do and worked every room of politicians. MCEC pulled down millions in welfare funds, with even more funding directly appropriated to them by the legislature, despite little experience managing antipoverty programs. The truth was that the lobbyists had no clue — or were willfully ignorant — of the fact that so few people were helped.

I also viewed the payments to lobbyists and politicians — along with the lawyers from at least four of the largest firms in the state — as a form of insurance. The News were buying cover in the event that someone questioned what they were doing. The biggest corporations in Jackson, like utility companies, didn't keep four of the ten biggest law firms in the state on contract. But Nancy did. Even years after my office arrested Nancy, the occasional big-firm lawyer would murmur in my ear that they didn't think Nancy was all that bad. She was signing the welfare checks over to them, after all.

Capital cities around the country are built on a foundation of influence and power. Jackson was no exception. But our culture of influencers lived — thrived — inside a city buckling under its own mismanagement and, as we learned with the DHS case, corruption. The state's capitol building sat across Mississippi Street from a church that ministered to the homeless. It was painful to think of one of Nancy's hired guns pushing a lawmaker to cut another check to her across the street from a soup kitchen filled to the brim.

Doling out welfare money in the way Nancy did was downright Machiavellian. I suspected, though, that there was a more vapid explanation, too. Nancy just liked being in the limelight. She took pictures all over town at charity events, handing out cash. She clearly enjoyed rubbing elbows with the governor's family or a famous athlete. Free-flowing money gave her the ability to do that.

This wasn't novel. Other infamous fraudsters were so motivated by cavorting with fame that that banal act became the real reason for stealing in the first place. Jho Low, the thief behind the heist of Malaysia's state-owned economic development fund, used the billions he stole to pal around with Leonardo DiCaprio and Kanye West. Money was a powerful motivator, but for some, the chance to befriend stars was just as intoxicating.

And one frequent domain, full of celebrities, where Nancy's free-flowing money landed was sports. We already knew from Richie's work that Brett Favre moved in the same circles as Nancy. The DiBiases — if you could call being a television wrestler an athlete — were benefiting, too. But the depth of the misappropriation to famous sports stars that Stephanie found would land us back in the national headlines.

CHAPTER TEN

The Gunslinger

"You've got to be kidding me," I said, glaring at my laptop. Brett Favre, the legendary Mississippi quarterback, was on an ESPN radio station. The audio of his interview was playing on my computer. Talking with two commentators from the *Wilde and Tausch* show, Favre was teeing off on our audit — and me. Any fond childhood memories I had of watching Favre were melting away, fast.

Eleven-year-old me would've found this moment mystifying. Back then, in 1997, Favre was a superhero to every little boy in South Mississippi. He was raised in tiny Kiln, Mississippi (locals disappear the *n* and call it The Kill), starred at the University of Southern Mississippi about forty minutes from my house, and went on to achieve near-mythical status among kids throwing a football at recess. That year he won a Super Bowl with the Green Bay Packers. I still remember him ripping off his helmet and running down the field in celebration, looking as happy as my buddies and me in sixth grade when we threw a touchdown at the public school playground.

Part of the reason every South Mississippi boy identified so strongly with Favre was, when we squinted, tilted our heads, and looked in the mirror, there was a bit of Favre's reflection in all of us.

🏈

When Brett Lorenzo Favre was born, his parents brought him home to a one-bathroom house built by his grandfather deep in the Kiln bayou. The murky water rose so close to the porch that alligators were always eating Favre pets. Four dogs — Fluffy, Whiskey, Bullet, and Lucky — went down that way.

As a boy, Favre was typical: crooked teeth, brown hair, scared of everything from ants to creaks in the night. His dad, Irvin Favre, was tough on him, but that was normal in the South, too. Irv was softer on the women in his house but not Brett.

"It'd be hard for my brothers to know Dad loved them," said Brandi, Brett's sister. "That's just fact."

Perhaps the only thing remarkable about Brett was his mean streak, according to Favre's biographer, Jeff Pearlman. Brandi recounted for Pearlman how Brett once forced his younger brother to drink a mix of tobacco spit, Worcestershire sauce, cow manure, and Brett's urine.

"I'm not saying Brett's mean now," said Brandi. "But long ago . . . God."

But all that washed away when Brett reached the football field. There he had mama-there-go-that-man vibes — an early swagger, a confidence. As a middle schooler, Favre would emulate Dan Marino's gruff cadence.

"Blue 50! Blue 50!"

On the field, he seemed . . . adult. Composed. Destined for something.

And he was dedicated. Favre's average Friday night as a teenager was staying home, missing every party in town, and working out in the garage. The work paid off. By age fourteen, Favre could flick a ball fifty yards in the air.

The problem was that no one was allowed to see that arm in action. Favre's high school football coach, his father, never — well, almost never — threw the ball. Irv Favre liked to keep it simple: run left, run right, run up the middle. The offense was called the wing-T, but it may as well have been called the Brett Favre Disappearing Act. The local newspaper often covered Brett's high school games and failed to even mention him. They once identified him as "Scott Favre," Brett's older brother.

Favre was so overshadowed by the school's star running back, Charles Burton, that no college was interested in the Mississippi boy with the hidden cannon. Then one day a young coach, Mark McHale from the University of Southern Mississippi, showed up.

McHale was a new employee at USM. Desperate to learn South Mississippi and to land recruits — particularly quarterbacks —

McHale was scrambling from high school to high school looking for talent. He arrived at Hancock North Central at the end of his first, long day on the job with no real hope for what he might find. He asked about the team's signal caller.

Coach Irv Favre was excited to see someone — anyone — interested in his son. When McHale arrived, they settled in to Irv's messy office and popped Brett's "highlight tape" into the VHS machine. In clip after clip, Favre handed the ball to Burton and not much else.

At some point, McHale had seen enough and looked for an exit. Probably sensing the tape wasn't the most compelling sales pitch for Brett, Irv asked McHale to come back and watch Brett play in person.

One Friday later, McHale bit. He made the drive to Hancock North Central again. Brett excelled in warm-ups, spinning the ball in a tight spiral. When he threw the deep ball, McHale reported the pigskin "had smoke on it."

Then the whistle blew. Irv Favre knew his son's only shot at a college scholarship was in the stands. McHale needed to see Brett throw live in a game. But Irv couldn't bring himself to change. Almost every play was a run. Burton runs left. Burton runs right. Burton runs up the middle. Handoff, handoff, handoff. Irv's team won 53–14. Even with the victory secured, Irv called run after run, leaving no opportunity for Brett to showcase his talent. McHale — and likely Brett — left disgusted.

Still, McHale kept thinking about that something he saw. The zip when the ball left Brett's hand in pregame. The way he walked up to the huddle. The eagerness when McHale talked to the young man.

McHale came back the next Friday, and a minor miracle happened. Irv Favre started running the ball again (a lot), but as the game reached a crescendo, Charles Burton was ejected for an illegal hit. Now Irv had no choice. With no starting running back, Irv Favre had to call pass plays for Brett.

And pass he did. Brett Favre took his one shot and put on a clinic. He hurled the ball around the field and with twenty-nine seconds left, plowed through the line on a sneak to score and seal a win.

McHale was convinced. Brett Favre had the stuff to be a college quarterback. McHale just needed to convince his new colleagues at USM.

It was a no-go from the jump. McHale was too green and had not built the trust of the other coaches. They would not take a flier on a kid with a hard-to-pronounce name whose own dad didn't trust him to throw in games. McHale talked up Brett Favre, but to no avail. Favre was not coming to USM.

Then fate intervened. There was a coaching shake-up. USM's offensive coordinator took a new job at Ole Miss in a flash, and a new coordinator, Jack White, was appointed. And White liked to pass. McHale had a fresh audience. When McHale described Favre to White, White was intrigued. He needed something new to wake the sleepy offense USM had sported in recent years, and maybe Favre was that something.

White summoned the Favres to campus so White could interview Brett. After their meeting and watching Brett work out, White couldn't put his finger on what he sensed. The best word was *spark*, maybe. Brett had a spark. An extra helping of moxie. It was enough. White pulled the trigger and offered Brett a scholarship. It was Favre's only offer to play college ball, according to Pearlman.

Once he arrived on the team as a freshman, Brett changed his number from 10 (his high school number) to 7 and then finally to 4. Then he started throwing so hard he was breaking receivers' hands. Chucking deep balls all over the field. Winning. He became *the* number 4 and never turned back.

<hr/>

After twenty years in the NFL and three MVP awards, Favre's legacy — and power — expanded even more in retirement. He appeared in Wrangler commercials, made the Hall of Fame, and became a cultural icon. His everyman looks — always wearing a ball cap and T-shirt and sporting some gray in his beard — were made for television. He even dabbled in politics, endorsing the late senator Thad Cochran during Cochran's 2014 reelection run. Favre cut a high-profile TV ad that helped seal Cochran's narrow victory.

By the summer of 2020, though, I was raging at Favre's radio broadcast. Our May 2020 audit led to his radio interview. While New's behavior was the part of our audit findings that turned my stomach the most, the national media obsessed over what we'd unveiled about Favre.

Before the audit was released, the public already knew Favre was involved in our case, tangentially at least, thanks to his connection to the concussion scheme. Prevacus was mentioned in Jody's first indictment, and any curious person who Googled "Prevacus" and "Mississippi" would soon see a picture of Favre on their screen. It took our May audit to connect more dots, though.

Here's what we found: Back in 2017, when Favre's volleyball-star daughter graduated high school, Favre took an interest in building a deluxe volleyball facility at his alma mater. Incidentally, his daughter also signed to play at the university. Favre began searching for funders, and eventually he turned to Nancy, who was sitting on a mountain of money. Favre convinced her to spend some of the resources available to her on volleyball, and Nancy in turn won the favor of the famous athlete whose approval she craved.

There was a problem, though. Any lawyer worth his salt could read TANF regulations and see that welfare money cannot be used to build a "brick and mortar" facility. Nancy wasn't allowed to give USM her welfare money for a volleyball court.

"Nancy I spoke with [USM athletic director] jon Gilbert this evening and between you and I he is very Leary of accepting such a large grant. Got me very uneasy," Favre texted New. Favre mentioned USM's worry about breaking the brick-and-mortar rule.

So they came up with a plan. New would take her TANF funds, wash the money by giving it to Favre Enterprises, and then Favre would donate to USM. They would claim Favre was being paid for performing some sort of spokesperson role for Nancy's nonprofit. And just like that — presto! — they could claim the money was no longer welfare and no longer subject to TANF rules.

"Would this . . . solve the brick and mortar issue?" Favre asked Nancy.

"It will," Nancy replied.

Of course, secrecy was critical for keeping the public unaware of how and why the money was flowing.

"Will the public perception be that I became a spokesperson for various state funded shelters, schools, homes, etc . . . and was compensated with state money? Or can we keep that confidential?" Favre asked.

"It will be confidential that you are accepting payment," Nancy promised. "Zach, my accountant, John Davis and I are the only ones that will have that information on this end."

"So if we keep confidential where money came from as well as amount I think this is gonna work," Favre confirmed. He saw exactly how to run the play they were calling.

"The less others know the better," said Nancy.

Not satisfied, though, Favre checked one more time a few days later.

"If you were to pay me is there anyway the media can find out where it came from and how much?" Favre texted Nancy.

"No, we never have had that information publicized," she said.

Problem solved. USM would have its volleyball funds, shrouded in darkness, via Favre.

And Favre was pleased. He told Jacob Vanlandingham that Nancy "gave me 5 million for Vball facility via grant money," and he remarked in other text messages how much money the grant money saved him personally from having to donate to USM.

MCEC eventually found a credulous lawyer to sign off on sending the money directly to USM, too, as it turned out. In October 2017, MCEC gave welfare money to the tune of $5 million to the University of Southern Mississippi's Athletic Foundation with the imprimatur of Stephanie Ganucheau, a state attorney. All this money paid for a beautiful court, with new floors bearing Golden Eagle logos, so shiny the reflection from the lights in the ceiling above danced off the hardwood. It was the kind of court a varsity team plays on, but the contract providing the funds claimed the court would be used for an "underserved population." With a dash of legal creativity and a big helping of concealed transactions, Favre's dream was realized.

Until we showed up. But unraveling all this took time, of course.

The first fact we noticed was that a first-rate volleyball court had been built in violation of the brick-and-mortar rule. Moreover, it had likely never been used to help the poor, despite being built with TANF dollars.

Stephanie Palmertree's auditors then discovered accounting transactions showing that $1.1 million in welfare money had been paid to Favre Enterprises by New's nonprofit. When the auditors asked MCEC for documentation to justify the payment, MCEC provided precious few papers. One was an email written in 2017 from Nancy to Zach New. The body of the email said it was "To: Brett Favre" and his accountant, "Bobby Lculumber" (a misspelled version of Bobby Culumber, Favre's CPA). It described how Favre would do three public service announcements, make public appearances for special events, and provide autographs. In a second document, which looked a little more like a formal contract, a "scope of work" was described. Favre was to "speak at three (3) total speaking engagements," "provide one (1) radio spot," and "provide one (1) keynote speaking engagement." The contract was signed by Nancy New as head of MCEC and Bobby Culumber of Favre Enterprises.

We then asked New which speeches Favre had given to earn the $1.1 million. After all, in Mississippi, government funds could not be disbursed before work was done. And Favre had already been paid. He would have already had to have done the work by the time we found the payments in late 2019, two years after the first check had been cut to him.

MCEC responded by sending a list of six speeches Favre allegedly gave. It named events like "Jackson Healthy Teens" with dates. New probably believed our auditors would stop looking once they were given this perfunctory list, but we didn't. Stephanie's team searched media reports, social media posts, event agendas, and everything else they could find. The conclusion at the end was clear. Favre hadn't given the speeches. He didn't even attend the functions.

Aside from rewarding speeches that were never given, the whole contract seemed strange. For one, it was a haphazard way to formalize spending more than a million dollars. It was short on detail. For another, Bobby Culumber, Favre's CPA, misspelled his own name when he signed on the dotted line. He spelled it *Bobbie*. And to top it off, the signature for Bobby Culumber did not match his handwriting when we compared it with other documents bearing this person's signature, like Culumber's driver's license. This made me wonder if his signature had been forged. When auditors asked Culumber if that was his signature, though, he stated in an email to my auditors that it was.

Later, when an investigator came to his door, Culumber changed his tune. He admitted what he said was not true. Nancy supplied $1.1 million to Favre and then hastily called later to tell Culumber she wanted to "close out the grant." Culumber said Nancy signed his name on a contract she invented to substantiate the $1.1 million payment. Nancy misspelled Culumber's name in the process.

Culumber's lie was par for the course for how people treated our auditors in those days. At DHS and plenty of other places, my team would travel the state conducting interviews for investigations or audits. People brushed us aside, lied, and generally said anything to make us go away.

The DHS arrests changed that. It put the fear of God into people. After we made those arrests, people were nervous when we came to visit. In all honesty, if I had to choose between being a paper tiger or a bogeyman, I'd choose the bogeyman. At least it was a sign of respect. Everyone knew we were doing our jobs.

Our May audit made the $1.1 million payment to Favre public for the first time. At that moment, we hadn't seen all the controversial texts Favre exchanged with New, but we knew enough to call attention to the improper payment. National sports media immediately covered it. While Favre had a sterling reputation inside Mississippi, the national media still remembered the stories about his alleged pursuit of a journalist and the sexts he had purportedly sent her years ago. The welfare scandal fueled a slow-burning fire of criticism and suspicion about his character that had never gone out.

Favre came out of the gate saying he hadn't known the money he was paid was welfare money. But that wasn't enough to keep the media off his back. ESPN and the *Washington Post* picked up the story. Two days later a representative of Favre Enterprises reached out to me and said Brett wanted me to make a statement saying he had done nothing wrong. I told him I would not do that. Federal and state authorities were jointly investigating everything involving TANF spending during John Davis's tenure. Then prosecutors would determine who had violated a criminal statute. This wasn't some backroom deal you could cut. We were going to follow the law, and I wouldn't get ahead of the normal investigative process.

A few hours later, Favre's representative called back and said Favre would consider repaying the money. This made the situation complicated. Technically, I could not tell Favre he had to pay it back right now. Our audit simply "questioned" the spending of welfare money on Favre's speeches. Once we questioned this and the other $97 million in welfare spending, my team and I talked with the head of the Office of Family Assistance at HHS in Washington, DC. That was the office that regulated TANF. Their director, Clarence Carter, told me the next step was for federal authorities to review our audit and make some decisions about how much of the $98 million was actually illegal. This would then determine who owed what back.

In other words, we were in a holding pattern per a request from the federal government. I knew that holding pattern could last years while the feds parsed our audit.

I told Favre Enterprises all this and that we were waiting on the federal government before we made final decisions about who should make repayments. If they wanted to pay, though, I couldn't stop them. I would send an agent to retrieve a check from Favre if he insisted on cutting one.

A few hours later, Team Favre called back. Favre wanted to repay $500,000 now and then repay the remaining $600,000 in $150,000 installments over the next few months. By the end of the day, we had the first $500,000 of the $98 million in misspending in our possession.

I gave Favre public credit for paying the money back, but if I'd known at the time about the quiet machinations he and Nancy had engineered, I wouldn't have been so kind.

Then Favre went on the radio. Two days later Favre took to the ESPN show based in Wisconsin and said I was "wrong in [my] words" when I said he'd been paid for speeches he never gave. He claimed the story was "ridiculous." Favre said, "For [White] to say I took $1.1 million and didn't show up for speaking engagements is absolutely, 100 percent not true."

My team had no reason to believe Favre had ever even seen the sham contract where Nancy obligated him to give speeches. That didn't change the main point: Favre had never given the speeches his contract required. The whole thing was a farce designed to funnel money to a volleyball court.

When I heard Favre's comments, I was angry. I responded by telling the world, again, what his contract said and that he didn't give those speeches. "If Mr. Favre is stating that MCEC [or his own accountant] never informed him that he was required to be at those events as a part of their agreement, then this, of course, would be one of the many lies MCEC leadership told . . . through the course of our audit," I said.

After that, Favre went quiet.

Favre was a famous athlete with a huge megaphone. There was no way I could compete with the attention his comments received. I knew the facts were on my side, but that didn't stop people following ESPN that day from reaching conclusions based solely on Favre's account.

To add to the furor, a chorus of Twitterati attacked me for not arresting Favre. Favre had endorsed Republicans and taken pictures with President Trump, so that was enough for liberals on Twitter to hate him. Within days of our audit telling the world about the contract for the no-show speeches, the Twitter mob conveniently forgot that I was the one who'd told them about the payments. They also forgot that prosecutors are the ones who decide who faces criminal charges. In their minds, if I didn't put Favre in jail myself, then I was protecting him.

On the other hand, Favre and his fans were mad that I'd told the world about the million-dollar payment. I was going after "the great Brett Favre," one exclaimed. One of my campaign donors called me and said to "leave him alone."

Watching this unfold was a reminder of how toxic social media, and particularly Twitter, had become. Thankfully I had learned at the outset of my career to laugh off these attacks. One early, terrible experience came when my office released a report on how administrative spending in public schools was going up faster than spending on instruction. I was a graduate of Mississippi public schools, my mother was a thirty-five-year public school teacher, and two of my four grandparents had been public school teachers. I cared about our public schools, and making sure they spent money directly on students was important to me. Hence the report my office released, showing that the classroom was being shortchanged while administrator salaries went through the ceiling.

I knew the report would anger those administrators. The paid education "advocates" who made their salaries convincing their donors there was a secret conservative desire to gut public schools were incensed, too. But the rage of those smaller groups aside, I thought it was important for the larger number of teachers and parents to hear the data. More than that, the students — who deserved to have money spent on them instead of on the adults — should have someone to defend their interests.

Slim Smith, a well-known left-leaning columnist at one of the state's largest newspapers, apparently disagreed. Because of the report, he took to Twitter and called me a member of the White Citizens Council, a racist organization from the civil rights era. He didn't say I was *like* a member of the White Citizens Council; he said I *was* a member (I'm pretty sure that council formally disbanded around the time I was born, for the record). Smith had once been the managing editor of his newspaper and had made appearances on *The Daily Show* with Jon Stewart, so he had an audience. I decided to push back. I replied that my biracial child would probably be surprised to know Daddy was in the White Citizens Council. Racists weren't big fans of interracial marriage, to put it mildly. Smith then compared my wife to a slave and my daughter to the child born when Thomas Jefferson slept with an underage slave.

When my wife saw the tweet comparing her to a slave, she was ready to drive to Smith's house and settle the matter herself. I talked her out of that solution. Instead, we would just move on. I still spent most of the next week wanting to beat the hell out of Smith for what he said about my wife and daughter. But after that I realized I would have a heart attack before age forty if I let these sorts of comments affect me.

I learned to let it go, in other words. By the time the Favre story unfolded more than a year after Smith's racist word vomit, I was long past the stage where social media criticism bothered me enough to dictate my mood. I should probably send Smith a thank-you note at some point.

One year after the release of our Favre audit findings, Favre still hadn't fully repaid the money. ESPN wrote another round of stories. Anna Wolfe posted a picture of herself at the gate outside Favre's home, hoping to get a quote. My position was still that I could not force anyone to pay back any of the $98 million in questioned costs until the federal government told us what portion of that spending was illegal. At that stage, only Favre and one or two smaller organizations had paid back any part of what they received. While the feds made their determinations, I was going to have to listen to the boobirds on the internet chirp.

The Favre anniversary story prompted Favre to reach out to me. At the time, I was away for military training at a US Air Force base out of state. A strange number appeared on my phone. It was the first time Favre and I interacted directly instead of through intermediaries. Favre claimed he wanted to talk about what had happened and to try to resolve it. My take-away was that he wanted me to say publicly he had done nothing wrong. At least, that's what his high-priced public relations firm later told my chief of staff.

We told them the same thing again: I would not do that because a joint team of state and federal investigators was still trying to uncover all the facts. Then the prosecutors would decide who'd done anything criminal.

Even with a statement from me off the table, Favre still pressed to have a meeting to discuss the whole matter. I told them I would only do that if representatives from the FBI could be there as well. I was not going to cut the FBI out after announcing they would be privy to everything we knew.

As Favre considered the meeting, I dialed one of my agents. I'll call him Bulldog here. Bulldog was a special agent at the state auditor's office, but I'd assigned him to a task force with the FBI, which meant he went to work every day at FBI offices. He was gregarious, with a round face, short hair, and a quick smile — just the person you wanted easing tensions when agencies had to cooperate. He also seemed to know everyone in the state. After my office turned our evidence over to the FBI, Bulldog became our representative on the joint state-federal team of investigators looking at DHS.

I asked for Bulldog's advice on Favre and the idea of a meeting. I did the same with Assistant US Attorney Dave Fulcher, who'd been assigned to prosecute the case, and Pat Dendy, the deputy state auditor. They all agreed that Bulldog and his team should reach out to Favre. Then Bulldog should suggest that Favre and his attorney meet with Bulldog's crew.

Fulcher and Dendy also thought I should not be in the meeting. For one, when I didn't show up for the meeting, it would signal this was not going to be a cigar-filled room where some deal could be brokered. Second, Favre was going to be asked questions in the meeting that might later be used as evidence at trial. Everyone in the room could be called as a witness. Investigators should be the witnesses for the state, not the principal, the state auditor.

Not long after our strategy discussions, Bulldog called Favre, and Favre agreed to a meeting with Bulldog and the rest of the federal investigative team. In a stubby, unremarkable white building in Hattiesburg, the offices of Favre's agent, federal agents and Bulldog grilled Favre. After the meeting, our conclusions were the same: Favre hadn't given the speeches, but he'd been paid the money.

I think, at the time, Favre misunderstood the public's criticism about him. People were angry that a rich athlete had been paid a million dollars of welfare money in the poorest state in the country. The fact that he hadn't given the required speeches made it worse. But even if he had given the speeches or complied with a part of the contract, the public would still want him to pay the money back. Being paid welfare money wasn't the same as being paid by Wrangler in an endorsement deal. TANF was supposed to benefit the poor, and Brett wasn't poor. Most other athletes who did public service announcements for good causes did them for free.

But Favre didn't write the check repaying the full amount. As the months rocked on and that fact festered, the criticism of him metastasized. Every time Favre commented on sports in any way that was inflammatory, social media and reporters raised the welfare money. When Favre criticized tennis star Naomi Osaka for not wanting to speak to the press, they asked about the welfare money. When Favre said anything about COVID-19, they said "welfare." It was a ghost he couldn't shake.

And it cost him. Favre lost an endorsement deal from Odyssey Health, and SiriusXM and ESPN Milwaukee suspended his radio show.

Congressman Bennie Thompson, the Democratic representative from Mississippi's Second District and a key ally of President Biden, got in on the act, too. His staff filed multiple Freedom of Information Act (FOIA) requests with the Department of Justice asking for all of their files on Favre. The DOJ denied all of Thompson's requests. His staff, along with the public, would have to wait many more months for a resolution to the Favre matter.

During those long months, I was repeatedly asked whether prosecutors would charge Favre with a crime. It was their call, but the prosecutors knew Favre's main defense was ignorance. Favre would say he was not well versed in TANF grant rules, nor did he have a sophisticated understanding of securities law. He did not know, for instance, if the concussion company Prevacus could legally give money or gifts to public officials, and he said as much, repeatedly, in text messages to Vanlandingham.

On the other hand, Favre had been warned he could not spend welfare funds on a volleyball court, and he clearly wanted to hide his receiving public money. When he asked Nancy if "the media" would ever find out about him being paid by her, that could be considered evidence of an intent to conceal what happened. These were the points that a prosecutor would have to ponder taking to a jury.

The other, tragic sports-related part of the DHS case involved a man named Marcus Dupree. For Mississippians, Marcus was another cult hero. Born in rural Philadelphia, Mississippi, Marcus was one of the most sought-after high school running backs in the country in the early 1980s. Some said he was the most accomplished high school football player in state history. Marcus accepted a spot at the University of Oklahoma playing for famous coach Barry Switzer. Switzer said Marcus might have been NFL-ready from the first day he put on a Sooner jersey.

In his freshman year at Oklahoma, Marcus was a second team All-American despite playing less than a full season. After that his fairy tale soured. He surprised fans by leaving Oklahoma in the middle of his sophomore year. He attempted to enroll at the University of Southern Mississippi but then pivoted and played for the New Orleans Breakers, a professional team in the old USFL, an upstart league that was designed to challenge the NFL in the 1980s and folded after three seasons.

Then the injury bug bit. Marcus tore a knee ligament in a Breakers game, was carted off the field on a stretcher, and was never the same. He played briefly in the NFL but never achieved stardom. In 2010, ESPN released a documentary on Dupree's life called *The Best That Never Was*. Aside from sports, it chronicled his financial troubles; he was taken advantage of by a well-known Mississippi preacher and lost everything. He moved into a small house back in Philadelphia.

Since the 2009 documentary, Marcus was a household name among two generations of Mississippians. That meant he was exactly the sort of celebrity Nancy was attracted to. She hired him.

When Nancy first contracted with Marcus, it was unclear why he was at MCEC other than to be, perhaps, a celebrity endorser. Jack Bologna eventually reported that Marcus was paid more than $100,000 by MCEC to mentor young children. MCEC called Marcus a "community liaison."

The big money from MCEC came for the home Marcus was living in, though. Anna reported that, by 2020, Marcus was living in a $900,000 home, complete with a horse barn, in a wealthy suburb of Jackson. The mortgage on the house was paid by MCEC. Anna went to that home to try to get Marcus's side of the story. Marcus told Anna he'd been an employee of MCEC. Then he told her to leave. "You just don't walk up on my property without getting shot," he said.

Our audit later revealed the gritty details: MCEC used welfare money to pay for Marcus's house to compensate Marcus for "Equine Assisted Activities." He was supposed to use the farm on his estate to teach emotionally troubled children about horses. MCEC "rented" the house from him by paying Marcus's foundation the money he would need to pay his mortgage each month.

Marcus received a substantial benefit from the arrangement. His foundation was paid $171,000 in February 2018, which was almost the exact amount of the down payment on the home. The $9,500 monthly mortgage payments to the bank, paid with MCEC's TANF money, meant he received another $200,000 in total.

The way the whole transaction was structured was painfully illegal. When we asked for proof that the home had been used for horse-related therapy, MCEC provided my team with some grainy pictures of Marcus's family riding horses. Loan documents on the home said the payments from MCEC had been approved at an April 2018 board meeting, but MCEC had no April 2018 meeting. When we looked at the accounting entries for each of the transactions benefiting Marcus in MCEC's books, they were often originally coded as "Rent." But after my auditors asked to see the books, someone at MCEC changed the transaction labels to "Contractual Services" in the software.

Changing accounting entries is a red flag for potential fraud. It can be used as proof that a person described an expenditure accurately the first time they booked the expense, then realized that such an expenditure was illegal and tried to conceal the nature of the expense by changing its description. It can be a way to cover your tracks.

Nancy didn't financially benefit from handing Marcus money or by MCEC guaranteeing the home loan. But she did benefit from his celebrity. She also probably felt good for helping a hometown legend who'd always found himself down on his luck. She illegally financed those good feelings with taxpayer dollars.

We could never determine if Marcus knew he was being paid in welfare money or even why he was being paid. Sometimes athletes like Dupree assume they are remunerated for their celebrity endorsement for a product. In this case perhaps Marcus thought the product was Nancy's nonprofit. TANF dollars can't be used to pay for endorsements, though. The exorbitant fees paid to athletes like Dupree can only be justified if real work was done. There was no way to know if Dupree understood that about federal law. For that reason, the brunt of the legal responsibility for what was given to Dupree fell on Nancy and MCEC.

The System

"This is like being butt naked at the capitol!"

Representative Steve Holland, a Democrat and funeral home operator, and state senator Terry Burton, a Republican and professional beauty pageant announcer, laughed at Holland's joke during an NPR radio interview. The interview was about a new personal training program for state legislators. The trainer hired to whip the legislators into shape was Paul LaCoste, a thick-necked, charismatic former college football player.

Holland's joke was that LaCoste pushed the legislators so hard in their 4:00 AM workouts that they felt like they were "butt naked." It didn't make much sense, but the quip still earned a chuckle on the air.

Every morning of the legislative session, staffers and elected legislators gathered in sweat-stained T-shirts and shorts to be yelled at by LaCoste. In his first year, 2010, LaCoste said legislators collectively lost more than fourteen hundred pounds. The program was celebrated as a way for elected officials to send the message to Mississippi that it was time to conquer obesity. The underside of that story was that a group of influential lawmakers and journalists were receiving free exercise classes. And worse, in May 2020, our audit revealed that the free workout coach was paid for with welfare money.

There was little evidence that legislators knew their training was financed by TANF. In legislators' minds, I'm sure, this was just another free perk that came with the job. In Mississippi, lobbyists routinely paid for lawmakers' meals and drinks while talking to them about their clients' concerns. Though few lobbyists would admit it, many hated the system. Some legislators grew so accustomed to free stuff that they'd drink at a bar, run up a tab, and then have the bartender send the bill across the restaurant to a lobbyist who was having dinner with a separate party. If free alcohol and meals were the expectation of the evening, why would it be a surprise to have free personal training sessions the next morning?

We found that LaCoste's company pulled down a $1.3 million TANF grant to pay for these boot-camp-style lessons from 2018 to 2019. On top of that, LaCoste's company purchased a $70,000 vehicle, a $20,000 trailer, and plenty of other equipment and materials with welfare money. Jack Bologna found proof of welfare payments to LaCoste's company for steak dinners, too. Interestingly, while the legislative boot camp was free to elected officials, other participants at other welfare-financed LaCoste camps had to pay. No one could determine whether any participants at any of the camps were TANF-eligible.

It's hard to know what was going through John Davis's mind as he spent this money on Mississippi's political elite. Lawmakers said LaCoste would yell at them to support John's agency as they did laps, but most of them apparently took it as a joke. Perhaps the legislators knew John was paying, and they assumed it was legal. The arrangement was odd, and the only conclusion we reached was this: John, and Nancy for that matter, liked keeping powerful people happy.

It also worked, professionally speaking. John and Nancy rose to the top of Mississippi society — one the head of a large, well-funded state agency and the other a big-time campaign donor and business owner — by building and working their networks. The way to build a network was to keep important people on your side and have their numbers in your phone.

But if the powerful are the priority of a decision-maker, then Mississippi's poor and her taxpayers, by necessity, have to come second. That was the story of Davis's welfare spending.

It was a story that repeated itself in other non-welfare cases during my tenure, too. Each was more infuriating than the last. Tunica County was an example. In late 2019, we began investigating a man who was running a house-repair program for the poor. The idea behind the program was simple: Tunica County would use taxpayer dollars to repair homes — fixing floorboards, patching windows, adding wheelchair ramps — for run-down residences that were sinking into the delta mud.

There was a need in Tunica County, no doubt. The people there were excruciatingly poor. In 1985, Jesse Jackson came to Tunica County and declared it "America's Ethiopia." The poverty rate around that time was more than 50 percent, which, according to the *Washington Post*, was "extreme even by the standards of the Mississippi Delta."

Then, in the early 1990s, the county became a casino destination. Positioned in Mississippi's northwest corner and driving distance from Memphis and its airport, high-rise casinos sprouted in Tunica's chlorophyll-green cornfields. With the towers came visitors and money. A lot of money. One county administrator estimated the county raised a billion dollars of new revenue over the course of the next twenty years. It would have been enough to pay for every child under the age of eighteen in the ten-thousand-person county to go to Harvard.

Instead of Harvard, the money evaporated on projects that, though well intentioned, didn't fundamentally change the lives of the residents. Money was poured into an Olympic-sized swimming pool, a fancy event venue, and a museum.

One of Tunica's casino-fueled programs was the housing program. When the county decided to create the program, a local mover and shaker named Mardis Jones presented at their door. He was ready to help — for a fee. Jones promised to run the program through his nonprofit. He would accept applications from impoverished local homeowners, select winners, find contractors to make repairs, and then pay the contractors through the funds set aside for the program.

After a few years, with only a few houses fixed by the program, people asked the same question they had been asking since the casinos first arrived: Where had all the money gone?

One person asking that question was Linda Fay Engle-Harris, a retired schoolteacher. Chico Harlan, a writer for the *Post*, penned her heartbreaking story. Her home was falling apart. She'd stuffed paper in the cracks of the floorboards to keep them sealed up. Slugs still entered and crawled around the house. So Engle-Harris applied to be part of the housing repair program. Jones gave her the runaround. Jones told her at the time, in 2015, that it was a five-year wait to have a repair. Given the condition of her house, he may as well have given it a death sentence.

The reason Jones could not fix homes was he was allegedly stealing from the program. By the time we investigated in late 2020, Jones appeared to have stolen nearly 40 percent of the total spending of the program. He took another 40 percent or so legally in the fees he'd negotiated with the county. That left about 20 percent for repairing homes.

Investigators found that the 80 percent Jones walked away with was spent in casinos and on a variety of other personal expenses. When we finished the investigation and arrested him, my agents served Jones with a demand for more than a million dollars.

Tunica County had a golden opportunity to address a variety of social maladies with their casino revenue. The Jones case and the quality of life in Tunica after twenty years of spending led to an inescapable conclusion: Not many people had been helped at all, aside from Jones.

Maybe no amount of government spending could correct basic social issues like broken families and endemic poverty. The Brookings Institution has shown that, if you finish high school, obtain a full-time job, and wait until age twenty-one before marrying and having children, then it's nearly impossible to find yourself in poverty. Statistically, more than 70 percent of people who do those three things even land in the middle class. Those were simple choices but hard to instill. If you could break the culture of poverty and teach people to make these choices, though, you could change more lives than even a billion dollars spread across ten thousand Tunica residents.

On the day I announced the Jones arrest in Oxford, Mississippi, I turned these thoughts over in my mind on the way back home. When I reached my office back in Jackson, three hours later, the front desk secretary Belinda said the phone had been ringing off the hook. Residents of Tunica County saw the news. They were calling and asking, now that we'd seized the money, how long it would be before their homes would be fixed. Belinda wanted to know what to tell them.

My heart hurt for those callers. I told Belinda we would never recover the lost cash, and the expressions on both of our faces sank. We knew she would spend the afternoon explaining that heartbreaking fact on the phone. In this case, and in many others, all we could do was mete out punishment to the responsible parties.

I reflected on these two cases after we finished our work on them. In the case of LaCoste, government was working well for connected folks because the person overseeing the government spending, John Davis, wanted it that way. It was rigged by design. But in the case of Jones, it seemed that he was a connected player who benefited from others' incompetence. The county put too much trust in him too eagerly, with no oversight.

I once heard a political commentator ask whether problems in government happened because everyone was in an episode of *House of Cards*, where murderous operators planned how to manipulate the world to their advantage, or an episode of *Veep*, a show where every character working in the White House was a bumbling idiot. To me, these two fraud cases showed that the outcome wasn't much different either way. Normal taxpayers suffered, and insiders like Nancy New and Mardis Jones came out on top.

It's easy to say that those in charge of government should do a better job, but running a government office in a competent and fair way is hard work. It's much easier not to monitor spending, or to let your office fly on autopilot. Case after case proved that the result of autopilot was often waste or fraud.

One audit we did of Medicaid, the health insurance program for the poor, proved this point. The premise of our audit was straightforward: We would take the income that a Medicaid recipient claimed on their state income tax return and compare it with the income the recipient claimed when they applied for Medicaid. We believed some applicants might be lying to Medicaid about how much they made. Tax returns were a good way to see if this was the case.

To do the audit, though, I had to ask the legislature to change the law and allow my team to see state income tax returns. State auditors have broad authority to look at all sorts of documents, all the way down to individual health records and federally protected public school student information. But tax records were considered sacrosanct.

Still, Medicaid was the largest federal program operating in the state (about half of federal spending in Mississippi went to Medicaid), and the state itself spent hundreds of millions on the program. Fixing small errors could save millions. That meant millions more for people who were eligible for the program, or public schools, or whatever else lawmakers deemed appropriate. So we had a good argument to make for more scrutiny of Medicaid.

When I asked for the legal authority to look at returns, I'd hoped a bipartisan group would support the measure for that reason. Instead, the bill caused a fight on the floor in both chambers. One House member, who would later go on to run the state's branch of the ACLU, asked for a meeting with me to discuss it. I agreed, because I was willing to talk about any of our proposed laws with any member at any time.

On the day of the meeting, the member and two of his colleagues walked over from the capitol. In my conference room, he spent most of the next few minutes accusing me of trying to take Medicaid from children. I explained that the children I know don't file tax returns.

At some point I stopped his rant and asked him: "Do you think it's possible for a Medicaid applicant to lie about their income to be put on the program?"

"That's not happening," he said. "There's no one like that."

I was amazed at the naïveté. And maybe more than naïveté, he wanted to ignore potential fraud because he didn't want anyone questioning the program. It hurt his argument for more spending.

Despite this opposition, and thanks to a few brave bill authors like state senator Josh Harkins, Representative Joey Hood, Representative Trey Lamar, and the leadership in both chambers, the bill passed and was signed into law by Governor Reeves.

For the next two years, we used that legal authority to audit. We found that around 5 to 7 percent of Medicaid beneficiaries, depending on the year, told Medicaid they made one amount while their tax return suggested a higher one — too high to be eligible. Five percent may not sound like much, but it meant somewhere between $64 million and $144 million in improper Medicaid payments per year.

In a state where we struggled to find enough money to pay public school teachers what they were worth, saving another $100 million per year seemed like a no-brainer to me. And Medicaid dollars shouldn't benefit the rich. Two of the ineligible people identified in the audit were on Medicaid despite owning a million-dollar, seven-thousand-square-foot home and reporting six digits in income on their most recent tax return. Federal prosecutors later found they either owned or had an interest in forty-eight gas stations. Prosecutors forced them to repay $130,000.

By the time we showed the Medicaid staff our findings in mid-2021, I'd been around the block enough to expect what was coming. They were not happy. Some Medicaid employees didn't care that we handed them potential savings to pump back into their program. They instead wanted to fight. They feared being publicly embarrassed. And they complained that Medicaid didn't have the legal authority to look at tax returns like we had. I told them that was the point — to give them ammunition to ask lawmakers for that right.

That didn't calm the waters, though. Some of the bureaucrats continued to withhold information from us. They also suggested to the public that tax returns were not that useful, despite stating in internal policies that the returns were needed.

The head of Medicaid in the state at the time, Drew Snyder, was a friend of mine. He was a few years ahead of me at the University of Mississippi. We were kindred spirits in that we were both younger than your typical agency head, and we'd both left Mississippi for a period — him for the University of Virginia — before coming back home.

Drew was a good guy and smart, but he was fighting an army of longtime state employees more concerned about being right than finding efficiencies. When that army worked around you all day and became your colleagues, it was hard to trust someone from the outside if the army said the outsider was wrong. In this case, I was the outsider.

This all taught me an important lesson: People who worked in government for several decades weren't going to put a stop to waste. They often had little incentive to try anything new or admit mistakes.

It also became clear that bureaucrats who stand for the status quo often find a willing ally in belligerents on social media. Perhaps I should have anticipated this after our study of outside-the-classroom spending and Slim Smith's tirade about my wife. His rant, I'm sure, was applauded by the school administrators who didn't like me pointing out that their salaries kept increasing while teachers' salaries, adjusted for inflation, seemed to be going down.

After the Medicaid audit, the ACLU and their band of Twitter followers predictably accused me of trying to hurt the poor and called me a racist. Never mind that our findings helped guarantee that only poor people would benefit from the program. They could not allow someone to suggest there was fraud at all.

The day after the ACLU attacked me for the Medicaid audit, a Black pastor from rural Mississippi called the office and asked to speak to me. He thanked me for excising some of the fraud from Medicaid. He didn't like people who lied to get benefits, he said, and he especially didn't like it if they were wealthy. He told me to ignore the criticism and keep going.

The next morning I was dropping my daughter off at daycare, and the daycare's security guard ran over. She said, "I'm so proud you are stopping people from lying just so they can live off the system." These comments buoyed my spirits and kept me going, regardless of the front-page stories full of ACLU quotes.

Yet despite my optimism, there was a sad truth underlying my experiences. There were insiders, and they were powerful. Whether the insiders were connected lawmakers, the local power player in Tunica, or entrenched bureaucrats, and whether or not they were backed by a bunch of self-appointed internet activists with an outsized megaphone thanks to social media, the bottom line was that so many of our institutions were not operating well thanks to them.

Alone

Bob Anderson stood before the media and introduced himself as the new permanent head of the DHS. He baked in the glare of blinding studio lights. Behind him were the navy curtains of Governor Reeves's press briefing room, a large state seal, and the governor. Squinting behind his glasses and looking uneasy, Bob appeared washed out on camera. As I watched him speak on TV from across town, I felt a flicker of optimism, though. Tall and with a salt-and-pepper beard, Anderson had a monotone voice and barely ever cracked a smile. He seemed low-key. No-nonsense. Down-to-business.

Maybe I can work with this guy, I thought.

His voice shaking, Anderson said, "I want folks to know, I'm not unfamiliar with the unique role that DHS plays in helping people with crucial needs at crucial times in their lives." He reported how his own family, during his formative years, had to rely on welfare for a period.

Bob had his work cut out for him. After we made our arrests, DHS as an institution was quivering in anger at my office. DHS staff were embarrassed, and some probably feared they might be next to see handcuffs.

Bob was also inheriting a staff that was still largely John Davis's staff. When Davis resigned, months before his arrest, no one else went with him. When retired FBI agent Chris Freeze took over for Davis, Freeze fired some of the brass who were appointed by Davis, but not many. Freeze told me the story of one employee who, on Freeze's first week, pledged her undying loyalty to him. She said she would do whatever Freeze wanted, even if it was unethical. He fired her a few days later. That was the culture Davis had created.

One of the cardinal rules inside that culture was that the auditor's office should be shut out. We knew from our audits that DHS directors told lower-level employees to avoid creating paper trails for our auditors to follow. In interviews with my team, those same DHS employees repeatedly denied there was fraud in the agency when we asked if they'd seen any wrong-doing in the past year.

And culture is hard to break. One change agent coming from the outside would be met with the same sorts of problems Drew Snyder experienced at Medicaid. Moreover, Bob had a strong background in government programs, but DHS was a complex animal. Bob was going to have to rely on the only people with expertise — John Davis's former staff — even if they'd been complicit in Davis's activities.

With all this in mind, I obtained Bob's cell number and sent him a text as the press conference wound to a close. "Bob, this is Shad White. Congratulations. Give me a call when you get the chance."

I followed up by asking Bob to come to my office, by himself, when convenient for him. I'd drafted a short PowerPoint deck, written for someone at the executive level, to convey all the work we'd done auditing DHS.

Apparently, I didn't move fast enough. By the day after the press conference, it started to feel like Davis's old staff had recruited Bob into their anti-state-auditor cult. Bob recoiled at the idea of coming to a meeting with me alone. He wanted to bring Davis's old counsel. When I suggested it might be better for him to come without her, he texted back that he'd "need a thorough explana-tion about the General Counsel's not being there."

What in the world? I thought. I obviously wanted Bob to come alone because some of my presentation might make exist-ing staff, including Davis's counsel, look bad. They had just overseen the loss of nearly $100 million of welfare money. It baffled me that Bob would offer a cold response to a meeting offered out of courtesy. I was under no obligation to give him an update and had suggested the meeting because my office wanted to help him right the DHS ship.

Bob eventually arrived alone. Stephanie and I briefed him.

He was nonconfrontational but seemed ill at ease. At the end of the meeting, I said, "Bob, we didn't bring you here to screw you. We wanted a meeting with you because we thought it'd be helpful for you to hear this. We wanted you to hear it without staff around. We wanted you to know who on your current staff was in key meetings with John Davis when money was being handed out. If we conveyed that information with Davis's old staff in the room, it might get a little awkward. But really this is your agency. We're just here to offer facts about what happened." He nodded, said some words of appreciation, and left.

Over the next two weeks, Bob sent emails to my auditors complaining about how rigorous they were being. He was taking advice from the staff who'd watched Davis squander millions. He accused my team of going beyond normal audits of DHS and doing an "investigative audit." He also questioned whether we were auditing in "an attempt to frame a narrative."

I sighed when I read the emails. Within two weeks of starting, having no idea about the depth of the problems he now owned, Bob was willing to ignore six arrests and a mountain of improper spending and instead assume we were being bullies. *Has he already downed the Kool-Aid?*

I sent Bob an email and said, "Over the course of the last few years of auditing DHS, auditors on my staff have been kept in the dark, at best, and at worst, lied to. When we asked DHS employees for information about misspending or fraud, they repeatedly, over years, looked at auditors and said they had nothing to report . . . You have been [at DHS] two weeks. You have not been at DHS long enough to understand what an unfair narrative would even look like."

Next, Bob filed a public records request with my office. It was unusual. The auditor's office had never received one of these FOIA-style requests from another agency. But Bob had a right to information from my office just like any other citizen, so we complied. The nature of the request was aggressive. He demanded to see any documents we had given to newspaper reporters regarding the DHS case. It was clear the staff at DHS were embarrassed by the raft of negative headlines about how they'd handled money. This was a way to hit back.

It bothered me that Bob was more interested in figuring out whether my office was talking to reporters than in changing how DHS awarded TANF grants. I called Bob and told him that I would give him all of the documents (there was only one single sheet of paper) that we had given to reporters, but that I was confused about why this request was worth our time. He told me that he was looking for "leakers" to the press. I told him if that was his priority instead of fixing the TANF grant system, he was lost.

"And Bob, if you want to find some leakers, start with your own staff," I said. The news stories I saw were based on documents his staff had given reporters after the reporters filed normal public records requests on DHS.

Then the DHS staff started claiming they were the whistleblowers in the entire matter. It felt like they were asking to be congratulated for discovering fraud of their own doing. The truth was that a DHS staffer had approached the governor's office with a one-page document back in the summer of 2019. The short document only had information suggesting that Davis and Brett DiBiase were engaged in fraud, and it was fraud related to Rise in Malibu. The document never mentioned the News or their nonprofit, MCEC. And they never sent it to a law enforcement body.

In other words, the only DHS tipster — allegedly Jacob Black, the deputy executive director — disclosed just enough to try to get John Davis fired and nothing more. Back then, Black was the front-runner for taking John's place, so long as no one looked any further than the information in his "internal audit." Unfortunately for Black, Governor Bryant forwarded that document to the proper law enforcement authority for public funds, my office. We did not take the document as the full truth. After more digging, we realized many DHS staffers had sat in meetings where John did much more than just misspend in Malibu. And his staff helped him.

I'd seen this movie before. Steven Soderbergh's film *The Informant!* tells the story of real-life whistleblower Mark Whitacre. Whitacre tipped off the FBI on price fixing by the top executives at his company — just enough information, Whitacre believed, to kick the executives to the curb. Once the executives were out, Whitacre's goal was to become CEO himself. Unfortunately, when he talked to the FBI, Whitacre conveniently left out his own embezzlement. He went to prison for nine years for the theft.

There was never going to be a ticker-tape parade for the hero staff of DHS.

These kinds of incidents — where Bob hesitated about meeting alone with us, where he complained about how deep our auditors were going, where he spent time probing for "leakers," where his staff tried to mislead the public about their alleged role as whistleblowers — were minor annoyances in the grand scheme of things. The important events were happening in the offices where prosecutors prepared for trial and the audit rooms where my team was plowing through documents. But the incidents still revealed a deep-seated antipathy by DHS staff toward my team, and they previewed future battles that would be even more pitched.

The biggest of those battles came when DHS finally, a year later, decided to have a private firm audit its full TANF spending. At last and after two years of me begging, there would be a full, penny-by-penny picture painted of Davis's work by a qualified outsider. Our main request was that we serve as a third party on the forensic audit. That meant we would not perform the audit work, but we did want to receive regular updates and help obtain documents if the outside firm had trouble.

I tried to secure funding from lawmakers for this forensic audit in early 2020, but they rebuffed me. Some of the rumors about why they objected reached me. Some legislators were concerned about what an exhaustive audit would find — which meant some were nervous that their names might surface. Some said they wanted the audit findings to be made secret. After my failure to obtain the funding, only DHS, with their large budget, could choose to pay for a forensic audit of this size.

Bob eventually agreed it was worth it, but there were some big caveats. Someone at DHS was trying to cut us out of the process. In the contract with the outside audit firm, for example, we wanted language saying that any criminal activity discovered by the outside firm would be reported to my office. Someone at DHS struck that language from the draft contract.

Even worse, someone also wrote the contract to limit what the outside auditors could look at. We knew DHS had misspent money in programs outside TANF, but Bob only wanted TANF money reviewed.

Pat Dendy reviewed the draft contract and reported to me. Holding the document in his hand and peering at it under his glasses, he said, "This is just an attempt to whitewash" the misspending. He'd later put his opinion in writing in an office email, just to solidify the point. In other words, it felt like an audit contract entered into with the objective of producing a clean audit that would make DHS staff look good.

Bob and I, surrounded by staff, held a video conference to clear the air. My team and I were angry at the entire DHS building for being a roadblock. I was frustrated that Bob had been recruited to their cause. And I was incensed that DHS was issuing public statements claiming to be working well with the state auditor's office but behind closed doors was waging a bureaucratic knife fight. Instead of doing their jobs, they were spending their creative energies boxing out my team.

At that point I was also, admittedly, feeling isolated. We'd made arrests at DHS and audited them, but few others had done anything to help. The federal investigators (Bulldog and his team) were in early days and had not made any arrests. Mike Hurst seemed more interested in re-litigating whether I should have given him the whole case in the beginning. District Attorney Jody Owens was preparing for trial but had not tried anyone yet.

I had also failed to convince anyone to seize the property that MCEC and the News had acquired with TANF money. By the terms of the News' grant agreement with DHS, anything the News purchased with welfare money belonged to the State of Mississippi. It should have even been marked with a sticker or wrapping saying it was owned by the state. That included the cars (an Armada, a Chevy Silverado, and an F-250) the News drove and technology (cell phones, computers, televisions) purchased by the News.

When new attorney general Lynn Fitch was sworn in, I took that matter to her and her two deputy AGs. High in their office building over the Jackson skyline, I suggested that one of her attorneys should file a motion in court to commandeer that property before it vanished. My office had no authority to do it.

It would take a year and a half before the AG's office took any kind of action. When they did, they simply told Bob he could hire private lawyers to make seizures if Bob wanted to. Paying those lawyers would cost the state a nice pile of taxpayer dollars while the state attorneys in Fitch's employ sat on their hands.

Most of the property bought with TANF money "walked away" during that year's wait. I tried to quiet my mind when it suggested the AG's office was going light on Nancy because of a personal connection between New and Fitch. Fitch had spoken at the opening of one of Nancy's facilities, so I knew they were acquainted.

In other words, it felt like my team and I were screaming, alone, into the wind that something wasn't right. We also had to endure constant murmurings about how we were the only ones who'd found a problem at DHS and speculations that we were probably mistaken. That feeling of isolation would change over time, but on the day of the video conference with DHS, I felt like the odd man out.

For the call, Stephanie and I sat on one side of the table in what we called the War Room, staring up at a mounted camera and TV screen. Pat sat off to the side, out of frame. Bob and his general counsel were on the call from their office and on the right side of the screen. The outside CPA firm chosen to do the forensic audit appeared on the left side of the screen, from hundreds of miles away. That firm — a reputable team from Baltimore, Maryland, with no real connections to Mississippi — likely wondered what sort of redneck shooting match they'd walked in to.

As Stephanie ticked through the issues we had with the contract, Bob grew more agitated. The cauldron bubbled over. There was no yelling, but we were close. The TV speakers buzzed and popped as our voices grew louder and louder.

I said, "Look, I don't understand your position. Either DHS

wants to get to the bottom of everything here and you are willing to let us see the results, or you're not. Which is it?"

Bob pushed back. There was tension on his end — a desire for the public to think DHS was working closely with us but an impulse to keep us at as great a distance as possible. I didn't like that DHS was not willing to let us look at everything the Baltimore firm found and that Bob wanted final say over what made it into the Baltimore team's report. I said if that was their position, then they should "stop saying to the media and the public that you're working well with us."

Bob lashed back and said I should stop telling the world DHS staff played a part in the misspending.

I laughed and said, "Due respect, I'll say whatever the hell I want to, Bob, because I'm telling the truth."

Then Bob's counsel stepped in. She realized I was close to walking away from any role in this outside forensic audit. If I had, it would not help DHS restore the public's faith in their agency. They wanted to be able to say the state auditor's team was happy with their progress.

Bob and the counsel asked to go off camera for a moment, and then came back. They would back down on most, but not all, of our objections to the contract that we were all about to sign. I consulted Stephanie and Pat to see if they were comfortable with where that left us.

"We can handle that," Stephanie said.

This wasn't our last fight, though. Two years later, still frustrated that DHS staffers had lied to my auditors, I asked the legislature to pass a bill requiring DHS's fraud investigation unit to report any suspected fraud or embezzlement to me and to the attorney general. Bob wrote a letter to lawmakers opposing my position.

I found out about Bob's letter and called a legislator to discuss. "Yeah, I threw his letter in the garbage," he said. "I don't think you have to worry." The bill passed with one nay vote in the House of Representatives and unanimously in the state senate. Governor Reeves, Bob's boss, signed the bill into law, notwithstanding Bob's opposition.

Ultimately, this part of the story is not about a fight between

Bob Anderson and me. It's about how entire institutions can obstruct accountability. Not everyone at DHS was a fraudster. I felt confident at the end of our investigation — an investigation by federal authorities (under two different presidential administrations), a review by three different prosecutors, and an audit by an out-of-state independent CPA firm — that every salient fact in the case had been unearthed. Many DHS staffers came out looking fine. But some of them still, for whatever reason, showed their teeth every time an auditor came by.

Perhaps they believed John Davis was being unfairly targeted or that what he'd done wasn't that bad. That level of cognitive dissonance was amazing to me, if that was what they believed. The DHS staff would have had to ignore the poor who were suffering all around them while watching John pay to have his friend Brett treated at a Malibu resort.

Or perhaps the DHS staff just didn't like reading bad things in the newspaper about their workplace. I don't know why the DHS well was so poisoned. Regardless, this battle of institutions should serve as a warning to all future white-collar investigators: When you find a scheme, you may be wrestling with more than just the target of your inquiry. You may be fighting an entire office.

You may also have to go it alone for a while to do the right thing. That period, where my team felt like we were the only ones working on the case and the only ones being criticized, reminded me of my time at the US Air Force Officer Training School (OTS) at Maxwell Air Force Base. During OTS, I was the leader of our flight, a group of sixteen trainees, for a week. The job of the flight leader is to march your group of pilots, JAGs, and other officers-to-be around the base. You ensure everyone completes their training exercises on time. You also learn some leadership lessons along the way.

One day I was forming up the flight outside our classroom to head to the cafeteria. It was hot. The first few members of the flight out of the classroom door were, admittedly, not moving with enough urgency. The drill sergeant saw them walking slowly and came at me like a cruise missile.

"OT White!" he yelled behind his wide-brimmed hat, chin

out. The sergeant was a few inches shorter than me, but at the moment I felt like I came to his chest. For the next few minutes I took a tongue lashing, nose-to-nose with him, for our failure to assemble quickly. It didn't matter that *I* was moving at good speed. I was responsible for everyone — and that was the point. When you're the leader, you're accountable for the actions of everyone in your unit. You take the heat alone, standing by yourself.

I knew as the auditor's office made our findings public, I would have to own any work done by the group. I was prepared to do so, for better or worse, standing there by myself.

But I also trusted my team. They did good work, as both criminal investigators and auditors. I knew, too, they were leaders with my same mind-set. They were willing to go it alone, and face off against any institution, if that's what it took to do the right thing.

"What were they thinking?"

While the public continued to digest the news that $98 million in welfare money had likely been misspent, I met with Brad White, chief of staff to Governor Reeves, and David Maron, the governor's chief counsel. Brad was a longtime player in Mississippi politics, known for his rural Mississippi accent and ability to tell a good joke behind the smoke of a cigar. He'd been savvy enough to work his way to the top of national politics, too, as a former chief of staff to the head of the US Senate appropriations committee. His aw-shucks manner aside, Brad was skilled. At his side was Maron, who'd walked straight out of a white-shoe law firm to work for Governor Reeves. A brilliant litigator, David looked the part with slicked-back hair and an ever-present dark suit.

At the time, I was still hearing rumors that Mike Hurst was telling people I'd handed the DHS case to state prosecutors instead of the feds to protect Governor Bryant. I knew Brad and Mike were close. Mike's kids even called the governor's chief Uncle Brad. I figured if Mike was telling his tale to anyone, he was probably telling Brad.

Brad and David came to talk about DHS. As the meeting went on, I could tell there was some tension on their side of the table, so I cut through it.

"Look, if someone told you I cut Mike out to protect Governor Bryant, they are out of their minds. Why would I give our files and full access to the FBI and other federal investigators if that were true? Why even tell the world about the case at all, back when we arrested Nancy and John? If that's your definition of a cover-up, it's the worst cover-up in history," I said.

Maron smiled across the table. *Those rumors don't make a lick of sense*, his grin seemed to suggest.

Brad said he understood, but he also added that he didn't like the fact that I had referred to Governor Bryant as the whistleblower. It was well known that Reeves's crew didn't like Bryant, but I'm not sure why my statement rubbed Governor Reeves's team the wrong way. Maybe it was because Team Reeves resented being handed this big a scandal in their first few months.

I'd already said it publicly, but I said it again to Brad: I acknowledged Governor Bryant was the whistleblower because Governor Bryant *was* the whistleblower. Statute defined *whistleblower* as the person who brings a tip to a law enforcement agency. The statute lists the state auditor's office as an example of law enforcement. Bryant was the only one in the case who reported the fraud to criminal investigators.

Beyond that, whistleblowers cannot be fired for turning over evidence, and no DHS staffer deserved that legal protection. They'd lied to my auditors' faces about what was going on and withheld information about the depth of the corruption.

Not long after the meeting, activists from every left-of-center organization, from the NAACP to the Children's Defense Fund, held a rally at the state capitol building to talk about DHS. As if on cue, they proved my point about the danger of handing the case solely over to Mike. The head of the Children's Defense Fund, Oleta Fitzgerald, sounded off. Fitzgerald, when talking about whether a Republican US attorney like Mike would fairly prosecute the case, said, "We don't trust that if that case goes federal that it won't go any higher than what it is."

Mike's friends could complain all they wanted about him not having exclusive rights to the case. But handing the case to Jody, along with the FBI (who would ultimately have to deliver their findings to Mike's office), was the way to show the public we weren't burying anything.

If I'd wanted to, I could have sown even more doubt about Mike's office handling the case fairly. Just before Stephanie's audit showing the welfare misspending, Mike's office asked us to not release the results. They made some claim about how it would hurt their ability to prosecute a DHS case one day. But federal law required us to audit federal funds (like TANF) in Mississippi each year. There was no clause in that requirement allowing us to hide the results. If Oleta Fitzgerald had known that Mike didn't want the full facts out there, there would've been more rallies.

At this point, I was jaded about Mike's motives. The most cynical parts of my brain told me that he wanted to hide the audit findings because, once the findings were out, there would be pressure on him to prosecute every nugget in there. Or because the audit would reveal something untoward about a friend of his. Or because he now saw me as some sort of rival; a good news cycle for me was a bad one for him. But I told my team we would continue to share information with Mike and the FBI in good faith. Finding the full extent of the fraud was more important than what Mike or I thought about each other.

Across town from my office, Nancy and Zach New were talking to their lawyers. They hired expensive attorneys, including a former army JAG who'd defended Sergeant Bowe Bergdahl. Bergdahl became famous after leaving his army unit in Afghanistan and being captured by the Taliban. He returned home after a Guantanamo Bay prisoner exchange. Then questions arose about why he'd left his unit in the first place. The well-known podcast *Serial* chronicled his case, and Bergdahl was the subject of frequent discussion on cable news. His lawyer, former lieutenant colonel Frank Rosenblatt, was now the News' lawyer.

I wondered where the money was coming from to pay for that high-priced representation. MCEC had almost no funds of its own, aside from taxpayer money. We also knew that the defense team had hired a forensic auditor, a former IRS agent. I didn't blame them for that, because it's what I would have done if I were representing them. But I hoped the News weren't paying for their audit with TANF money.

The News' team of lawyers went right to work. First, they convinced the judge to unfreeze the bank account holding MCEC's TANF funds. The News said a state auditor couldn't halt spending in a private account. Only the AG could do that, and the AG had not asked to lock the account. The News won that argument.

Next, the News argued to the DA that no one should be allowed to discuss the case in public. The defense attorneys also tried to suppress (prevent us from using in court) communications between Zach New and his brother, Jess. They argued that those communications were protected by attorney-client privilege, as Jess was an attorney. But I knew from hearing about the texts from investigators that there were plenty of communications between the two where Zach was not asking Jess for legal advice. Those should not be privileged.

Jody's team of prosecutors went into the trenches every day to fight back. Attorney General Fitch's office should have been helping by filing papers in court to refreeze the MCEC account that held the welfare money, and I said as much to the AG's office. That was a common move in white-collar cases — preventing stolen funds from being used for the defendants' legal defense — dating back to insider trading cases in the mid-1980s.

But the AG's office never pitched in. Instead, Fitch filmed a video around that time with Brett Favre (where he called her "Lynn Finch," with an *n* in her last name) discussing COVID and promoting her office — all after the public knew Favre was enmeshed in the scandal. Perhaps Favre believed it was important to stay in the good graces of the attorney general, and that led to the video. Or perhaps Fitch was wagering it was better for her long-term political future to align with Favre. However the video came about, Fitch was firmly on the sidelines in the case.

While Jody waged legal war, I sought to stave off any attack on my office. I worried that politicians sympathetic to New might try to remove some of my office's legal authority. Every quote to the press from Mississippi's lawmakers expressed outrage, but I knew not all of them felt that way. I'd seen too many people, oftentimes those in power, who didn't want auditors to tell the world how the government spends taxpayer money.

For instance, when COVID-19 hit, Congress sent billions of stimulus dollars to the states. Mississippi received $1.25 billion for the legislature to spend. In a typical year, Mississippi's state budget is around $6 billion, so the new $1.25 billion was a substantial shot of adrenaline for appropriators. It was also a significant amount of additional money to audit. So I asked for $3 million of the $1.25 billion to audit that $1.25 billion.

To sell the request for $3 million, I put on a suit, and Stephanie and I walked to the capitol building. With an explanatory memo in hand, my wood-heeled black dress shoes clicked and clacked up and down the white ceramic floors. From one meeting to the next, the reception was positive. No one opposed spending some of the stimulus money to catch potential embezzlers.

Then the capitol fell quiet as the final versions of the appropriations bills were written. Key decision-makers went behind closed doors and hashed out the final compromise. Our request was a rounding error on $1.25 billion. I assumed we'd receive the money.

After the internal debates, legislators emerged from behind their barricades. They walked their spending bills to the lawyers at the foot of the antique wells in each chamber. Bills moved fast at this point. Votes were taken quickly with the staccato chiming of "All in favor? All opposed? The ayes have it, the bill passes." This happened over and over until the spending was done.

A few hours later, once the bills were posted online, my staff and I had our first look.

No money for auditing.

I was incensed. I called legislative leadership in both chambers. Staff from one side didn't return the call. The other chamber's head policy staffer called me back.

"The decision was made above my pay grade," he said.

"I was under the assumption that that's *exactly* what you were paid for," I replied. The staffer recommended that I ask Governor Reeves, to whom the legislature had awarded $50 million, for some of his money. *Go beg someone else*, in other words.

I stared down at the capitol building from my eighth-floor office across the street. *If I throw my phone through the window, I wonder if it will hit someone on the street*, I thought. *That would be bad.*

I calmed down, and instead used the phone to call the governor's team and, well, beg. Governor Reeves agreed that auditing was a necessity. Within forty-eight hours we were given $3 million of his $50 million in discretionary stimulus funds.

I don't mean to demean all legislators. The good ones are some of the finest public servants I know. They think hard

The author as a little boy fishing in his neighborhood. *Emily White*

The author's grandfather
in his truck. *Bob White*

The author's father working in the oil field. *Emily White*

Brett Favre receives a call in 1991 from his childhood bed informing him he'd been selected by the Atlanta Falcons in the NFL draft. *Getty/Tim Isbell/Biloxi Sun Herald/Tribune News Source*

The author's grandfather in his earlier years.
Bob White

The author, the week he graduated from law school, preparing to move back home.
Mallory White

Brett Favre running down the field after winning Super Bowl XXXI. *Rogers Archive/Getty*

Finishing a round of military training at an F-16 installation. *Shad White*

The author inside the Mississippi governor's mansion in 2018 on his swearing-in day. *Knox Graham*

Brett Favre. *AP/Rogelio Solis*

Teddy Dibiase Jr. during his wrestling days.
Wikipedia user Sayuncle via Dibiase's wikipedia entry

Nancy New and John Davis pose with Brett Favre, Zach New, Teddy Dibiase Jr., and others at the University of Southern Mississippi. *MCEC*

Mississippi's governor's mansion. *Crystal Marie*

John Davis during his time as head of DHS. *State of Mississippi*

The Woolfolk State Office Building, where the gears of government turn quietly and home to the Office of the State Auditor. *Shad White*

Former Governor Phil Bryant. *US Dept. of Energy, via Bryant's Wikipedia entry*

A view from Rise in Malibu, the luxury rehabilitation center attended by Brett Dibiase.
Yelp user

Dr. Jacob Vanlandingham testifies before Congress about his experimental concussion
treatment. *C-Span screenshot*

Nancy New's home at 1800 Sheffield Drive in Jackson, which she financed partly with government dollars. *Office of the State Auditor*

District Attorney Jody Owens and the author the day they announced the arrest of the DHS Six. *AP/Rogelio Solis*

Mississippi's capitol building. *Crystal Marie*

Mugshots of the DHS Six. *WLBT*

Attorney General Lynn Fitch. *AP/Rogelio Solis*

Former US Attorney Mike Hurst. *US DOJ*
via Hurst's wikipedia entry

USM's volleyball facility, paid for with TANF dollars. *Clarion Ledger/Chuck Cook*

Reporter Anna Wolfe.
Wolfe's Twitter account

Deputy DHS
Director Jacob Black.
State of Mississippi

DHS Director Bob Anderson at the press conference announcing his appointment.
Governor Tate Reeves is behind him. *AP/Rogelio Solis*

Belinda Gartner, tireless front-desk secretary and merciless gatekeeper. *Shad White*

Nancy New in court
shortly before her
guilty plea.
AP/Rogelio Solis

Zach New in the
courtroom awaiting
his plea colloquy.
AP/Rogelio Solis

The author testifying before the US House Ways and Means Committee (subcommittee
on work and welfare) in Washington, DC. *US Ways and Means staff*

Vandalism on a building in South Mississippi falsely blames Governor Tate Reeves for the TANF scandal. According to WDAM-TV, this was one of multiple instances of graffiti fingering Reeves for the fraud during the 2023 gubernatorial campaign. *WDAM staff*

The staff of the Office of the State Auditor. The author is standing in the center of the first row with Stephanie Palmertree and Charles Woods on his right and Larry Ware on his left. *State of Mississippi/Gib Ford*

about how they're voting and try to solve problems by improving the law. But others are there to "big dog" it — enjoy the trappings of the office, slap their buddies on their backs, go out to paid-for dinners, and, to the extent they ever do anything of substance, protect their friends.

Whatever some folks' reasons for opposing transparency, I couldn't let that stand in the way of telling the public what happened. That instinct came from my grandfather. I spent a couple of summers working in the oil field with Papa while I was in high school. Other than me dragging heavy black hoses up the flights of metal stairs on two-story oil tanks in the Mississippi heat, my chief recollection of that time was that my grandfather could not stand a man who would shrink from saying the truth. He must've had Matthew 5:37, which says to let your yeses be yes and your nos be no, bolded and double-underlined in his Bible. "Tell it like it is," in other words. He also practically raised me and my cousin, a marine veteran, and being a wimp in the face of pressure — especially if it was pressure to hide the truth — wasn't a trait he would tolerate in his young men.

Yet a lack of transparency and a desire for an auditor who would back away from a tricky issue is exactly what some in the political world wanted.

When the legislature decided not to fund the DHS forensic audit and the COVID stimulus audit, I knew it was only a matter of time before that news was made public, and the lawmakers would get defensive. They would be angry when taxpayers and the media asked questions about why they wouldn't fund these projects. Some legislators might then turn their ire on my office.

I received a few threats in my time as state auditor — it's never fun to read that someone thinks you belong at the bottom of a lake in "concrete shoes" — but the gravest existential threat to a state auditor's office is lawmakers cutting your funding or taking away your legal authority. The thought that it could happen was enough to curdle my faith in representative democracy.

I saw this scenario play out in North Dakota. In 2019, the North Dakota Legislature had had enough of their state auditor's performance audits. They passed a law taking away the auditor's ability to independently launch them. It would have crippled his office. He fought back and won a decision saying the change was unconstitutional.

The lesson of North Dakota was clear. Probe too hard, and you may have your power stripped. I was not going to let that threat soften the blows I'd strike when there was misspending, though. I had to be prepared to fight for the right to audit.

One of the biggest advantages state auditors who are elected, rather than appointed, have in a fight like that is their independence. The legislature may try to hurt you, but if you have a following of taxpayers who know and have voted for you, you can raise a stink. An unelected bureaucrat might not have as much luck.

In the end, despite my fears, the Mississippi Legislature had enough good members to not take any action against my office. There were some stalwarts in both chambers who loved accountability, and I knew they would be on my side if there were a call to arms.

As for the death threats, I had a group of investigators with guns who were about as protective of me as a team of big brothers. I didn't lose sleep over them.

One reason it was hard for lawmakers to train their fire on me was the steady drumbeat of coverage about the DHS case. Newspaper articles covering portions of our audit trickled out each week. Journalists were overwhelmed when the audit was first released. There were too many examples of waste to cover in a thousand words — or even ten thousand. But bit by bit, they unpacked the DHS audit for the world.

The results stretched forever. MCEC paid John Davis's brother-in-law hundreds of thousands of dollars to illegally lease a property that wasn't even ready for use when the payments started. The brother-in-law was also paid $150,000 to be a "Leadership Outreach Coordinator," whatever that meant. At the time, Davis was living with him.

Davis's nephew, Austin Smith, was paid almost half a million dollars by MCEC and the Family Resource Center, combined, to teach at coding academies, even though they had to pay the nephew to be trained on how to teach coding. This was on top of the salary the nephew was paid as an employee of DHS. In a one-year period, the twenty-two-year-old was paid more than $300,000 — more than twice the governor's salary.

Any relative who could find an excuse to be paid TANF money made out like a bandit. A relative of the DiBiases convinced MCEC to buy tens of thousands of dollars' worth of a flimsy children's book she'd written. The author's own description of the book online was filled with typos and grammatical errors, but the book was good enough for Nancy.

Waste was rampant. More than a million dollars from MCEC and FRC had been given to "consulting" firms, often without a contract or a clear work product to show at the end.

An obsession with sports was present throughout. MCEC rented baseball fields with welfare money and let a private travel softball team called the Mississippi Bombers use the field. There was no evidence that anyone on the Bombers qualified as "needy" in order to receive field time paid for with TANF money.

MCEC spent substantial sums of welfare money to advertise at out-of-state NCAA basketball tournament games and a college football bowl game. I wondered how they thought a Mississippi welfare recipient would make it into the stadium in another state to see the advertisement.

Thousands were spent on sports coaches to mentor Mississippi young people, but, again, there was no verification that the young people were TANF-eligible. Thousands more were spent sponsoring a high school football all-star game.

To be clear, some of these beneficiaries, like the softball team of young women, probably never knew they were receiving welfare money. Or they assumed DHS and the nonprofits knew what they were doing when they provided cash. For instance, MCEC paid a respected Mississippi virtual reality company nearly $800,000 to train sixty students on how to build a virtual reality experience. No one could show that any of those sixty students were needy. But the VR company employed experts in VR, not experts on federal regulations. They performed the service they were hired to perform, so it was hard to blame them.

Others were more suspect. DiBiase businesses benefited while Brett DiBiase worked at DHS, so they should've understood the rules. The DiBiase funding was also for positions or projects so vague that they were meaningless. For example, Ted DiBiase Jr., through his businesses Priceless Ventures and Familiae Orientem, was paid to work as a "Leadership Outreach Coordinator" (another one!). Priceless Ventures was given money to put on workshops "intended to help you understand — at a greater level, yourself, your values, your significance, and your potential." I'd never heard a better description for a pile of hot garbage. It cost taxpayers $3 million. Jess New helped them along, too, by filing the corporate paperwork for the DiBiases.

Ted Jr. had his travel paid out of welfare money through MCEC, too. His business would bill MCEC for first-class air travel, expensive hotels, and nice meals, including one spectacular $607 steak meal. Brett DiBiase did the same through his company Restore. All told, the DiBiases pulled down more than $5 million in TANF over the last two years of Davis's tenure.

One pattern with the spending that bothered me as a public school graduate was the money handed to private, tuition-charging schools where there was no evidence that the spending reached a needy child. Nancy's own private school drew down money for textbooks and plenty of other costs without showing whether poor children were served.

Another trend was the heavy-handed use of faith-based initiatives. The News paid for Christian singers to perform at churches around the state and dropped more than $60,000 to establish a "prayer council" for mayors. There was no evidence that poor folks attended the concerts or the mayor meetings. Thousands more in welfare dollars went to a church and a religious mentoring service with no real work product demanded.

The media's hands weren't clean, either. Mississippi's biggest newspaper, the *Clarion-Ledger*; a local television station; a talk radio station; and a few other outlets were sent checks backed by welfare funds to run ads that did not comply with federal rules.

And from time to time, Michael Torres, the agency auditor Stephanie assigned to oversee this project, saw expenditures that defied any explanation at all. One example was a $3,000 cash payment from MCEC's welfare fund to John Davis. Michael was the quintessential auditor — detail-oriented and with a voice that never went above a few decibels. He would furrow his dark eyebrows and say, sotto voce, "What were they thinking?"

In 2018, this misspending was happening at FRC and MCEC. Then, in 2019, John drastically cut FRC's grant.

Christi Webb, FRC's director, explained why. She told my agents that John always demanded to control where some of the spending went after it reached MCEC and FRC accounts. He loved spending on the DiBiases, for example. FRC knew some of the pet projects John demanded violated federal law, so, at some point, Webb told Davis she would not comply. According to Webb, the day she told Davis he cursed and screamed. Then Davis realized this wasn't a problem; he just cut FRC's funding and handed even more to MCEC. Nancy found her pas de deux with John even more lucrative. That year, Nancy pulled in more than $20 million in funding from DHS.

To conceal the arrangement, MCEC swept the floor behind their steps every time they tracked mud. They falsified information in their reports to DHS staff about how they were spending money. They wrote contracts with DHS staff that said they would spend money one way, but then actually spent it a different, illegal way. They forged signatures on documents.

Following our audit, only one institution that received Nancy's money fired a salvo suggesting the audit was wrong. That institution was the agency that ran the state's public universities. Their executive director, Dr. Al Rankins, knew politicians bowed to him because they loved staying in the good graces of the universities. He wasn't accustomed to being told he'd done something wrong.

Rankins didn't like the audit results, so he sent out a letter claiming auditors should not have questioned the welfare spending on Southern Miss's volleyball court. He also demanded that I tell the public our audit finding was wrong.

I wrote Dr. Rankins back. I pointed out that he knew Southern Miss's Athletic Foundation was being paid in DHS money. His own internal documents proved that. I also told him that, rather than asking for retractions to our audit and making flaccid arguments, his time would be better spent providing the public with a plan for the volleyball court to be used by the at-risk community.

Part of the point of my letter to Rankins was to let others know that, if they were considering questioning my team's work, it would be like challenging a Weed Eater to a boxing match. It wasn't going to end well for them. My crew documented everything we wrote in the audit. And we were right.

Beyond the audit, reporter Jack Bologna kept pushing. Jack filed a public records request with DHS to put his hands on the "internal audit" that DHS employees wrote to Governor Bryant. That was the key document, according to DHS staff, that showed they were the ones who should be credited with uncovering the fraud.

The reality was that DHS knew they couldn't disclose the one-page document without destroying the narrative that they were heroes. The document was too thin and said nothing about the News. So they told Jack to buzz off and file a complaint with the state ethics commission if he wanted to see it. Jack was no fool. He probably knew the "internal audit" wasn't all the DHS staff had made it out to be.

I'd been impressed with Jack's ability to fight through the state's bureaucracy. He was not from Mississippi, but he'd learned the lay of the land quickly. He had boyish looks, a big head of black hair, and a slight frame. You could catch him running forest trails on the outskirts of Jackson if you went at the right time. Underneath the baby face and skinny frame was a pit bull who wouldn't let go of an important story.

After Jack's columns, my auditors went on to ask DHS employees directly why they'd never raised the facts described in the internal audit — or any of the other fraud related to the News, for that matter — to the state auditor's office. The answer was alarming: They claimed they did not believe there was a place to report fraud. They assumed the questions my auditors asked every year were pro forma. According to them, no one in Mississippi actually investigated white-collar crime involving public funds.

You will be getting paid regularly

By mid-2020, the cat-and-mouse game between prosecutors and defense attorneys was in full swing. Jody's team in the district attorney's office was waiting to see which defendant would be "first on the bus," in prosecutor-speak. Being first on the bus referred to the defendant who agreed before the others in a conspiracy case to admit guilt and cooperate. They often received the most favorable treatment from the government.

Nancy, meanwhile, was in no way signaling a desire to ride the bus. MCEC released a statement suggesting that John Davis had signed off on all MCEC's spending. The statement also implied that my office should audit FRC, MCEC's rival.

We were looking at FRC just as closely as we had MCEC, but that aside, the stupidity of MCEC's statement was astounding. MCEC came close to admitting that money had been misspent, and their only excuse was that someone told them to do it. That wouldn't fly in front of a jury. Murderers can't prove their innocence by claiming someone else told them to pull the trigger. It also wouldn't fly because the News made so much money, personally, off MCEC's welfare spending. And they'd misled DHS staff about how they were spending.

MCEC's deflection to FRC was worse. It implied that what MCEC did was justified because others did it, too. No murderer was ever acquitted with the defense of, "Well, sure, I killed the guy, but plenty of other people have committed murder, too."

No good defense attorney, and certainly not the skilled attorneys the News had hired, would sign off on a statement like that. The statement suggested that Nancy was calling the PR shots herself. Some time later, we learned that their defense team had quit, including the attorney who'd defended Bowe Bergdahl.

Nancy was proving to be an enigmatic person. She had enough brains to build an empire large enough to enrich herself. She had the charm to build a network that included the biggest celebrities and politicians in the state. But she did not have the sense to avoid giving the media evidence of her own guilt.

I searched my mind for an analogue to her. There were parts of her tale mirroring that of Ken Lay, the former CEO of Enron. In its heyday, Enron's stratospheric valuation defied common sense. Lay ignored that fact or maybe didn't understand enough about what his underlings were doing, which led to fraud. He was making too much money to ask hard questions.

Nancy also seemed to have ignored the way her nonprofit defied the laws of financial gravity. They were supposed to be running a school serving special needs children in the poorest state in the country. But that school could afford a campus in Costa Rica and could finance a nice life for Nancy and her children. Maybe she was making too much money, and having too much fun being patted on the back, to ask questions about why their bank account was so full.

If Nancy was like Lay, then Zach was similar to Andy Fastow, Enron's CFO. Fastow created the side businesses and subsidiaries to hide Enron's faulty accounting. He also took a big cut of the money that went through those subsidiaries, which allowed him to play the Houston socialite. He hired his dad to run the foundation that was financed by his ill-gotten gains. Like the Fastow Foundation, Nancy and Zach's nonprofit enabled their philanthropist lifestyle and provided money for the family.

Exploring these analogues was helpful for thinking about how the DHS corruption was allowed to happen. One striking similarity: Just as there was little oversight of Fastow's subsidiaries by Enron corporate leadership, there was also little oversight of Nancy's nonprofit by DHS staff.

In addition to the lack of oversight, John Davis ruled DHS through fear, just like Enron's management. In Kurt Eichenwald's book on Enron, *Conspiracy of Fools*, Eichenwald wrote that, at one point, Ron Astin, an attorney hired by Enron, was asked to do something unethical. He yelled at Fastow, "Andy, I don't represent you! I represent Enron!" I wish someone at DHS had had the courage to say that to John — that they didn't work to please John, they worked for the taxpayers — even if it meant losing their job.

John's heavy hand was on display at meetings he led. Once during his tenure, DHS held a conference for agency employees. John decided the room should sing a chorus of "Amazing Grace" (for some of the trainings, John even hired an expensive violin and harp duo to add a little class to the room). Standing in front of the crowd, a group of five women went onstage, microphones in hand. As they nervously crooned, John became upset that the staffers in the audience were not singing along with enough gusto. "I can't hear you!" he said, looking around the room. "Do you want three days off?" he asked, threatening a three-day suspension. Stilted laughter trickled through the hall. One of the women singing onstage, her eyes wide, waved her hands at the crowd nervously, trying to encourage more volume.

At another event, John was speaking to a hotel conference room full of his team members and decided to end every other sentence with the question "Amen?," beckoning the crowd to affirm what he was saying. When the attendees didn't answer with a loud enough "Amen!" in reply, John puffed up. His chest, adorned with a gold tie against his black dress shirt and black suit, pushed out a few more inches. "You gotta learn something about me," he said. "When I say Amen, you better say Amen back to me big time, or I get disappointed, and then I get really mad. *Amen?*" The employees parroted back, "Amen!"

He closed the session by saying the attendees were having a banquet-style event that evening where they could "dress up," but if they didn't want to dress up, he promised not to fire them. "But I will tell you this," John said, "if you're in this room and don't want to be here, get the hell out." More awkward laughter. "*Amen?*"

One person's leadership style doesn't usually create fraud, though. A fraud as big as Enron, or even DHS, is like a plane crash. For a plane to crash, multiple redundant systems have to fail. For the DHS scandal to happen, the federal government first had to decide to place the onus on the states to spend TANF money correctly and then back away. DHS's monitoring of the nonprofits had to be shut down. And MCEC's private auditors needed to ignore what was happening.

All that happened here. The forms that DHS was supposed to submit to the federal HHS were often incomplete. They were allowed to continue operating with few questions asked.

Davis also did not monitor the nonprofits that received the funds. He handed them cash-upfront grants and allowed them to spend away, subject to his occasional demands.

Then there were the private CPAs hired by MCEC to review their books. MCEC was audited by a small, private firm called Williams Weiss Hester and Company from Jackson. The firm gave MCEC a clean audit for years.

There is a deep, dark secret in the private accounting industry: There are good CPAs and there are bad CPAs, just like there are bad doctors, lawyers, and zookeepers. Bad CPAs lived off "drive-by audits." Clean, hassle-free audits kept their clients happy and meant the CPA would continue to be hired. Think Arthur Andersen, the once-prestigious firm that audited Enron and WorldCom.

I don't know if Williams Weiss Hester and Company actually did drive-by audits (that is, if they were derelict in their professional duties) or if they were kept in the dark by MCEC, but after Nancy was arrested, she seemed to think they did shoddy audits. In 2021, Nancy and Zach sued the CPA firm, claiming they did not have the required certifications to perform audits of federal funds. The firm also should not have told MCEC they had a surfeit of "unrestricted" assets and should have stopped the News from spending money, the News said. Apparently cars, cell phones, rental contracts, Nancy's house, consulting payments, money for investments in experimental drugs, retirement accounts, and everything else that benefited the News — none of which MCEC could afford with its paltry budget before DHS grants — didn't make it obvious enough. Their accountant should have told them they weren't supposed to get rich, the News protested.

With the landing gear, warning lights, and autopilot broken, still another system had to fail here: The agency that should have been regulating private sector auditors needed to fail to do its job. In Mississippi, that agency is the Board of Public

Accountancy. It's the definition of a sleepy bureaucracy. The tiny board, populated by CPAs, is tucked away in state government and was run by a man named Andy Wright. He had a staff of four people. They were charged with investigating private CPA firms that should have their licenses revoked for failure to audit to accounting standards.

The truth was that Andy, like many other bureaucrats, was trying to get to Friday each week. He seemed to fear going too hard on CPAs, perhaps because the CPA community was so small and tight-knit in Mississippi. Disciplinary action against anyone might mean hurting an influential CPA and jeopardizing Andy's job.

Andy was unaware of just about everything around him, almost by design. Four months after the arrests of the DHS Six, and one week after our audit revealed $98 million in questioned spending, there were rumors that some accountants from outside Mississippi might file complaints about the work of Williams Weiss Hester and Company. The complaints would go to Andy's board for Andy to enforce. Andy called Pat Dendy.

"Pat, has the auditor's office ever thought of looking at those nonprofits that get TANF money?" he asked. "There may be something fishy going on over there."

Pat practically fell out of his chair. Andy was living under a rock. Apparently the underside of the rock didn't accept deliveries of the *New York Times* or any other outlet that covered our arrests. My guess was that life under Andy's rock kept him safe over the years. Under it, he could see nothing, hear nothing, and keep his job.

A week later, a group of Texas and Virginia CPAs, alarmed by what they'd seen in the private audits of MCEC and FRC by Mississippi firms, filed complaints with Andy against the firms. Andy freaked and called Pat again.

"Pat, what if the press finds out?" he exclaimed. Pat gently suggested that Andy just do his job.

"Well, what are y'all going to do about it?" Andy asked. Pat explained that the state auditor's office didn't regulate private CPAs. That was his job. We performed audits of government money.

The press found out about the complaints and asked to see copies of them. Andy refused. He was spending time researching the out-of-state CPAs to see why they were playing in his backyard, and, according to him, he was thinking about filing a complaint against *them* at *their* own state boards of accountancy to scare them off.

Back inside his cave, Andy would successfully hide out for the rest of the DHS case timeline. As far as I know, the Board of Public Accountancy never took a license away from any CPA involved in auditing MCEC or FRC. Andy made it hard to tell if firms had had licenses revoked because, if it ever happened, he didn't put their names on the board website. Arthur Andersen, by comparison, was put out of business by the Enron scandal. To this day, I'm not sure if Andy ever read our audit of TANF funds.

Finally, there was a lack of regulatory oversight for nonprofits themselves, like MCEC. Nonprofits everywhere are walking fraud risks. The Association of Certified Fraud Examiners (ACFE) has said, "Nonprofit organizations can be more susceptible to fraud due to having fewer resources available to help prevent and recover from a fraud loss. This sector is particularly vulnerable because of less oversight and lack of certain internal controls."

In Mississippi it was as bad as it gets, because no government agency probes nonprofit operations. The Mississippi Secretary of State's office required all nonprofits in the state to register with them but didn't ask for much else. That office had been given no investigators to go around looking at nonprofits for illegal activity. One experienced private CPA who counted several nonprofits as his clients told me the clients were often unaware their charities were not their own private fund. Some didn't even have boards. That meant the nonprofit was little more than a bank account belonging to an individual or a family. If they were dishonest, they could lie to the world about why they were raising money and then spend the money as they wished.

"Charities are not personal piggy banks for their founders to tap into for pet projects," Laurie Styron, the executive director of CharityWatch, has said. One example of this problem was Favre4Hope, Brett Favre's charity. His nonprofit claimed that it raised money "for disadvantaged and disabled children and breast cancer patients." Instead, most of its big contributions from 2018 to 2020 went to the USM athletic foundation or the high school booster club where his daughter played volleyball. "If the charity told donors it was raising money for breast cancer but then spends the resulting donations on an athletic facility, the people running the organization are not fulfilling their obligations to spend the nonprofit's donations the way its donors intended," said Styron.

In any event, all this created a perfect ecosystem for fraud. DHS and MCEC were what our hothouse produced. It made me wonder what other corruption lurked out there in the night, undiscovered, and how to get at it.

⚖

While the criminal cases marched toward trial, a new investigative team puzzled with the same questions that Richie and his crew had worked to unravel. Bulldog, the task force officer on my staff whom I'd assigned to work with the FBI, was now on that team with an FBI agent (I'll call him Ryan) and an investigator from the OIG (I'll call her Lopez).

Bulldog, Ryan, and Lopez spent hours talking with my investigators, looking through our files, and leaning on Stephanie Palmertree's and Michael Torres's extensive knowledge of federal regulations. We invited them to work from our office, which was especially convenient for them when part of my team had to be sent home during the COVID-19 pandemic. The federal team had the run of the place.

Their goal was clear: to get all the evidence necessary to indict new people beyond the DHS Six if more crimes had been committed. The reason new charges against new people were the priority is something federal law enforcement call the Petite Policy. This policy states that federal prosecutors should avoid prosecuting defendants for federal crimes if the defendants have already been prosecuted in state court for the same actions. The federal government didn't want to waste limited resources on holding someone accountable for something they'd already been punished for.

Bulldog was a talker who could build rapport with any potential witness. Ryan was a young, straightlaced, rail-thin marine. And Lopez was a committed, incisive OIG agent. Backing them was a team from the Department of Justice. That team scheduled the payments flying around more than a hundred bank accounts. I knew if we'd missed anything, they'd find it.

Seeing them work together reminded me of stories about the old days, when employees from the Mississippi state auditor's office worked with the FBI on Operation Pretense. This was a mid-1980s sting operation where FBI informants, pretending to be vendors to county governments, recorded dozens of local elected officials accepting bribes. The tapes from the wired-up conversations led to more than 50 of Mississippi's 410 county supervisors being charged with corruption. Some of the dollar amounts on the cases were small, but the number of corrupt officials caught in the net of Pretense reverberated around the state.

While the FBI supplied the informants who recorded the incriminating conversations, state auditors gathered financial documents for the FBI. Auditors also testified in some of the cases about the shady fiscal practices of counties that often accompanied criminal activity.

State auditors' work back then showed that a small number of highly motivated law enforcement officials could break the back of a long-standing culture of corruption. The key was cooperation across multiple offices. With our partnership with Jody and Bulldog's joint state-federal team in place, we now had that.

As the federal investigators shook the bushes, the DiBiases grew nervous. One of their attorneys requested a meeting with federal prosecutors and asked that my team be excluded. The prosecutors alerted us, and I told them I had no problem with them talking to Ted Jr.'s lawyer without Bulldog or anyone else from my squad present.

In the meeting with federal prosecutors, the lawyer sketched out a grand conspiracy theory in which Governor Bryant had orchestrated all the spending to benefit the News, and I was the pawn in the cover-up.

After the meeting, the prosecutors told Bulldog what was said. Bulldog told me. I'd had enough of the innuendo. "Then tell the lawyer to put up or shut up," I said. "Show some proof of this crazy conspiracy. If the feds can find proof on more people, then good. Everyone who did something wrong should go down. If the feds suspect Bryant of telling Nancy to go get rich off this money, or if they think Bryant benefited, then tell them to do the work we've been doing. Investigate! Reach their own conclusions! Tell them to do their jobs!" Mike Hurst was in charge of those prosecutors, and he could dive in to any potential wrongdoing as much as I could.

Bulldog passed that word back to the federal prosecutors. A few days went by, and then Bulldog called again.

"The prosecutors talked to Ted Jr.'s lawyer again," Bulldog said. "It's been a colossal waste of time. He offered nothing of value to prove this conspiracy theory. I think they were embarrassed for him. Probably shouldn't have even sat down with him."

Passing the buck would always be the name of the game for the defendants. In November 2020, the journalists covering the story, Jack and Anna, saw an interesting social media post: Nancy was having a yard sale. On an unseasonably warm Friday, they both walked up Nancy's manicured lawn and asked her for an interview.

Anna would later write that Nancy "declined to answer most questions." But when she was asked whether she was told to spend some of the welfare money the way she did — such as on the Prevacus treatment — Nancy said, "Absolutely." No more details than that. Just enough to keep the public guessing.

That weekend Anna did unearth details of a meeting among Davis, Nancy, Dr. Vanlandingham (the founder of Prevacus), and Favre (who owned a large piece of Prevacus). According to Ted Jr.'s lawyer, Vanlandingham came to Favre's home to pitch the concussion treatment as an investment. Vanlandingham didn't understand the relationship between Davis and Nancy, but he said Davis appeared to be Nancy's boss. Ultimately Vanlandingham would walk away with more than $2 million in welfare funds funneled through MCEC.

Later Nancy and her lawyers would claim that despite the fact that they gave a boatload of TANF money to Prevacus, they never intended to take any income earned from the investment for themselves. They were just following instructions. That claim was belied by Zach's text messages to Vanlandingham, though. In texts, Zach made it clear that he wanted payouts from the investment to go to the family's private LLC.

You will be "getting paid regularly," Vanlandingham told Zach.

"N3 llc will be the name we use" for the account receiving the returns, said Zach. "That is me, mom and my brother Jess."

The scheme to pay the News was also confirmed by texts between Favre and Vanlandingham. "Nancy did get approval now to take 50k in shares from Prevacus. I gave her the good shares that won't cost her or have a tax requirement," Vanlandingham texted to Favre.

"Now that's awesome," Favre replied. It would be hard for Nancy to run from that evidence.

The fact that the defendants were trying to throw around the hot potato of guilt was a bad sign for them. They'd gone from admitting no wrong to finger-pointing about who was at fault. That, again, came close to an admission of guilt. The Hinds County judge assigned to Nancy's case had seen enough. Six days after the yard sale interview, Judge Faye Peterson issued a gag order telling everyone to stop discussing the case for fear that Nancy might convict herself in public.

The vise tightened on the defendants again when Bulldog's team made their first public move: putting a claim on Ted Jr.'s home. When the team served the notice (called a *lis pendens*), a realtor was in the middle of showing the $1.5 million, six-thousand-square-foot dwelling, with its pool and boathouse, to potential buyers. DiBiase had purchased the home in 2018, right around the time he was paid by DHS.

State and federal authorities working together in this way thawed my relationship with Mike and the US attorney's office. I stopped hearing rumors about what Mike was saying around town. I sensed they were pleased at how the team was looking at the case. In addition, we continued to send other good cases

Mike's way. When we found that the mayor of the town of Moss Point had thrown a gala to raise money for local schools but instead used the dough to buy a dog and a car for his family, we worked it jointly with the feds. It was narrow enough to share with them and be able to close out quickly. Mike was grateful. He called — the first time in a while — to say our team had done a bang-up job.

In state court, though, Jody's progress ground to a halt due to COVID. The pandemic made it impossible to assemble a jury. Trials were pushed deeper down the calendar. The only silver lining was that the delays gave Jody and Jamie McBride, his chief deputy, time to negotiate plea deals.

On December 17, 2020, Brett DiBiase walked into open state court and pleaded guilty for his part in the DHS scandal. He accepted his share of responsibility for using welfare money to go to the luxury rehab facility in Malibu while claiming to teach classes. He cut a check that day for a first payment on the money he'd have to return. Of all the money he made off DHS — his salary at the agency, his $200,000-plus salary at MCEC, the money paid to Malibu — he was only responsible for paying back the $48,000 for the treatment. The rest, like so much of the welfare money, was just waste. It was the first guilty plea in the case, and Brett pledged full cooperation with the prosecution.

Meanwhile Nancy's school, New Summit, was falling apart. Teachers noticed that their paychecks were short. They complained to local bloggers and on Facebook. Bulldog and his team noticed, too, and started interviewing some of them.

As it turned out, the paycheck issue was part of the school's death rattle. People discussed conservatorships, lawmakers talked about a state takeover, and some of the wealthy around the state mentioned buying the school. In the end, though, the school just collapsed. By the middle of 2021, teachers would be laid off. When fall 2021 arrived, no children with backpacks scurried through the doors. The school didn't reopen.

DHS, as an institution, marched forward. Notwithstanding my frustrations with him, Bob Anderson made moves around this time, late 2020, that made sense. Bob asked Attorney

General Fitch to provide attorneys to help seize property belonging to DHS in the possession of the News, and when the AG's team refused, Bob allegedly tried to hire former attorney general Jim Hood, the Democrat who'd just lost the gubernatorial race. Fitch's crew fired off a pugilistic response saying Bob had no authority to hire outside counsel. Eventually the two sides settled on an outside attorney who was acceptable to all.

Bob's staff were still a hindrance to us, though. The Baltimore CPA firm started their forensic audit of all the TANF spending during Davis's tenure but quickly became stuck in the mud. DHS staff didn't know how to pull basic financial documents needed to help the firm do their audit. We stepped in where we could to access and provide the necessary ledgers.

The recipients of TANF money like MCEC were fighting the CPA firm, too. Nancy claimed publicly that the forensic audit would exonerate her, but privately she refused to provide the Baltimore auditors with the documents they needed. Heart of David, a Ted DiBiase welfare subrecipient, did the same. They were so obstinate that we subpoenaed their documents, and Heart of David's lawyer fought the subpoena. In the end, a judge had to rule that Heart of David was required to give us the documents so we could transmit them to the CPA firm.

On January 19, 2021, Mike Hurst left his position of US attorney. After nearly a year at work, the federal team had not finished their analysis of the accounts. Mike's office had filed no charges, served no indictments, and arrested no one in the DHS case. If I'd handed Mike the full DHS case, the News and MCEC would still have been drawing down money all that time.

"It's not time to worry"

Jody and his team netted their second plea deal, this time with Anne McGrew, the accountant, in January 2021. Anne was prepared to testify about the financial maneuvering that happened at MCEC and New Learning. She was the one who changed all the accounting entries to camouflage which money was used to pay for which expenses.

We expected Nancy and Zach to blame Anne for all the welfare money being misspent. The problem with that defense was that Anne made her modest salary and nothing more while she worked for the News. The News walked away richer.

But then Anne's judge rejected the plea deal. Without much explanation, Judge Adrienne Wooten decided Anne's deal was not stiff enough. It was Jody's first real setback in the case. I called him. "We will keep working on it," he said. "Anne knows she did wrong, and she wants to be helpful. We'll get a deal done."

Looking around the office that week on the eighth floor of Woolfolk, I saw concerned faces. Accountants and investigators are smart people, but they're not lawyers. They don't always see the inside game being played in courtrooms.

"It's okay," I assured them. "There will be another deal. It's not time to worry."

I reminded some of them that we faced adversity every day in our cases. Maurice Howard came to mind. Howard was a young preacher and the mayor of Aberdeen, Mississippi. He was popular in his area and, while he was a Democrat, had won some plaudits from conservatives for carrying a gun on his hip to city council meetings.

Based on a tip, we investigated him and found that he'd lied to the city council about attending conferences on behalf of the

city. Howard would tell the council he was attending conferences, and they'd pay him in advance for his expenses on the
trips. When it was time to go to the conferences, we tracked
Howard's location to everywhere on God's green Earth except
where he was supposed to be.

On the day of Howard's arrest, Richie pulled on a STATE
AUDITOR raid jacket and drove to Aberdeen. He wanted to
accompany the agent in charge of the case, because the agent
was still wet behind the ears. When they arrived at Howard's
home to arrest him, the younger agent walked to the front door
and knocked. Richie, waiting in the car, then realized Howard
was in the backyard — and was sprinting toward the house.
The younger agent at the front door hadn't seen this happen.
Richie's first fear was that Howard was running to the back
door to grab his gun from inside the house and start shooting.
Without Kevlar on, Richie jumped out of his car, ran past the
young agent at the door, who was stunned to see Richie sprinting past him, and beat Howard into the house before he could
do anything rash.

Back at the office, Richie called me and told me what
happened. "Good job," I said with a lump in my throat at the
thought of losing him. "Now don't ever do that again."

Richie laughed and said, "Sure thing, boss."

Following the arrest, COVID shut down courtrooms around
the state. Howard's trial was delayed indefinitely, so he decided
to run for reelection. In his campaign he called me every name
in the book. He said he was being accused of an "embezz-lie,"
which I thought was creative. One of his allies on the council
went on television and said I was a "straight up racist," because
Howard is Black. Howard also hired a celebrity defense attorney who'd been on *Real Housewives of Atlanta*. The mayor won
reelection. Prosecutors wondered if a local jury would convict
him. My investigators were crestfallen.

We powered through, though. I spent time on the phone
talking to the district attorney for the area, John Weddle.
Together we came to the conclusion that we couldn't let this go.
Weddle was one of the best DAs in the state, and he was angry
on behalf of the taxpayers of Aberdeen. Once COVID abated

he marched Howard into court. Dressed in all black and flanked by his two TV attorneys, Howard walked in to the courtroom, sat down at counsel's table, and pleaded guilty.

Obtaining a felony on a man who'd just won an election in the jurisdiction in which he was going to be tried was a challenge. But we were challenged all the time. Every auditor who ever walked into a building where she wasn't wanted faced a challenge. Every time we finished a big case someone called my team and me liars, or worse. Every time an auditor signed an audit and put his license on the line for what he wrote, and every time I put my name and reputation at stake on our work, it was a challenge. Every time we were peer reviewed by other state auditors' offices, which was required every three years, it was a challenge.

We accepted all this as an opportunity to prove ourselves. I told my crew we would not back down, and we would document and prove everything so no one could question our work. And at the end of the day, that will make the difference, regardless of the speed bumps along the way.

As Jody reworked his Anne plea deal, I met with the new acting US attorney (Mike's replacement), Darren LaMarca. LaMarca had serious, dark eyes behind his glasses. He leavened his serious mien with colorful socks that featured patterns of beer steins and the like. Darren had been involved in some high-profile white-collar cases in Mississippi already, and I liked his style. The purpose of the meeting was to discuss another case, but I used it as a chance to tell him my thoughts on DHS.

"Darren, my hope is that you or Jody will be able to put every single person who did something criminal in this case in jail, no matter how high up. Everything we have is yours, and anything you need we will try to go get," I said. LaMarca said he agreed and that the Bulldog-Ryan-Lopez team, who would report their findings to LaMarca, was working to reach that goal, too.

It didn't take LaMarca long to get in the fight. He and his assistant prosecutor, Dave Fulcher, unveiled the first federal indictment against the News on March 18, 2021. In addition to the TANF fraud, the Bulldog team discovered that the News lied to obtain money from the Mississippi Department of Education. Specifically, they defrauded something called the 504 program, which was intended to provide private teachers for students needing a psychiatric facility or hospital setting.

To draw down the money, Nancy and Zach had to submit the names of teachers and students who were being served. The federal indictment said the News lied by claiming children who'd never attended their school were going there. They claimed students who no longer attended the school were still attending. They said people who no longer taught at New Summit School still worked there and that people who were not teachers were working as teachers. They claimed a person who'd never worked at the school was working there and that some teachers had certifications that they didn't hold, which resulted in a higher reimbursement than was deserved. In other words, the News submitted lists as fake as three-dollar bills so they could be paid 504 money.

The indictment said the News bilked public education funds to the tune of $2 million. That number would grow to $4 million once Bulldog's team finished reviewing all the false rosters. After the arrest, Anna reported that the News accounted for the vast majority of the entire state's 504 spending. In one year they received 74 percent of the 504 funds handed out by the state education department. The other recipients of the funds were typically psychiatric clinics. How no one at the education department noticed that a single school seemed to be serving such a high number of students with acute mental health needs was anyone's guess. The bureaucrats hadn't made a peep.

Federal agents called the News' lawyers and told them the News should immediately come to the flagpole outside the federal courthouse to turn themselves in. Once inside, they pleaded not guilty and walked away.

Shortly after, Lopez, the OIG investigator, asked me to meet. We connected at a quiet coffee shop near where I lived, midmorning, after the rush of commuters had already passed through.

"I wanted to say we're very impressed with your team, particularly Stephanie Palmertree," she said. I thanked her. We chatted about a few additional types of skills she thought my office should add based on her experience at the OIG, and then we got to the meat of the matter. She'd come, in part, to set some expectations about what the federal investigation could achieve and its timeline.

"How long do you think you'll need to investigate all this?" I asked. Not only was the misspending massive, but it also seemed to grow every time we looked behind another pile of debris.

"I'm thinking about retiring in five years," Lopez said. "I fully anticipate we will still be investigating this matter when I retire."

I hung my head. This was going to be a long haul. I was prepared to hear that news, but having it confirmed was dispiriting.

I'd require some new faces to endure that long haul. In the summer, Richie walked into my office with less energy than usual. Closing the door behind him, he sat in the chair in front of my desk.

"I've done something," he said.

This was a man I would have trusted with my life. *Whatever he has to say can't be that bad*, I thought.

"What's that?" I asked.

"I've taken a new job." Richie explained that, when I hired him, I knew I was getting someone at the end — I would have characterized it "the peak" — of his law enforcement career. Richie wanted to use everything he'd learned — the lessons from chasing cold leads in the clay hills of East Mississippi to build a long-forgotten civil rights case, the experience of slicing through the schemes perpetrated on consumers when he was at the AG's office, the reps he earned managing a city police force — to do one, final good piece of law enforcement work. He'd found that final project here, at the auditor's office. And now it was time to leave.

"I don't know what to say, brother," I said, looking back at him. It wasn't a total surprise to be hearing this. Richie had a daughter at the University of Mississippi and a son not far behind. The cost of college would be easier if he were making a corporate salary. But it didn't change the fact that hearing the words was hard.

"I'm always here for you, brother. It's just time," he said. He told me about his offer to go work as director of security at a large bank, and I understood. As he stood up from the chair, I gave him a bear hug and sent him on his way. He'd been the first big hire of my career, and it turned out to be a great one.

Not far behind, Bo Howard took a job as an IRS agent the following month. Each job meant a big pay raise. I was proud of the two. Losing good senior people because of the lower pay that I could offer at a state agency was a perennial problem.

My choice to replace Richie was Larry Ware. Larry left the attorney general's office, where he was director of the public integrity division, to come work for me. We hit it off right away. He was a cerebral and dedicated investigator, a man who thought about cases at nights and on weekends like I did. When you listened to him talk, you could tell every word was methodical. He had a steely-eyed aura, like his pulse never ventured north of fifty beats per minute. He was only two years older than me, too, so we shared a similar energy.

I also added Charles Woods as my new chief of staff. Tall and affable, Woods was younger than I was — youth was starting to be a theme around our office — and razor-sharp. I poached him from Capitol Hill, where he'd been a deputy chief of staff frustrated at Washington's sclerotic policymaking. Aside from being one of the best strategic thinkers I'd encountered, he had a servant's heart. He served as a captain in the National Guard and had deployed to Syria, leading 150 soldiers in a hot zone.

The Mississippi Legislature and Governor Reeves made changes for the long haul, too. They passed two laws in response to the DHS scandal around this time. The more important of the two expanded the capabilities of the internal fraud investigation unit inside DHS.

Also that summer, Stephanie's team released another audit of DHS. This one covered the tail end of John Davis's time as executive director, along with Chris Freeze's and Jacob Black's tenures. During that year, DHS and its grant recipients likely misspent another $10 million, taking the total questioned costs to more than $100 million. DHS even gave money to MCEC just days before the arrests of the DHS Six, despite knowing they were under investigation.

And Nancy, regardless of the impending trial and the new indictment, continued to hustle. She managed to talk a bingo hall director in rural North Mississippi out of $25,000. She and the bingo hall had a previous relationship. MCEC once claimed the bingo hall as a subsidiary that fed MCEC revenue, though the hall always seemed to lose money. As we'd seen in our audits, when the News came under scrutiny and wanted to use the bingo hall as an alleged source of money, they would change accounting entries to suggest that the bingo hall provided the funds instead of TANF.

After her arrest, Nancy told the media she'd stepped down as head of MCEC. Old habits die hard, though. Nancy was still moving large sums around and texting former vendors to MCEC about the nonprofit's work. One of those money moves was to call and convince the bingo hall director to wire her cash. The bingo director was duped by the same sorts of student lists that Nancy fabricated in the 504 scheme. But the director decided that he should keep $1,000 of the funds he sent her as "seed money" for a new nonprofit he was thinking about starting. He did so without telling the bingo hall board members.

Once the transfer happened, the Mississippi Gaming Commission heard and dragged the bingo hall director in for a hearing. They stripped the hall of its gaming license. The state's patience for Nancy's stratagems was running out.

In the heart of summer, Jody and I sat down to lunch to review. It had been three years since I'd taken office and almost two since Jody had won his election. We both had a few more scars than when we'd broken bread at Steve's Deli at the onset of the DHS case. An editor for the *Clarion-Ledger* told me my audits had made me the most "polarizing figure" in the state. Jody was trying to survive a crime spree, and he was mediating between a beleaguered police force and a group of tired judges. I could see a few more gray hairs on both of us compared with last time.

Jody walked me through his case strategy, in terms of both personnel and argument, as we munched on chips and salsa at the Iron Horse Grill. After ruminating on what he said, I recommended he call Stephanie Palmertree as a witness. Aside from Brett DiBiase, Anne, and the investigators who handled the case for our office, Stephanie would add the most to a case because of her extensive knowledge of federal grants. She'd also worked for a nonprofit before coming to the auditor's office, which gave her expertise in how MCEC *should* have been functioning. And she was decorated, too: Her audits of DHS resulted in her winning the American Institute of CPAs' top national award for state-level auditors, which is like winning an Oscar for accountants. She could tell a jury what was a routine bookkeeping mistake and what was not.

With that, Jody and I parted ways, back to our offices where a hundred murders or corruption cases waited for us. It was a long, hot July.

The Demands

Around the time the first breeze of late summer cut the Mississippi heat, the Baltimore firm hired by DHS finished its forensic audit. The results were a disaster for the News. The firm found that the News alone misspent more than $52 million. That finding was on par with ours. In total, when you added in the money to the Family Resource Center, the Baltimore auditors found that DHS oversaw the misspending of nearly $77 million in TANF funds. When you consider that my team looked at every DHS program — TANF, SNAP, childcare subsidies, everything — and found more than $100 million in illegal spending, and Bob only allowed the Baltimore firm to look at TANF, the conclusions looked similar.

What was worse for the News was their failure to cooperate. Zach claimed in letters to the independent firm that he wanted to sit with them and explain why my office was wrong. But when the Baltimore firm called him, Zach and his lawyers refused to answer. Same for Nancy. By failing to cooperate, the News sealed their fate. Two independent audit teams now said they'd wasted a tragic amount of welfare funds.

The new penny-by-penny audit also shed more light on some of the previous misspending we'd identified but hadn't explored in depth. For instance, our audit noted that a company called NCC Ventures was improperly given money by MCEC. By the time the Baltimore team conducted their audit, the head of NCC Ventures, Nicholas Coughlin, was working as a deputy division director for Attorney General Fitch. He was a close friend of the DiBiases, a tall former reality television star, and had received DHS money to "create opportunities for conversations with industry leaders and potential employers for indiviudals [sic]." For "creat[ing]" those "conversations," Coughlin was paid more than $168,000 in welfare funds. He had little work product to justify the payments.

A few weeks before the release of the Baltimore audit, Stephanie and I spoke on the phone to HHS representatives in Washington who ran the TANF program again. Since our first audit showing that DHS likely misspent millions, we needed these federal employees to tell us how they would decide what was and was not spent legally. Now the feds made it plain: The Baltimore audit would be the critical evidence that would help them make their determinations. It would also dictate, in part, what the State of Mississippi would have to pay back to TANF. The size of those penalties was likely going to be "unprecedented," according to one HHS employee on the call.

My team had seen enough. We'd made our arrests nearly two years ago. It was time to request repayment — to issue "demands" — of the misspent welfare money, including the misspent funds that hadn't led to criminal charges.

To reach final conclusions about who owed what back, I gathered Stephanie, Larry, Charles, Pat, and a new employee, Jim Bobo, in the conference room. Bobo was a seasoned lawyer with a southern gentleman's goatee, glasses, and a long mustache. He was also one of the savviest attorneys I'd ever met. He'd been a defense attorney for part of his career before working in the attorney general's office. A devout Catholic who attended daily mass, he'd built a reputation as an aggressive advocate in his time with the AG and was promptly fired when Attorney General Fitch took office. Their loss was my gain.

Our first task was to take what our previous audits of DHS showed and compare it with what the Baltimore firm found. If there was a Venn diagram where one circle represented the money we thought was misspent, and the other circle was what the Baltimore firm thought was misspent, we wanted to collect the money in the overlap.

Next, we decided who would pay this money back. Anyone who authorized improper spending can be held liable, so big demands would go to John Davis, the News, and the leadership of FRC, the North Mississippi nonprofit.

Many of the people who received misspent funds could be

asked to pay money back, too. But in some cases, a vendor who was improperly paid could fight off such a demand if they did the work they were required to do. The *Clarion-Ledger* was a good example. MCEC placed an ad in the newspaper and paid for it with welfare money. Spending TANF money on that ad was not allowable. The *Clarion-Ledger*, of course, didn't know TANF money was being used. They took the money and placed the ad in the paper. If the state sued the paper asking for the ad money back, the paper would likely claim they were a "good faith vendor." They'd done what they were paid to do in their contract. And they'd win.

Because of this "good faith vendor" principle, we only demanded that the vendors who had not met the terms of their contracts pay back what they'd received.

Nailing down the exact amounts of each demand took multiple meetings and a ton of man-hours by Stephanie's team, Larry, and Bobo. In our final meeting, I looked around the room. Stephanie, still wearing black, had eyes that looked hardened compared with when we'd started investigating DHS. Pat was tired, too, but was nearing retirement and the rewards of dedicating more than thirty years to the office. Larry and Charles were fresh, ready to provide one more burst of energy to end the case. Bobo stroked his gray chin, a sly grin on his face, knowing years of legal experience led him to this moment where he could shut down a massive misspending scheme.

This was a top-notch group. They would be our closers. If I had to put the intellectual horsepower between those four walls against any room I'd ever been in, including the classrooms at Oxford and Harvard, I'd bet on my audit team.

Before the demands were released, I called Bob Anderson to discuss what he thought about recouping funds. I told him I'd asked Attorney General Fitch to task one of her lawyers with this after we'd arrested the DHS Six more than a year prior. Nothing came of that conversation.

Bob had had a similar experience. He'd asked the AG for an attorney to be assigned to re-collect misspent TANF money. According to Bob, Fitch's chief of staff said that wasn't a good use of taxpayer resources.

When Bob shared the story with me, his voice was as animated as I'd ever heard it. "I considered asking her if suing China" — Fitch had filed suit against the People's Republic to hold them responsible for the coronavirus leak — "was a good use of tax dollars," he said.

Bob eventually convinced the AG to let him hire Brad Pigott to enforce our demands. Pigott was no slouch — a Duke and University of Virginia graduate who'd served as US attorney for seven years in the 1990s. Beyond our demands, Pigott could go after any additional welfare money we hadn't demanded if, upon further review of the evidence, he deemed it necessary.

Then, at last, the demands were done. On October 12, 2021, we served notices on John Davis telling him he owed Mississippi $96 million. That was what DHS misspent in TANF during his tenure, plus interest. It was the largest demand ever issued by the Mississippi Office of the State Auditor.

Nancy, Zach, and Jess New, along with the other MCEC board members, were ordered to repay $68 million. FRC's leadership owed $15 million.

As for the vendors paid by the nonprofits, Brett Favre was told he'd have to repay the remaining $600,000 for the speeches he hadn't given. Adding interest, his demand reached $828,000. Davis's nephew and brother-in-law were served demands for the coding classes and other work they didn't do. AG employee Nicholas Coughlin would have to repay the money he was given for "creat[ing] opportunities for conversations" with businesses. Marcus Dupree needed to return the money paid to "rent" his farm that hadn't benefited welfare recipients. And, of course, the DiBiases were told to repay the millions they'd been given.

Once the demands were served, the recipients had thirty days to repay. If they didn't, it was the responsibility of the attorney general to enforce those demands. They passed that responsibility to Pigott.

Around that time, I drove across the hot, flat cotton fields of the Mississippi Delta to give a speech about our recent cases. Standing behind a decades-old microphone at the Greenwood Country Club, I told the audience about the ups and downs of our work. At the end, I opened the floor to questions. A reporter jumped to her feet, straightened her glasses, marched awkwardly to my podium to confront me, and fired away.

"Mr. White, would you reflect," she asked from just a few feet away, "on the Nancy New case and the fact that her school for the disabled has been closed in light of . . . um . . ."

As she stumbled, I jumped in. "Nancy New's fraud?" The crowd snickered.

"Well, I wasn't going to say that," she said.

"I will," I replied. With that, I explained I had no reason to feel guilty for the collateral damage of the misspending. *What does this reporter want?* I thought. *For me to ignore Nancy's wrongdoing?*

🏈

While the civil demands would take time to be enforced by Pigott, the criminal trials were bearing down. The judge accepted Anne McGrew's second plea deal. McGrew agreed to testify against Nancy and Zach. In cases like this, everyone — even Hollywood — knew the accountant was pivotal. Brian De Palma's *The Untouchables* was a film about Eliot Ness finding, and keeping alive, Al Capone's bookkeeper so he could take the witness stand. In the real world, mafia accountants were brought before the US Senate in the 1950s, showing that a few accountants working for multiple mob families understood the corruption better than nearly anyone else.

Meanwhile, national media bellowed at Favre after the $828,000 demand. This second round of coverage was more vituperative than what had followed our first audit's disclosure of his involvement. Now the *New York Times*, the *Washington Post*, and *Sports Illustrated*, among others, called him out for having had a year to repay the money and failing to do so. An electrician friend of mine was on a job in rural South Dakota, and he sent me a message that workers on his crew were talking about a state audit of Brett Favre all the way in the Mount Rushmore state.

Two weeks after we issued our demands, Favre repaid the final $600,000 he owed from the original $1.1 million he was paid. He did not pay the interest.

On the night of Thursday, October 28, 2021, Logan, Charles, and I returned late from a trip to recruit accounting students at the University of Mississippi and an evening speech I'd given in North Mississippi. My head hit the pillow around midnight. In what felt like a millisecond, my eyes were open again, with the alarm clock blaring and showing 4:30 AM. Our toddler had a morning surgery to put tubes in her ears. Unshaven and wearing some old Levi's and a neon-green MISSISSIPPI ASPHALT hat, I helped my wife bundle up our girl in her pajamas and went to the hospital. By six fifty-five, we were in the waiting room outside the OR.

My daughter was wearing a tiger-print miniature hospital gown and watching Disney on the television above her bed, happily awaiting the procedure she didn't know was headed her way, when my phone lit up. My friend Suresh sent me a screenshot of a Facebook post from Brett Favre's account. "I would never accept money for no-show appearances, as the state of Mississippi auditor, Shad White, claims," Favre barked. Favre suggested he reached out to me and the office seeking "clarification" about what we meant when we said his contract required speeches, but that I'd "never granted a call back or a meeting." "For Shad White to continue to push out this lie that the money was for no-show events is something I cannot stay silent about."

Within seconds, many of Favre's 1.1 million Facebook followers grabbed their digital pitchforks and came for me. Their reaction was brutal. I was inundated with comments. The mildest called me a fraud; the most aggressive was a woman who threatened to castrate me in front of my family.

Dear God. Favre had questioned my honesty and the validity of the work we'd done in front of a national audience. And he'd left no choice but for me to respond. I started typing a statement into the Notes application on my phone. As Rina snuggled with our tyke, I handed her the phone and asked her to review my statement.

Her dark eyes scanned the text. "Move this part up," she said, scrolling. "This should be your main point." She pointed.

After I made those changes, I sent the statement to Logan, my office's communications and press secretary, and told him what I was about to post. He said the media were already asking for comment.

"These are lies, Brett Favre," I wrote. "I am not going to hide how much you were paid, why you were paid, or conduct backroom meetings to make this go away." Favre knew exactly why he'd been paid. Bulldog had handed him his contract when they met. Favre knew the contract said he was supposed to "speak at three (3) total speaking engagements," "provide one (1) radio spot during the contract period," and "provide one (1) keynote speaking engagement."

It also bothered me that Favre acted as if we had not explained this to him. "To suggest my office has not met with you is a lie as well," I typed. "You have met with agents who work for me. They showed you the contract. They showed you the emails confirming the contract quoted above is how you were paid. To suggest I have only communicated this to you via the media is wrong."

As the old saying goes, "A lie will go 'round the world while truth is pulling its boots on." Favre's cock-and-bull story quickly earned more than a thousand shares. My rebuttal never reached more than a hundred.

A couple of hours later, I drove my wife and daughter home from the hospital. Logan and I strategized by phone as I made my way along the highway. "Every reporter in the state is going to want an interview," he said.

"I know," I replied. "This is not pretty, but the integrity of everything we do in the office has been questioned now. I don't think I have an option. I'll stand up and answer every question they have." This was the only way to stem the tide of damaging commentary rolling our way. I knew Favre would not have the courage to do the same.

Once home, I cleaned up, shaved, threw on a blue suit and tie, and went into the office. At 1:30 PM, I held a press conference on the first floor of Woolfolk. There I could go into greater detail on why we handled Favre the way we did. "We don't treat anybody with special treatment when they reach out to the auditor's office," I said. "If he had been the mayor of a small town who'd benefited from misspending, what we would have done is, we would have linked him up with the case agent who investigated this.

"We don't do . . . backroom deals, where one person gets to come in and meet with me and slap me on the back and then act like everything should go away," I added.

I also described the meeting with Bulldog in which Favre was shown his contract and where he admitted he hadn't given any speeches. "One of two things is true," I concluded. "[Favre] was either lying to those agents in that room when he saw the contract and said that he didn't do the speeches, or he's lying this morning when he says that none of this has anything to do with speeches. Personally, if I were Mr. Favre at this point, this afternoon I would probably be in a room with my lawyer trying to think of an answer to that question."

Favre never responded.

A few hours later, I went back to my family. I didn't relish how any of this played out. It's not beneficial to take on someone who is a hero to many, especially in Mississippi, and it's even less fun to stand up to a million belligerents who want your head on a pike. But it had to be done. Some days I gripped the steering wheel a little tighter on the drive home and thought, *To hell with this job.*

The next week, I happened to run into a veteran politician in the state who pulled me aside. "I didn't like the way you handled the Favre thing," he said. "We have some sports-crazy people in our state. They're not going to believe you."

My facial reaction betrayed my thoughts. *Do I look like I care?* In the words of the apocryphal quote attributed to legendary football coach Nick Saban, "If you want to make everyone happy, don't be a leader. Sell ice cream."

If nothing else, the Favre back-and-forth brought my office closer together. They were glad someone defended their work. On Monday morning, an angry Packer fan called the front desk.

"Tell your boss he should not be going after Brett Favre," the caller raged.

Belinda, the front desk secretary who wore glasses and a permanent smile, had the patience of Job. In a calm voice, she intoned, "Thank you for your opinion, ma'am. Of course, you probably know my boss is just doing his job."

"Well he shouldn't," the caller said.

Belinda waited a beat. "Well, just out of curiosity, when do you think he should do his job, and when should he not?"

"It depends on who he's going after!" she yelled.

"I rest my case," Belinda said with a smile and hung up. We all understood it. The law didn't change depending on the subject of the investigation, no matter how popular they were. That was a core value to which every person in the agency held tight.

The Governor

In April 2022, Charles, my chief of staff, walked into my office. "Anna Wolfe has a story on Governor Bryant. It's a long-form piece. Maybe a bunch of articles."

It had been several months since the judges issued their gag orders. During those months of silence, the only news about the case was a new, and much longer, indictment of the News and Davis that Jody's team issued. The defendants weren't just on the hook for embezzlement now. The News were indicted for bribing John Davis and on RICO charges (the crime of participating in a larger criminal organization), among other things. While the new charges ratcheted up the pressure on the defendants, they'd been met with limited coverage in the media. The silence was about to be broken by Anna's new article.

"Good for her," I said. "What's she writing about?"

Anna was sitting on a treasure trove of text messages between Bryant, Favre, the concussion doctor Vanlandingham, and others. She'd filed a public records request with my office to obtain those same texts weeks prior, but like all investigative records in every case, we never gave them out. Standard practice was that evidence like the texts would not be made public until a trial — that is, unless one of the defendants with access to the texts volunteered them to her.

"Sounds like Governor Bryant granted her a really long interview," said Charles. In fact, once Anna had the damaging texts, she demanded a sit-down with Bryant, and Bryant agreed. Wolfe drove on a Saturday, palms sweaty, to the offices of Bryant Songy Snell, the former governor's consulting firm, and was granted a three-hour interview. The governor's new office wasn't as big as his former haunt in the state's tallest office building, but it was elegant. Floor-to-ceiling windows, showcasing a verdant view of Mississippi flora, served as the backdrop to the meeting. Golden shovels — awards for Bryant's work attracting industry to the state — hung on the walls alongside pictures of Bryant with various dignitaries.

With the microphone hot, Anna confronted Bryant with the messages, including the one where Vanlandingham offered Bryant a "company package" (equity in his business) as thanks for what Bryant had done for them during his time in office. After reading Vanlandingham's offer, she reminded Bryant that he said he would "get on it hard."

"Can you explain that [offer] for me? And what does 'I am going to get on it hard' mean?"

"I think I was open to hearing what he had to say," replied Bryant. "But I had no desire to own stock. Now, 'get on it' would be, 'I'm going to get on an opportunity for us to come and meet. I'll get on it right now.' My normal responses to everyone is, 'Let me get on it. Let me check and see.' And I know this probably doesn't sound right, but it's just the truth. I would just say, 'Fine. Come and see me. That sounds great. Let's get together.' But he did call me, and I just said, 'This is not the thing I want to do.' And I think the proof of this is I didn't join them. I didn't take stock."

When her article was published, the contents were not a surprise to my team. We'd seen most of the texts long before then. The feds weren't surprised, either. To the public, though, the texts and Bryant's explanation constituted a bombshell. No one outside of law enforcement knew about the Vanlandingham offer before that.

The obvious next question was, had Bryant committed a felony? Prosecutors, not auditors, decide who to charge with a crime, but I knew enough prosecutors to know how they were thinking about it. They were reading the statutes closely, like the state embezzlement statute. The most salient fact when they analyzed the case under that law was that Bryant had never actually accepted anything of value. If he had, he might have been guilty of using his position in government to enrich himself. They were also looking at the federal bribery statute. It said a person who "agree[d] to receive" a bribe in exchange for "being influenced in the performance of any official act" is guilty.

Prosecutors also knew that, if they took Bryant to court, he'd point out evidence like the fact that he'd hired a former FBI agent to uncover all of Davis's misdeeds after Davis retired, for example. And he'd reported the original DHS tip to law enforcement.

These were the kinds of conversations happening behind closed doors at the US attorney's office and at the Hinds County DA's office. Political pressure on them to act was immense. After the story with the text messages broke, the NAACP called on the Biden administration's Department of Justice, the US attorney, and the FBI to move. The NAACP said, "The Mississippi Office of the State Auditor determined that more than $94 million in federal funds were used for 'questionable' expenditures in 2017, 2018, and 2019. The audit report noted that its findings and all related information had been referred to the U.S. Department of Justice. However, nearly two years later, despite the overwhelming documentary evidence of fraud, forgery, and abuse in this matter, DOJ has not yet launched a criminal investigation."

National media noticed the NAACP's missive. Rumors rippled through Jackson that the letter was being taken seriously by the US attorney general. Jody said his constituents were imploring him to act, too.

The NAACP's statement that the "DOJ has not yet launched a criminal investigation" was not true, but the feds were moving slowly. My only agent assigned to their team, Bulldog, kept me apprised of their progress. It seemed like they were constantly sidetracked, chasing four rabbits at once. One minute they were trying to prove fraud with the welfare money, then tax evasion, then bank fraud, then the 504 Plan cases, and so on.

Another reason progress stalled on the federal investigation was that federal prosecutors were approaching a May trial date for the News over their theft of the 504 education funds. The prosecutors were hoping for a plea, so the federal investigators let off the gas on the welfare fraud while the negotiations stretched on. Those negotiations lasted longer than expected.

State prosecutors were also trying to come to terms with the News on a plea. Both state and federal teams said they preferred a "global" resolution, where both sets of prosecutors agree jointly as to what punishment is fair and see if the defendants take it. Communication was strained, though. Jody and his top ADA, Jamie McBride, were buried under a string of homicides in Mississippi's capital. There was little time for discussion. Federal lawyers were under more pressure to seal a plea agreement fast because their trial would come in a matter of weeks, not months like the state prosecutors. They all reached a bottleneck. No deal could get through.

And then the dam broke.

"What are you doing tomorrow afternoon?" Bulldog asked on our daily update call.

I was driving home from a long day, unbuttoning the cuffs of my shirt, and listening to my daughter hum "Let It Go" from the car seat in the back. "I've got a speech at the Westin with the state chamber of commerce. What's going on?" I said.

"That's the Westin in front of the federal courthouse?"

"Yep," I said.

"Across the street, while you are doing that, Nancy and Zach New are going to be pleading guilty to federal charges," he said.

I was skeptical. "I've heard this before, Bulldog . . ."

"I know, I know. But it's happening. Unless they change their mind at the last minute, it's happening." I felt a jolt of adrenaline. Bulldog sounded convinced. After more than two years, this might be real.

"What do you need from me?"

"Nothing. I'll be there in the hearing. I'll brief you when I know something. Go give your speech. Don't worry about it."

I laughed at the thought of "not worrying" about this case. "I'll do my best, brother."

The next day I wrapped my speech and walked out of the Westin, staring up at the imposing federal courthouse in front of me. Behind those closed glass doors and the space-age architecture, our case was either revivifying or taking a body blow.

I went back to the office and tried to busy myself. Staff filtered out to go home for the evening, but I was staying, come hell or high water. To occupy my mind I was reading *Fraud* magazine when Bulldog appeared in my doorway. He was wearing a new blue suit, something he'd purchased for this occasion, and had bags under his eyes.

"We got 'em."

Bulldog recounted how, with the trial date bearing down, Judge Reeves, the federal judge hearing the case, gave the parties a deadline to change their plea. If the News did not change their plea by that date, Reeves would lock in the trial on his calendar and refuse to hear any admissions after that.

Zach was on perhaps his third or fourth set of lawyers at the time. The most recent was a seasoned former white-collar federal prosecutor from Birmingham. The truth must have set in for Zach after hearing it from enough attorneys: He was going to have to plead guilty.

Prosecutors then suggested to Zach that he might receive the lesser of the two sentences between him and his mother. With that, he sat down in the back office of the federal courthouse and disclosed everything he knew about what happened at DHS and MCEC. He admitted to committing wire fraud with $4 million in public education dollars. That statute said he was eligible for five years in prison. The judge delayed his sentencing until November.

Nancy proved harder to crack, but hours after Zach folded, she followed suit. She also agreed to sit for multiple sessions over several days, telling federal prosecutors and investigators everything she knew. She then acknowledged she was guilty of wire fraud to conceal money laundering. The evidence that cooked her had been her home on Sheffield Drive and the rapid movement of government money from MCEC, through several transactions in a short time, to a quarter-million-dollar check that provided for the home's down payment. She was eligible for ten years in prison. The judge pushed her sentencing to the fall as well. Federal officials moved to seize the Sheffield home.

As Bulldog told the story in my office, my phone rang. "It's Dave [Fulcher, the assistant US attorney]," I said.

Take it, Bulldog mouthed silently.

"Dave," I said, answering.

"I don't know if Bulldog has told you or not, but I have good news," he said. As he conveyed the day's events, I paced in a circle around the upholstered chair Bulldog was slumped into.

At the end, I said, "Dave, congratulations, my friend. That's great work. I've told you again and again, but I'm grateful for you, and we're here to give you anything and everything you need to keep the case moving forward."

"The next thing I need to keep the case moving forward is a beer," he said, laughing. He and Ryan, the FBI agent on the investigative team, were en route to the nearest cold beverage.

As we hung up, I looked past Bulldog's chair at my reflection in the glass bookcase in my office. I've always been thin, but the past few months had taken a toll. I was just plain gaunt.

Bulldog and I walked out of the office. We were the last two to leave the building, turning off lights behind us. Outside, it was starting to rain. We parted ways, and I sat alone in my truck with water running down the windshield. I did the sign of the cross, acknowledging to God that only He knew what true justice was, but today felt like justice, so I thanked Him.

The lightning strike of a plea sent Jody's team into a frenzy. On my ride home, he called me.

"I guess you've heard," Jody said.

The pressure on Jody to land the plane was heightened now that the federal prosecutors had their first scalp. I could hear stress and a twinge of anger in his voice. There must have been a part of him that was frustrated with the feds for steaming the train out of the station without him aboard. Moreover, Nancy had just admitted to money laundering in open federal court. It opened her up to even more state charges, beyond the dozens of counts she was already facing. Jody wanted to act quickly.

"Why won't the News plea for you?" I asked.

Jody posited that the News might think they had enough incriminating evidence on Governor Bryant that they deserved a sweetheart deal for the ages. In a way, this was part of the game plan from the beginning: indict the players where we knew we could prove felonies and then see whom they squealed on while cooperating. "Start at the bottom and work your way up," as Jody put it.

"If they do, then get the info out of them and run with it, regardless of who they talk about," I said.

Jody didn't need my advice, but I told him this: If the News give you something of value, share it with the feds. Don't sit on it. That way, if there was a higher-up whom the News could implicate, the two teams could coordinate on how to prosecute. Working together maximized their chances of success at this point. If the News gave them a bunch of embarrassing stories about Bryant but nothing that substantiated a charge, Jody and the feds could mutually come to that conclusion. Two separate teams of prosecutors coming to the same decision would insulate both of them from any allegation that they were overlooking something.

Despite their hesitancy, the News had jumped the psychological barrier preventing them from admitting fault. They had told a federal judge they were guilty. A state judge wasn't much different. Less than forty-eight hours after the hearing with Judge Reeves, Nancy and Zach's attorneys called Jody and told him they were ready to plead guilty to state charges and end the ordeal.

By the time they did that, I was in Arkansas for work, preparing to walk into a meeting with Governor Asa Hutchinson. Jody called and, as was often the case with him, started talking in the middle of a sentence.

". . . so Zach's coming in at seventy-five years, seventeen to serve, which we think sends a strong message." The words were coming out fast.

"Jody, pause. Are you telling me Zach New has pleaded to state charges?"

"And Nancy."

"Hot damn!" I yelled. My friend Winston, who was driving me in his black F-150 to the Arkansas capitol, jumped in his seat.

Jody said the agreement was cemented. The judge would hear the pleas next week. The News would admit to nearly $8 million of criminal, fraudulent TANF spending and would be ordered to repay at least $3.656 million each. And they could still be on the hook civilly for the remaining tens of millions that were misspent without an associated criminal charge.

Those numbers were massive — the largest public fraud ever — by Mississippi government standards. Some of the more infamous Mississippi public fraud cases, like the kickback scheme at the Department of Corrections, or the scandal at Mississippi's Department of Marine Resources, or a fraud scheme involving a large publicly funded beef plant, all had perpetrators who walked away owing less than $2 million in restitution.

Here the combined state and federal cases had much bigger losses due to fraud. On top of that, the defendants and John Davis had likely evaporated more than $100 million in welfare money. While they hadn't stolen all that money, the state's poor saw little, if any, benefit from it, because it was spent in violation of TANF regs, and they could still be sued in civil court for it.

I tried to compose myself and straighten my suit as I leaped out of Winston's black truck. A weight was lifted off me. I thought back to the donor who told me he would never donate to me because my team had arrested the News, about the threats I received in the wake of the Favre demand, and about the woman at church who questioned my character because we'd taken down Zach, her friend. It all now seemed worth it.

"Good news?" Winston asked.

"Brother, if I get any more good news today, Arkansas will be my new favorite state." Winston laughed. "Well, maybe second favorite," I conceded.

We walked into Governor Hutchinson's office. I looked around as Hutchinson finished a call with the White House. The office was small and ornate but dimly lit, with all its windows blocked by thick blue drapes. The governor's desk sat to the side. From that tiny space, Bill Clinton had launched a successful presidential campaign thirty years prior.

"Mr. Auditor!" he beamed. "Sit down." Hutchison was tall and thin, with an avuncular bearing and an easy manner. After some chitchat, he said, "I've been following some of your work."

"Yessir. That welfare case has gobbled up a lot of our time," I said.

"I saw that one! I mentioned it in our staff meeting last week. We have to avoid big mistakes like that in my last year . . ." He trailed off and then looked up again. "Anything new there?"

Hutchinson was a former US attorney — once the youngest in the country — so I figured he liked a good fraud case. On the wall behind me was a framed jury verdict from his last criminal trial before he ran for governor.

"Well, Governor," I said smiling, "have I got a story for you."

The Pleas

"All rise!" Judge Faye Peterson, the state court judge hearing the News' cases, walked into her courtroom. She was a smaller woman but carried herself like a judge — straight posture in her chair and a commanding voice. She was wearing all black save for a diamond brooch on her robe.

The courtroom was long and narrow, with just two long benches behind the counsel tables. The walls and benches were dark wood, as was the backdrop behind Peterson. It smelled like a library full of dusty books. Nancy and Zach New were pleading guilty in this courtroom.

I sat behind Jody and Jamie, with US Attorney Darren LaMarca and one of his chief assistants, Pat Lemon. Across the room, a woman sitting behind Nancy was ignoring the proceedings and contorting her head and neck in our direction. She was staring straight at me behind her protective face mask, her gaze locked in.

Larry Ware leaned over and whispered in my ear, "That's probably Nancy's sister. I think she likes you." I chuckled.

Investigator Jerry Spell overheard us and said, "If she needs to be mad at anyone it's her own sister."

Jamie rose from behind the prosecutors' table first and recapitulated the counts to which Zach was pleading. Zach stood in his suit and tie listening calmly, his hair swooping down onto his forehead.

Bribery of a public official. "Guilty," Zach said.

Fraud against the government. "Guilty."

Wire fraud. "Guilty."

Zach's plea deal went into detail about what he was copping to. Zach admitted he bribed John Davis with purchases paid for in TANF money so John would give MCEC big TANF grants. One purchase was an "off the books" black GMC Yukon. Zach also bribed John by paying John's friend Brett DiBiase $250,000 in salary and a travel allowance, giving John unrestricted access to MCEC's Amex card (which was fueled by welfare money) and cash, and hiring John's nephew Austin Smith for hundreds of thousands of dollars of welfare money to teach coding classes Smith was unqualified to teach.

There was also the fraud against the government. Zach knew he could not use welfare money to pay for Paul LaCoste's workout classes for politicians. He did it anyway because John demanded this as a condition for giving MCEC big grants, according to Zach.

Importantly, Zach admitted that the secret maneuvering to push money to the volleyball court — Brett Favre's pet project — was a felony. Back then, Favre told Nancy the money's arrival felt like a gift from "Santa."

Nancy cooed back that Santa "felt you had been pretty good this year!"

Zach pleaded guilty to "knowingly transferring" that money to the volleyball court and intentionally circumventing the grant's prohibition against brick-and-mortar spending. He did so with "John Davis and others."

Zach worked with John to disguise these uses of welfare money by running the expenditures through MCEC and then mislabeling expenditures in public documents and ledgers. The same was true for their spending on a "virtual reality center" in Jackson. They knew they could not spend money on it, but they helped John do it and disguised the expenditures by calling them a lease.

Finally, there was Prevacus. Zach admitted they knew Prevacus was not a proper recipient of welfare money. The News still moved welfare money from MCEC's account to their private business account and then to the concussion treatment company. The proceeds from any return on that investment were going to the News' private LLC. If John was getting his cut of the welfare money as a bribe, then the News must have thought they should have a take, too.

Nancy then stood and walked to the microphone for her turn. Zach sat back down at counsel's table, facing forward but staring obliquely.

For the most part, Nancy looked the same as she did before her arrest, when her nonprofit was hauling in cash and she was in the company of famous athletes. She'd always been slightly heavyset, though not beyond what was typical for her age. She kept her familiar, serious-but-upbeat look on her face. Her hair lay a little flatter in the courtroom than in the posed pictures she'd taken when promoting her school at a press conference or attending a banquet. One of the federal prosecutors muttered, "You know, she looks remarkable for a stroke victim." The feds obviously doubted the veracity of the claim that Nancy had suffered a serious stroke the year prior, believing it to be a ploy for sympathy from the court.

Nancy pleaded to the same schemes as Zach and then a few more. She admitted they'd given welfare money to a man named Jesse Pearce for his personal training business while knowing that was not allowed by TANF regulations. The Pearce admission was a revelation to me. I'd never even heard his name. But Bulldog had. Bulldog explained that Pearce was another handsome young man in John's circle. Investigators called Pearce "The Body" because of the skintight T-shirts he wore in pictures on social media. John told the News to send him money.

Nancy also confessed she knew she wasn't allowed to spend money on the children's books they'd purchased but did so anyway at John's insistence. She conceded she engaged in "criminal fraud and forgery" by paying for Brett DiBiase's stay in Malibu. And she admitted that all this was part of what was considered a criminal enterprise when she pleaded to the RICO charge.

When you strip away the complexity, their scheme was simple: pay to play. John Davis gave the News tens of millions of dollars of welfare money. In exchange, they had to do what John wanted with it. Sometimes that meant helping John's friends and family. They were able to do this by running the money through the News' nonprofit, where there was far less oversight than the oversight on a state agency. All that was left was to lie on some official documents about how the money was spent. When the News realized no one was watching the money, it was easy to also decide to treat the slush fund as their own. That led to all the spending on the News' salaries, the house, the cars, the leases, the withdrawals from the retirement account, and everything else they pocketed.

The charges meant Nancy was eligible for a hundred years of prison, with the state recommending she serve twenty-five. The caveat, prosecutors said, was that the judge should consider reducing that number to whatever prison sentence the federal judge imposed. If Peterson followed that recommendation, Nancy would spend all her time in federal instead of state prison.

After all the maneuvering, Bo Howard's original prediction was right: The News didn't want to spend a day in state prison, so they brokered a deal on every charge against them, all within a matter of days, for the chance to serve their time with the feds.

With that, the hearing was done. The judge delayed sentencing until November, when John Davis's trial would take place. The expectation was that the News would cooperate against him through the summer. Somewhere Davis's attorney must've felt the noose tighten. Nancy, Zach, their two relatives, and their attorneys made their way past the TV cameras and out the door.

Jody turned to look at Darren and me. "Congratulations, my friend," I said, shaking his hand.

"We need to explain this to the press. The judge just quashed her gag order in this case back in chambers," said Jody.

I looked at Darren, who seemed a touch nervous, and said, "We'll follow your lead, Jody."

The three of us walked outside to face a bank of cameras and spotlights. Darren and I sat behind each of Jody's shoulders as he explained the pleas.

"We will not tolerate the powerful preying on the weak," Jody said.

Ross Adams, a local reporter, said, "Auditor White, will everyone, including Governor Bryant, be thoroughly investigated?" The answer was an easy one: yes. My agents and I would uphold the oaths we all swore to do our jobs. If for some reason anyone doubted my commitment to investigate the case to the fullest extent, I'd given the FBI access to everything we had more than two years prior. I'd also let them physically work from my office. They could, literally, stand over our shoulders and check our work or work the case on their own.

We'd also proved our commitment to transparency. The biggest questions about Bryant revolved around his relationship to Prevacus, and we were the ones who told the world about the Prevacus scheme. No reporter or citizen had ever heard of the concussion treatment until we unveiled the results of our investigation. We showed we were not covering up the concussion scheme; we were the ones telling Mississippi about it.

We'd also been the ones to tell the world about the $1.1 million payment to Brett Favre ostensibly for speeches. Then we went out and recovered that $1.1 million. It proved we were willing to take on anyone, no matter how politically popular, who owed the state money.

In the parking lot of the courthouse, out of view of the press, the investigators and I celebrated. I grabbed Jerry around the neck in a headlock, careful not to muss his gelled hair, and thanked him. Richie McCluskey took some time away from his bank job to come back and watch the proceedings. We shook hands and congratulated each other. Bo Howard was graduating that week from training at an IRS academy in Georgia, but he was there in spirit. Larry couldn't wipe the smile off his face. It was the most important step toward justice for the taxpayers that I'd been a part of.

In the fall of 2009, I was holding my grandfather's hand. He was dying. After smoking during his military career and for most of his adult life, cancer was ravaging Papa's lungs and bladder. Lying in a bed in his home, he looked at me with weary eyes. I knew it might be my last chance to hear his stories, so I started asking him questions about his life. My mother sat behind him, outside his field of vision, jotting down names and dates of events with a pencil and pad as he spoke.

He'd lived a simple life, one marked by a lack of access to the power or money that I'd later see among others in my time as state auditor. At eighteen, he'd left home without a penny in his pocket to serve his country. He loved his wife, whom he'd rescued from a previous abusive relationship. And he worked — day in, day out, often seven days a week — in the oil field. He'd plugged along, putting food on the table for his family in a world that sometimes felt rigged against men of his station. But in all that he proved a commitment to the most important things, like family and community — things far more important than influence or riches.

At some point as he talked, I could tell he was exhausted. His breathing was labored. I tapered my questions. He looked me in the eye and said, "You know, your dad and I raised you to be a good man. If there's one thing I'm sure of, it's that you are a good man. Always do what you think is right, and you will be okay." I smiled and squeezed his hand a little tighter, feeling his rough, brown skin that often had streaks of oil in its crevices. His hands were cleaner that day than I'd ever seen them.

It was the last time I spoke to him. It would be the challenge of a lifetime to meet his expectations for me — to always be a good man, always do what I thought was the right thing — but I would damn sure try.

The White Whale

John Davis was the white whale, the final objective in a years-long quest. To reach our goal we'd have to solve a growing disagreement between the state and federal prosecutors, though.

The pleas should have ushered in an Era of Good Feeling in which we could work together. Instead, tensions were high. State prosecutors had promised the feds that the feds could handle any new indictments past the original six people Jody indicted in state court in February 2020. The logic was that Jody and his team would focus on convicting the original DHS Six. The feds would target new people. No one would waste resources on a redundant prosecution. But after nearly two and a half years, the feds hadn't indicted a single new person.

Jody was frustrated because, as his team started "proffer-ing" the News (interviewing them per their cooperation agree-ment), the News spilled the tea on DHS underlings like Jacob Black. They also talked about Christi Webb, the head of the nonprofit in North Mississippi who received welfare money just like Nancy. As the News turned state's evidence, Jody became convinced that some of these new people had violated criminal statutes. They should be indicted and made to cooperate against John, too.

"Why hasn't Christi Webb been indicted by the feds?" Jody asked me. "Why hasn't *anyone* else been indicted?"

"I don't know why, Jody," I said. "I've been asking similar kinds of questions for a few months now."

"This is hurting our ability to get John. Trial is in November. Why is this taking so long?" he asked.

We were back to square one, facing the same old question: Do you want to give a case to federal authorities and watch it languish? They are skilled, but boy, do they take their time. And Jody and I answered to the voters. We didn't have the luxury of unlimited time. Our bosses, the taxpayers, expected us to move faster than that.

On the other side of the fence, the feds believed Jody had been lucky with the News' guilty plea. They didn't want Jody charging new people, because they thought he would lose. This was the same argument Mike Hurst had made at Primo's two years ago — that Jody was incapable of convicting the News — but Mike was wrong then. I suspected the feds were underestimating Jody's ability to close the door on the smaller fish like Black and Webb. If he could, the smaller fish might cooperate and generate new evidence on bigger fish.

I'd often joke with my staff that we should scratch off the words STATE AUDITOR from my office door and put THERAPIST in their place. State and federal prosecutors needed a mediator — someone to listen to their feelings, and positions, and try to find common ground. I proposed a meeting between them.

"Is there an appetite for all of us to sit down and discuss where the DHS case might go from here?" I asked the group via email. "As information comes out of the defendants who've recently pleaded guilty, I know we all want to be on the same page about how to use that information to maximize our chances for success."

All the lawyers were open to it, but even in the replies there was a snippiness. We started debating times for a come-to-Jesus meeting at my office.

Around the same time, Brad Pigott, the attorney hired by DHS, filed suit in civil court to collect money from those who owed the state for the welfare spending spree. It had been two years to the week since we outlined the tens of millions of losses in Stephanie Palmertree's first audit findings.

Pigott's complaint in the suit was lengthy. It stretched sixty-seven pages and sued everyone from John Davis and the News to the Northeast Mississippi Football Coaches Association and Rise in Malibu, the resort Brett DiBiase visited. Brett Favre, Jacob Vanlandingham, and Prevacus were named. All the DiBiases were defendants, as were the other beneficiaries of

John's largesse, like the nephew and would-be computer coder Austin Smith; Davis's brother-in-law; Marcus Dupree; and Paul LaCoste, the college-football-player-turned-workout-coach for politicians.

In the complaint, Pigott called the arrangement between Davis and Nancy an "illegal *quid pro quo* agreement and conspiracy." The suit attempted to recover $24 million of the $96 million in total welfare misspending.

Just before the suit was filed, I'd started to worry that the attorney general might not greenlight Pigott's action. I'd hoped for years that the AG's office would sue the DHS culprits to recoup lost money and property. Much of the property, like the News' cars, had long since been sold and driven away.

My concern was informed by a pattern I'd noticed since Attorney General Fitch took office: We'd demand someone repay money to the taxpayers, the person would refuse, we'd send the case over to the AG for enforcement, and then . . . nothing.

One of our investigations stood out as an example. We found that a well-known Republican woman used her position on the state parole board to obtain tens of thousands of dollars in unallowable travel reimbursements. When we checked with the state's Department of Finance and Administration, they agreed the woman could not be paid the money she'd received. The legislature's investigative board conducted their own inquiry and agreed, too. We served a demand on the woman, and she declined to repay the money. The task of suing her fell to the AG. The AG never filed a complaint. The woman kept the money. The AG confirmed in a letter that her office had no intention of seeking repayment.

Regardless, the News' pleas must've shocked the AG into action. Or at least shocked the office into allowing Pigott, a private attorney acting on behalf of the state, to sue.

Two weeks later, both teams of state and federal prosecutors gathered in my office for our kumbaya session. In our refrigerated conference room, Jody's state prosecutors sat to my right, feds to my left. The state side was lit with energetic chatter, the federal side marked by short haircuts, cinched neckties, and quiet whispers. Jody's team had more of a swagger than before. They'd booked big DHS guilty pleas that some had assumed they'd never earn.

The meeting, I said, was as much about reigniting conversation between the two sides, which had grown frosty, as it was coming to definitive conclusions about what would happen next. Jody then went to the heart of the matter.

"We've got our November Davis trial bearing down, and we've got to build our case. I feel confident we could try it today, but we still don't have guilty pleas on everyone else." In other words, he wanted the feds to indict people beyond the DHS Six who could cooperate and testify against John.

Darren LaMarca and his lead DHS trial attorney, Assistant US Attorney Dave Fulcher, stared back. Dave had a contented look on his face, but under it was a deadly seriousness. Darren looked up behind his glasses, his voice soothing. He said he understood and that his team was optimistic they'd be able to show progress in the next few weeks.

"Well, I can give you guys sixty days — starting two weeks ago," Jody said. He was saying that in sixty days (or forty-six, to be precise), the "deal" to let federal prosecutors take the lead on indicting new defendants would be off. Jody would consider charging anyone he needed to advance his case against John.

Jamie McBride fidgeted with his pen and pad. Dave's stare didn't change. Darren said he understood. In truth, Darren couldn't tell Jody what he was or was not allowed to do. But he did hold a trump card: Federal authorities, in rare circumstances, could file motions to stay all proceedings in all courts around a case they had. This was a power imbued by the supremacy clause in the Constitution, the clause that said federal law took priority over state law. And it was a nuclear option that would permanently taint relationships with local prosecutors.

Jody was pressuring federal prosecutors to act and, if they didn't, he was telling them he didn't believe they'd use the nuclear option to shut him down.

"And I don't mind going to trial," Jody added. "The public might even need that."

Thus far the guilty had all acknowledged they'd done wrong

through pleas. None had gone to trial. That meant the public hadn't seen any of the evidence against them. As a result, Jody thought a trial, where all the evidence came out and where everyone was allowed to testify about other parties involved, would release the valve on the pressure the media were applying. The public might find it cathartic to know the truth, warts and all.

The risk was that trials were unpredictable. If Jody chose to go that route it might end in an acquittal. Nevertheless, he wanted to send the message to Darren that he wasn't afraid of the courtroom. Showing the public the evidence in a state trial would ratchet the pressure on the feds even more.

"Look," I said, turning to Darren, "you have to understand the constraints Jody and I are under. Voters won't give us five years to let this thing play out."

I knew Jody's calculus from our conversations. He believed that if he could show convictions on the first DHS Six by the end of 2022, the voters would see that as progress. He just needed Darren to give him enough momentum, and witnesses, to secure a Davis conviction in November.

Darren acknowledged the different incentives each side of the table faced. The more he talked, the more his velvet words assuaged the lingering distrust. I could feel the mood in the room growing warmer.

"Give us two or three more weeks," Darren said. Even if nothing happened in the next three weeks, at least they were talking again, I surmised. And at least federal prosecutors wouldn't be surprised in forty-six days if Jody charged a new defendant or two.

Jody paused for a moment. "Makes sense. We'll keep working," he said. We all stood up and shook hands, parting ways. As everyone made for the elevators, I hoped we'd purged some of the animosity between the teams.

Then three weeks passed. No new activity from the feds. *Jody might be on his own,* I thought.

The Plan

As we waited for Jody's forty-six-day clock to expire, Jim Bobo and Larry called me back to the investigations division. I scanned my badge and walked through their locked glass door, passing by the division's black plastic gargoyle mascot — the beast that perched on a castle watching for evildoers below.

"CLA has a new report," said Jim. CLA was the private Baltimore CPA firm hired to audit DHS. While their main report had been issued in 2021, they were now releasing smaller deep dives into specific parts of what had happened at DHS with TANF money. "This one has to do with Jacob Black."

Black had been John Davis's deputy and, according to some, had helped author the "internal audit" that was taken to Governor Bryant in 2019. My staff had always been skeptical about Black based on the fact that the internal audit omitted any information about the News. It had just enough dirt to try to have the governor kick John to the curb but not enough to overturn the entire agency.

Prior to that betrayal, Black and Davis had been close. Black was tall and built like a former high school athlete who'd let himself go a bit. Despite his youth, he had wispy blond hair and a puffy face; he still sported Costa-style sunglasses with a strap retainer around his neck. He had a serious, ambitious demeanor. For a time, he must've assumed Davis was his ticket to the top.

Thank you for "always thinking ahead," John texted him once.

"I am just trying to keep up with my teacher," Black replied. "Thank you for being that teacher."

Black's proximity to Davis also meant staying close to the News. We'd seen emails where Black was managing the details of the cash transfers to the News' nonprofit. In one exchange, he helped MCEC avoid audit scrutiny by telling them to call an expenditure a "lease" instead of what it was: the unallowable cost of building a brick-and-mortar facility at a local church. The closeness of the Black-New relationship and his willingness to help the News skirt TANF rules seemed suspicious.

Now it appeared that he helped another company sidestep regulations.

"CLA has laid out a case that Jacob Black should be held responsible for the money that went to NCC Ventures," said Larry. NCC Ventures was the company owned by Nicholas Coughlin, the man who'd recently been sent out to pasture by Attorney General Fitch. Coughlin had been paid to have "conversations" with businesses but produced no real work product. We'd already demanded that Coughlin pay the money back, but Black might also be jointly liable for the NCC contract based on CLA's work.

"What's the angle?" I asked.

Jim Bobo took a deep breath, his standard move before launching into a detailed legal explanation. "The contract that NCC had with the state was bogus. NCC needed to compete against other companies providing similar services in order to win its contract. It looks like DHS, specifically Black, helped them set up a fake competition against dummy competitors."

"Explain that, *dummy competitors*," I said.

"Companies that did not actually do work that was competitive with NCC. Like picking two high-priced law firms to compete against a low-priced accounting firm to win an accounting contract. It makes it so whoever was selecting the contract winner would have to select NCC," Larry replied. I later learned that sometimes dummy competitors don't even know they are competing. A person at the agency might just pluck some prices off the dummy's website and *wham!* — you've got a competing bid. It's all a ruse to ensure that a specific vendor wins the contract.

"If someone on the inside, like Black, helps break that whole procurement process to help a friend, they at least have civil liability. We can serve a demand on them," said Larry.

"What do you think?" I asked Jim. On tough matters of legal proof, Jim held as much sway as anyone in the office.

"We should serve a demand on him."

I thought about how this might affect the criminal trials. It was possible one of the two teams of prosecutors, or both, might be opposed. They might view it as a distraction. On the other hand, it was my job to demand back misspent money, and that job didn't pause for speculative reasons. One of the prosecutors would have to give me a concrete problem presented by such a demand to convince me to hold off.

"Let me call Dave and Jody," I said. "Go ahead and prepare the civil demand."

A few days later I'd been given the green light by the prosecutors. No one thought the demand created a problem. If anything, it might show John that others were facing pressure and could testify against him.

On a warm, sunny May day, Michael Guynes contacted Black and met him on the sidewalk on High Street in downtown Jackson. Michael put a $3.6 million demand in the hand of Black, who did not seem pleased, and they went their separate ways.

Interestingly, Anna Wolfe didn't cover the issuance of the Black demand despite writing in excruciating detail about everything else that happened in the DHS case. I wondered if a friendship with Black was the reason for her silence. We knew they were connected based on documents found on Zach New's computer.

Years prior, Zach had typed a Word document that set out his plan to push John aside and capture DHS. The piece read like a tutorial on manipulating a state agency. Clicking away at the keyboard, New described how Black longed to replace Davis.

"Main Agenda: 1. Remove John Davis from Office," he wrote.

"2. Place Jacob Black as ED of DHS.

"3. Position individuals to have job security if they are in support of Jim Hood."

Black was a fan of Jim Hood, the Democratic nominee for governor. The News may have been tired of Davis's bullying and demands about how to spend DHS money. Or maybe they thought Hood was going to best Reeves in the upcoming 2019 election and Davis would be out at DHS. Either way, Zach locked arms with Black and sketched out how Black might be put in as director.

The ultimate goal for Zach was clear: "4. Become the main provider for any and all contracts through DHS."

What was amazing about the document (aside from the fact that Zach put his plan in writing) was that Zach had collected dirt on everyone in DHS's orbit. Mid-level DHS staffers, John's family, journalists — no one was spared. He knew who was having an affair with whom, who had what ambitions and weaknesses, and who was connected to which politicians.

Zach said Black had "alternative control motives for outside partners," whatever that meant. Regardless, he was the man they wanted at the top.

Anna featured as an important player in the plan. Black was "leaking . . . information to Anna Wolf [*sic*]," said Zach. Ostensibly that information was the kind that would help bring down Davis. Wolfe was described as being "friends with Jacob Black."

In another cryptic passage, the document said an attorney in town — a relative of FRC's director — was "working behind the scenes with Anna Wolfe, Jacob Black and for financial gain." Anna's name appeared again, as either a pawn or a player in the charade.

Through Black's connection to Wolfe, it would be death by a thousand cuts for Davis. Each new Anna story would damage John Davis's career and lead to Black's rise — and give Anna more content to cover. After reading the document, one couldn't help but wonder if Wolfe was complicit in taking down Davis but protecting Black. How much had she known about Black's wrongdoing and failed to report? At minimum, Zach New's document raised these questions.

By the summer of 2019, with the Hood-Reeves gubernatorial race tight, the waiting was over. If Governor Bryant could not be persuaded to fire John based on Anna's negative stories, the anti-John faction would take matters into their own hands. There was no guarantee that Black's favored candidate, Hood, would win and name Black director, so Black sent what he thought would be a kill shot — the internal audit — to Governor Bryant. The plan didn't pan out as envisioned. Within two years, Black would be out at DHS, with Wolfe largely silent on his involvement.

𝕸

Just as things were heating up, I learned I was about to lose another integral team member.

"Sit down, man," I said, welcoming my 8:00 AM meeting into the office.

Bulldog plopped into the brown-striped upholstered chair in front of me. Over the past two years, he'd interrogated witnesses from entitled Davis relatives all the way to Brett Favre. He comforted teachers from New Learning Resources who'd lost their jobs and calmed tempers between investigators and prosecutors. The work came at a cost. His weight had been down, then up, then down again. It might have also cost him his marriage.

Bulldog reached into his smokeless tobacco tin and put a pinch in his lip. We reminisced about the last few months in 2022. We were both passionate about the case, and, as usual, I was keyed up, talking fast and loud about what we should be doing. Usually Bulldog mirrored me, but today I could tell he was withdrawn.

I paused when I realized he was taciturn. My look must've asked Bulldog to explain what was going on behind the tired eyes. "I'm going to resign," he said. He explained he needed a different pace and a fresh start. I could sympathize. If my time as state auditor taught me anything, it was that the dedicated men and women of law enforcement sacrificed a great deal to serve.

For the next few days, I tried to keep Bulldog by offering a pay raise, but he'd already decided.

All these events weighed on my team and me. It was mile twenty-five of our marathon. We knew we'd get to the finish line, but we were also near our breaking point. I decided it was time to take a breath. I invited everyone who participated in the DHS investigation — Stephanie's team; Michael Torres, who'd left for a private CPA firm; Larry's crew; Bo Howard, Richie McCluskey, and all the office veterans — for a meal. I bought a few pizzas, and we talked about how far we'd come. Of the original team of investigators who tackled the case, only Jerry Spell and Michael Guynes remained employed at the Office of the State Auditor. At the end of the reunion, I slipped both of them a bottle of their favorite liquor: Deep Eddy Vodka for Jerry and Johnnie Walker Black for Michael.

Reinforcements were coming for the final mile, too. Following pressure from the NAACP, Representative Bennie Thompson renewed his push on the DOJ to investigate DHS. The DOJ and FBI seemed to respond. DOJ put new attorneys based in Washington, DC, on the case — at one point as many as twelve in total. The FBI assigned two new agents to put fresh eyes on Bulldog, Ryan, and Lopez's work and to dig on their own, too. The marathon was starting to feel like a relay race, with fresh legs to carry the baton over the finish line.

To help them, I appointed a new agent to replace Bulldog as our task force officer assigned to the FBI. This agent, whom I'll call Operator (he was gregarious, built, and bearded, like a special forces operator), would now spend his time working the welfare case. Operator was a graduate of Jackson State University and a former member of their famous marching band, but he looked like he should have been on the football team. I joked that if we held an election for "mayor" of our office, he'd beat me in a landslide. He was liked by everyone he met. He was also our most productive agent. It pained me to take him off everything else he'd been doing, but welfare was the priority.

To break the news to Operator that we were pulling him off his other cases, I brought him and Larry into my office.

Operator sat on the couch, leaning forward, hands clasped. Larry relaxed into the chair beside me. "Thank you for doing this," I said. "You're going to meet your new FBI colleagues soon, I know, and when you do, Larry will have another full copy of every ounce of evidence we have in this case for you to give to them. Start by reviewing all that. It's going to take time to get up to speed."

I also explained to Operator that his main job was to do his job — "pull no punches and investigate everyone of interest," I told him. "And I mean everyone. Do you understand?"

"I do," he replied.

"I don't care if it's big-time politicians, athletes, or the pope. Everyone."

"We will go after them all"

Cindy Byrd was in a fight for her political life.

Byrd, Oklahoma's state auditor, claimed she'd discovered that a wealthy group of nonprofit executives had defrauded Oklahoma. The execs took millions, illegally, from the state for their online school, according to one of her audits. The owners of the nonprofit were influential and regular campaign donors to Oklahoma politicians. They launched a word-of-mouth and public relations campaign to discredit Byrd.

Then, in the middle of Byrd's 2022 reelection campaign, her worst fears materialized: A dark money political action committee, fueled by an estimated $1 million of donations from an unknown source, started spending against her. She would have to weather a torrent of ads supporting her opponent. For a while, she looked done for. Then, at the eleventh hour, Oklahoma prosecutors unveiled criminal charges ranging from embezzlement to racketeering on the nonprofit executives. Five days later, Byrd survived at the ballot box despite being outspent.

I knew those were the same stakes in my career. The easiest path for Byrd, me, or any other auditor is to hide from cases like these. Keep your mouth shut; get reelected. The consequence for angering wealthy donors was political decapitation.

And the culprits at the heart of the DHS scandal knew that, too.

Jess New — Nancy's son and attorney, who after Nancy's guilty plea was *still* the head of the state's oil and gas board — made it plain. "I want to go after EVERYONE responsible for [the investigation into us]," he texted Nancy. He'd been paid hundreds of thousands of TANF dollars, so Jess's motivation was both personal and professional.

The people who needed government licenses from his board knew his proclivities. One CEO of a large Mississippi oil company told me he could never support me because New would punish him for it. "It would kill my business," he said.

Jess's mother shared his same instincts. "It has passed [*sic*] time to turn the other cheek," said Nancy in a text to Jess. "First . . . we have [to] make it through this and get this stopped," she added, before being arrested. "Then we will go after them all."

"Hey, bub. Wanna hoop?" Drex asked me over his landline.

"Sure. C'mon over," I replied.

In seventh grade, basketball and soccer were the only things I cared about. I loved playing basketball with my friends on our school's team, where I was the only White boy on the court. I played point guard and couldn't score worth a lick, so my job was to get the ball up the court and to our star center, Alex. He did the rest. We were one of the best teams in the county.

Alex lived down the road from me in a trailer with his cousin, our team's small forward, whom I'll call Drex. Drex would occasionally call me and want to shoot on the rim in my yard. I didn't have concrete under the goal, so Drex and I ran, jumped, and pounded the ball into the patch of grass to try to turn it into compacted dirt.

After shooting for a while one hot afternoon, Drex and I decided to ride our bikes down the street to Bob's Grocery Store to grab a drink. At the store, we dropped our bikes, sprinted in, and split ways. I walked to one cooler and grabbed a Coke. Drex walked to another and nabbed a blue sugary drink in a round container that looked like a clear plastic barrel. I then went to pay. As I put my money into Bob's outstretched hand, I looked and saw Drex walk out the store's glass door without paying. Bob hadn't noticed. I stared back at Bob in silence, not able to muster any words. Back outside, Drex didn't seem to think much of it. We rode our bikes back home, Drex chattering away, me silent.

An hour or two later, after Drex had returned home, I sat at the kitchen table and told my mom what had happened. My eyes were hot with tears at the shame of doing nothing when Drex nabbed the drink.

Mom slid fifty cents, the cost of the blue drink, across the table.

"Go back over there," she said.

I scooped up the coins, remounted my bike, and slow-peddled back to Bob's. Bob, an older, terse man who owned the store and spent his time either carving meat in the back or at the checkout counter at the front, must've thought it strange to see me back for a second drink run. I don't remember what I said to him exactly, but I know I couldn't bring myself to say Drex stole the little barrel. I put the money in his hand and dashed off, red-faced.

I felt my silence was just as wrong as if I'd taken the blue drink myself. The shame from that small moment stuck with me. Better to learn the lesson of silent complicity early in life, when the only thing at stake was a cold drink, than later.

The silence of the welfare case was broken now, though. The News' guilty pleas amplified the media coverage about — and the pressure on — the two biggest names in the case: Favre and Bryant.

Favre attempted to push back on the criticism swirling around him, but each new argument he made backfired. First, Favre's lawyer went public and said Favre didn't know the money he received came from welfare funds. But Favre's text messages showed that, at minimum, he knew he was being paid government money. He repeatedly appealed to Davis (who handled all welfare money in Mississippi), New, and the governor for help — and received it.

"John mentioned 4 million [for the volleyball court] and not sure if I heard him right," Favre texted New. "Very big deal and can't thank you enough [smiley emoji]." In total John and Nancy would send $5 million for the volleyball court.

Favre showered gratitude on the people handling those public funds. "I love John so much. And you too," Favre texted New.

Favre was insistent on government funds being used to finance his fundraising commitments to USM according to

USM's president. "I've asked Brett not to do the things he's doing to seek funding from state agencies and the legislature for the volleyball facility," USM president Rodney Bennett told Bryant. "The bottom line is he personally guaranteed the project, and on his word and handshake we proceeded. It's time for him to pay up — it really is just that simple."

Once the public realized Favre knew he was being given DHS funds, Favre's attorneys pivoted back to the topic of the $1.1 million welfare payment, the money given to him for speeches. When Favre's lawyer was asked if this money had anything to do with fulfilling a volleyball donation commitment, he said, "No, no, no, it's nothing like that."

But again, Favre's own texts sank his case. "Hey brother Deanna and [I] still owe 1.1 million on Vball," Favre texted John Davis. "Any chance you and Nancy can help with that?"

Finally, Favre's lawyers tried saying the $1.1 million contract requiring him to give speeches was a sham document. As a result, he shouldn't be held accountable for not meeting its terms. But the problem there was obvious, too: If there was no valid contract justifying the $1.1 million payment to Favre, he could not legally be paid $1.1 million.

Eventually, Team Favre stopped trying, letting the bad headlines — many of which were self-inflicted — wash over them.

And of course, Favre's claims of being "honorable" were beset by an inescapable problem: He'd said in texts that he didn't want the public to ever find out about all this.

Bryant scrambled, too, as his texts showing communications with Favre became public. He eventually released a glut of those messages on a website called bryanttexts.com.

Bryant pointed out that during his conversations with Favre, Davis, and New about the volleyball court at his alma mater, he stressed following the law. As Favre badgered Bryant for help, Bryant said, "We are going to get there. This was a great meeting. But we have to follow the law. I am to[o] old for Federal Prison [sunglasses emoji]."

He warned Brett not to try to skirt DHS rules at the same time. "To override or not obey the law would be a potentially criminal offense. Neither one of us want an investigation by the Auditor. I promise you, there is nothing more I can do except follow the law."

And when reporters went too far, he shot back. Anna Wolfe's boss, the CEO of *Mississippi Today*, falsely claimed they were "the newsroom that broke the story about $77 million welfare funds . . . being embezzled by a former governor . . ." Bryant threatened to sue *Mississippi Today*, the CEO, and Anna for defamation, because he'd never been charged with a crime. They quickly apologized.

Watching court filings with text messages being released, followed by justifications, followed by rebuttals, made the whole case feel like a Ping-Pong match played off the table, walls, and ceiling at the same time.

Governor Reeves even stumbled into the crossfire when he and his DHS director, Bob Anderson, fired Brad Pigott, the Democrat and attorney they'd hired to recoup the misspent welfare money.

On a Friday afternoon, Pigott told reporters he'd been canned. The reason, he said, was that he'd tried to subpoena documents at the Southern Miss Athletic Foundation regarding Bryant, Favre, and the volleyball court that Favre's daughter played on. "All I did, and I believe all that caused me to be terminated from representing the department or having anything to do with the litigation, was to try to get the truth about all of that," said Pigott. "I am sure they can find a loyal Republican lawyer to do the work."

Reeves and Anderson quickly resuscitated the case, though, hiring a larger regional law firm — one with no real allegiance to any party — to replace Pigott less than a month later.

On the morning of September 2, 2022, I pulled open the heavy glass door that wore the state's seal and the words OFFICE OF THE STATE AUDITOR. I trotted into our reception area to see Belinda at the front desk already at work. I paused and grabbed a piece of candy from her dish, waiting for her to finish her current call.

"Good morning, state auditor's office," she said into her headset.

"You know what I'm about to say," the caller said.

"No, ma'am, I do not," Belinda replied.

"When are y'all going to prosecute Brett Favre?" the caller said. Belinda was taking about half a dozen calls per day like this at this point.

"Ma'am, my boss is the state auditor. He is not a prosecutor. He does not have that power."

"That don't matter. He needs to prosecute hi . . ."

"You must want to speak to the attorney general," Belinda said, cutting her off. "Transferring you!"

"No, that's not what . . ." Belinda punched a key on her keypad and sent the caller blasting into the ether in the direction of the attorney general's switchboard.

I chuckled.

"Good morning, Shad," Belinda said, looking up over her glasses. "Do you need something?"

"No, ma'am," I said, crunching the candy. "I just need to tell you to keep doing a good job."

"Yessir."

Back at my desk, I scrolled through a local blog. Rumor had it Zach New was preparing to sell his forty-three-hundred-square-foot luxury home in Bridgewater, an exclusive Mississippi subdivision inhabited by the founder of the state's biggest tech success and other millionaires. In looking to see if that news had been reported yet, a new headline hit my screen.

"Biden appoints new US Attorney who will inherit welfare scandal investigation," wrote reporter Geoff Pender.

Mike Hurst and Darren LaMarca's permanent replacement had finally been named. Todd Gee would be the new chief federal prosecutor for the southern half of the state. Gee's résumé had one line that stood out: former counsel to the US House Homeland Security Committee.

Gee had been Representative Bennie Thompson's point man when Thompson served as chair of that committee. And Thompson, who was the most high-profile politician in the state at the moment thanks to his position atop the January 6th committee, held massive sway in the Biden administration.

He'd also criticized the Department of Justice's lack of urgency on the welfare case.

The message from the White House was clear: Thompson would be in charge of the prosecution now. His lawyer would decide who faced criminal charges.

"Why did you do this?"

On September 21, 2022, my alarm buzzed, as usual, at 4:50 AM, and I got up for my morning workout. By 6:00 AM, I was making coffee for my wife and breakfast for our three-year-old. Rina and I scanned the morning news, fed our newest baby girl, and got ready for work. I left the house at 7:30, and by 8:00 AM, I put my truck in park at the Woolfolk parking garage.

Once in the lobby, Belinda gave me her usual bit of grandmotherly advice.

"Did you even eat yesterday? You look like you haven't eaten."

"Yes, ma'am, they let me eat!" I said, hurrying to return emails before starting the day's schedule.

A few hours later my new press secretary, Fletcher, drove me to tiny Collins, Mississippi, where I gave a lunchtime speech. On the way back to Jackson, my phone rang. The words JODY OWENS filled the screen.

"Mr. D-A," I said. "How are you?"

"Y'remember when we sat down at Steve's that time three years ago?" he blurted.

"Won't ever forget it," I said, laughing.

"That changed my life," he said. Then a pause. "We got John Davis."

The jolt of energy I'd felt when Jody told me Nancy and Zach had pled guilty didn't come this time. Just relief. My head dropped, and my eyes closed.

"State and federal charges," Jody added. Federal prosecutors, who were still waiting on their new boss, Gee, to arrive, had never indicted Davis. But facing mounting pressure, they'd worked with Jody in the early days of September to convince

Davis to plead guilty and then cooperate against anyone else involved in the case.

"Congratulations, my friend," I said.

"I'm tired, man," he replied.

"I know. I bet that lunch at Steve's took ten years off your life," I said. "You and I both know there were people saying you'd never pull this off. You proved them wrong. Incredible work."

"I was ready for the feds to do something," he said. "Up until this week, I've been the only one to indict anybody for TANF fraud. The feds helped here, and John knew he did wrong, but the fear of time in state prison sped the deal up."

"No doubt, Jody. Without you, this day doesn't come," I said.

Jody explained that the news would come out and the pleas would be heard in court, both state and federal, the next day. We made plans to meet at ten o'clock the next morning in his office and go into the courtroom together.

September 22 was my thirty-seventh birthday. I put on the same suit I'd worn to announce the first arrests of the DHS Six more than two years prior. At nine fifty, Larry and I hopped in the truck with Jerry, the agent who'd flipped Nancy's accountant in 2019, and drove to the state courthouse.

In Jody's office, the two of us talked privately about the next steps.

"The feds have to do more here," he said, leaning forward. "You've put thousands of hours into this. I'm working like a madman." Jody's calm look, eyes wide, masked frustration. "I've got these crazy death threats on this thing, too." He nodded to a bruiser of a bodyguard named Terrence standing outside his office door. I could tell that if I got into a scrap in a dark alley, I wanted Terrence on my side.

"They need to be looking at Florida," Jody added. By that he meant federal authorities needed to think about Prevacus, the Tallahassee-based concussion treatment company that Favre had promoted and that had been fueled by welfare dollars.

It was a natural place to continue the case. ESPN had reported that Prevacus and Vanlandingham had "overstated" their drug's effectiveness on programs like Megyn Kelly's NBC show. Vanlandingham told the public his drug could "reduce the secondary damage that occurs after [a] concussion." He said it was "unbelievable" at "stopping the advancement of a concussion." His investor Favre said the drug would "save the future."

In fact, there were no human trials to prove what Vanlandingham claimed. The drug hadn't been cleared to be safe or effective by the FDA. Vanlandingham likely needed increased interest in the drug to fuel his next round of fundraising, and he'd made big claims about the nasal treatment's efficacy to garner that attention. There were echoes of Elizabeth Holmes and her blood testing technology at Theranos. When Holmes falsely claimed that her machines could test for a variety of ailments with a single drop of blood, and when she promoted that story to raise cash from the market, she was convicted of wire fraud.

Holmes had also claimed in marketing documents that Theranos had relationships with big names like Pfizer and the Department of Defense, which wasn't true. Vanlandingham claimed in marketing documents that Prevacus had deep ties to the NFL Players Association and the NCAA — but those organizations later denied working with Prevacus. I wondered: If federal prosecutors decided Holmes should go to prison for misleading the public, would they see Vanlandingham in a similar light? Could they prove he intended to deceive? If so, would he agree to cooperate and provide evidence on other important people?

Or maybe federal prosecutors could show Vanlandingham's company believed they were trading campaign donations for their grant money? This was a federal crime, too. And clearly one member of the Prevacus team thought that's what they were doing. "Let me get this process down correct," a Prevacus board member texted to Vanlandingham. "We get $2 million from MS Gov Office and we ear mark some of the funds to the next MS Gov. Campaign fund. America at its best." Vanlandingham denied that's what they were doing.

Back in the meeting, Jody wondered aloud, "And where is Lynn in all this?" Attorney General Lynn Fitch had been quiet throughout the DHS debacle, failing to even register a meaningful comment on the largest public fraud scheme in the state's history. Whereas Jody and I faced criticism for moving too slowly — despite being the ones to uncover and serve the first indictments in the scheme — Fitch had escaped controversy by doing nothing at all.

At the time, Fitch was in another state speaking to a group of activists and pastors. Wearing her perpetual smile and a perfectly kempt sky-blue suit, she was working to become a national figure — and staying far away from the fray of day-to-day prosecution.

"I mean, she's got prosecutorial authority," Jody said with dismay. "She's the only one not here."

"And she's got the full case file," I said, meaning we'd given her a copy of all the evidence we had. "We started this thing, though, so we take the heat, I guess, Jody. No good deed goes unpunished."

Moments later, Jody and I followed Terrence's lead downstairs to the courtroom. The chamber had the feel of a reunion where both sides of the family — the ones you did want to see and the ones you didn't — had all gathered.

Richie McCluskey and Bo Howard, the former investigators who'd started this conflagration, waited just inside the door. Richie pounded my fist on the way in. Ryan from the FBI sat on a back bench, nodding in my direction. Reporter Anna Wolfe was on the edge of her seat in the first pew, dressed in earth tones from tip to toe. I took up a post behind counsel's table over the shoulder of Jamie McBride, Jody's top assistant who'd negotiated the pleas.

Bob Anderson sat glassy-eyed farther back. Within hearing distance of one of my agents, Bob had the following exchange with a federal investigator.

"Did you hear Shad's interview on the radio this morning?" the investigator asked Bob.

"I could barely listen to two words of it. *Boy wonder*," Bob hissed in reply.

John Davis and his attorneys entered the room. Davis was now a federal felon, having pleaded guilty to conspiracy and theft of public funds two hours earlier in a federal court appearance across town.

"All rise!" the bailiff called. Judge Adrienne Wooten strode to the bench.

Wooten was in her late forties, a former legislator, and demanded precision from the attorneys who appeared before her. She would even check the math of damages and restitution in plea agreements live in front of everyone. "I'm very good at math," she'd say.

Judge Wooten wouldn't hesitate to throw out a plea agreement if she felt it was too lenient. Plea agreements were just deals struck between prosecutors and defense attorneys — a recommendation to the judge for how she might sentence the accused. A judge could always accept a defendant's admission of guilt, throw out the agreement, and sentence the defendant to whatever she liked, within the bounds of the law.

Davis was slated to plead to five counts of conspiracy and thirteen counts of fraud against the government. By agreement between the lawyers, he would face up to thirty-two years in prison. The only question was whether Judge Wooten would find this punitive enough.

Wooten called the defendant to the podium. Davis stood with his two lawyers and walked forward. He was heavier than when I'd last seen him three years earlier, and his pants sagged. He hitched them up as he shuffled to the heart of the room. He was wearing a bright floral tie similar to others he'd worn for legislative testimony and press conferences announcing grant awards.

The charges to which John was admitting all involved Brett DiBiase, the wrestler whom John only described as a "friend." John acknowledged Brett was paid welfare money to teach drug rehabilitation courses while Brett was actually being treated for drug use in Malibu. He admitted Brett's Malibu treatment was also illegally paid for with TANF funds and that Brett was paid a $250,000 salary — more than even John made — for a job Brett was not qualified to do.

In a soft voice, John stated he knew Brett billed welfare for a stay at the Royal Sonesta Hotel in New Orleans, and he knew Brett was lying about what he did there. Brett and John claimed Brett was there to meet with a team from Louisiana

State University and learn to teach drug rehab classes. But the trip was just a vacation. John went with Brett and stayed in the same room, so he knew the nature of the trip. Finally, John admitted he used welfare money to pay for the cost of travel to see Brett in Malibu.

In total, John was pleading guilty to illegally spending more than $450,000 of welfare money for either Brett or his own benefit.

Once John recounted the charges in his own words, Judge Wooten looked at him from behind her glasses, perplexed. Why did John go to see Brett in Malibu? she asked. Why didn't Nancy New go to see Brett? After all, Brett was technically *her* employee. She seemed to be wondering why Brett was so important to John.

When Davis looked uncomfortable, trying to think of a way to explain, Jody rose to his feet.

"Your Honor, may we approach?" he asked.

"No," said Wooten. She wanted her questions answered. "Why did you do this?" the judge pressed.

John stopped and looked up. "Very very bad judgment," he said. "It was wrong."

While John would never elaborate on what drove him to help Brett, prosecutors said later that the charges all arose out of John's "personal relationship" with Brett. While John had overseen the misspending of more than $100 million in taxpayer funds, he was being held accountable for rigging state government to benefit his closest friend in the scheme. Those were expenditures where the benefit was so personal that John should be held responsible.

Judge Wooten accepted John's admission of guilt and then summoned the attorneys to the bench.

Joe Hemleben, one of Jody's assistant prosecutors, leaned over to me. "This is where anything could happen," he said.

Wooten was out of earshot, but she was enunciating so I could read her lips as she spoke to the lawyers in their huddle.

"He. Will. Go. To. Jail. Today."

The attorneys returned to their stations. Judge Wooten informed John that she would accept his guilty plea. John Davis was headed to prison, with a stop at house arrest first. We all wondered whom he might implicate on his way there.

Outside, on the same steps where Jody and I had announced the arrest of the DHS Six, Jody told the press the plea represented "justice delayed, but not justice denied." I reminded them that, had Jody not been willing to indict the DHS Six in early 2020, millions of additional dollars would have been misspent. His ability and willingness to move quickly saved the state a mountain of welfare funds.

Once the questions abated, Jody and I went back into the courthouse and in the lobby said our good-byes.

"Whatever you need from us, let me know," I said. "We just assigned Operator to the case, so he's your point person for whatever you need."

"Operator? He's your best agent. He's given us tons of good work on other cases."

"And he's yours for whatever you need on DHS."

⚖

"Auditor White, it's good to meet you," said Representative Brad Wenstrup of Ohio, holding out his hand and welcoming me to his Washington, DC, offices. Wenstrup was strapping and a little shorter than me. He sported a big smile and easy manner, though I could tell he was more laconic than your typical United States congressman — more of a quiet military officer than a cocktail party politician.

Wenstrup was also a senior Republican member of the US House of Representatives Ways and Means Committee. Ways and Means was what Hill staffers called an A-Committee. Its hearings were among the most high-profile in government. And the committee's Republicans, now in charge thanks to a string of election wins in November 2022, had their eyes on Mississippi.

Wenstrup and I sat down onto his plush furniture surrounded by moving boxes. They were filled with trinkets from his time in the service and pictures with dignitaries. The sunshine from big windows lit the blue walls. The Washington skyline was framed outside the glass. I'd been to Washington many times since winning the eighth-grade essay contest, but our monuments and capitol never ceased to take my breath away.

"Sorry for the clutter. Just moving in. Benefits of seniority I guess, right?" he said, gesturing to his new space.

Now that they were in charge, Wenstrup and the staff on his powerful committee wanted to dive in to the Biden administration's foot-dragging on government fraud. Mississippi's welfare case was top of mind. Wenstrup's crew wouldn't even wait to swear in their new members in January or take all the mementos out of moving crates. They wanted details on welfare, Favre, and what the federal government was doing about it.

Before our meeting, Wenstrup sent a letter to the Biden Department of Health and Human Services, who administered TANF. "The Mississippi case is emblematic of a systemic problem: TANF lacks necessary guardrails making it susceptible to fraud and abuse," the letter began. "As the scandal involving NFL-quarterback Brett Favre and the misuse of welfare dollars in the state of Mississippi makes clear, the Temporary Assistance for Needy Families (TANF) program needs serious reform . . ."

Wenstrup's team gave my office credit for uncovering the scandal and quantifying the loss, but they could not understand why the federal government had failed to take any meaningful action in response to our findings. It had been nearly three years since my office took our file to the FBI and federal prosecutors. The feds asked to be the lead agencies charging new people after the DHS Six, but there were still no new indictments. And it had been nearly two and a half years since I turned over our full TANF audit to the federal HHS, but that agency hadn't made a peep about helping to recoup money.

"Congressman, I'll be honest and say I'm a little frustrated with the feds," I said. "I've held my tongue in public, but it's been a long time." Back home, some reporters were taking their frustrations at the pace of prosecutions out on me. Rather than talk about how the Biden DOJ or Mississippi attorney general hadn't charged any new defendants, they painted me as investigator, prosecutor, judge, jury, and executioner. Any failure to prosecute Favre, Bryant, or anyone else was framed as my decision.

And that framing was nakedly political, in my view. The journalists left covering the case didn't seem interested in criticizing the

Democratic-appointed federal prosecutors who made charging decisions. They were much more comfortable excoriating a conservative like me. One newspaper even inaccurately called *me* the prosecutor.

All that aside, the focus needed to be on the future. "The important thing here is that HHS do something — anything — to make sure this doesn't happen again," I said. "Republicans can lead on this thing." Wenstrup nodded in agreement. I offered a few suggested changes to federal TANF law, like requiring state agency heads who handled welfare funds to sign financial statements under penalty of perjury. Wenstrup also wanted to use this as an inflection point to reevaluate welfare's effectiveness, which was long overdue according to most Republicans. The congressman closed the meeting by saying the Ways and Means Committee had a strong interest in having hearings on the scandal and that committee staff would be in touch.

The national attention created strange political crosscurrents, though. Republicans like Wenstrup were eager to point out that Democrats were refusing to act in the face of massive fraud. But three former-Trump-acolytes-turned-Twitter-trolls upset that narrative.

The new dynamic was probably triggered by Favre, who had shifted legal strategies. He fired his old lawyer and hired a former Trump White House attorney. Shortly after that, two Twitter personalities — baby-faced twenty-somethings who claimed to be political consultants to Trump — with hundreds of thousands of followers came at me with knives out. They alleged on social media that I was part of the welfare embezzlement because my office had drawn down TANF funds to do our annual audit of DHS and that I shouldn't be investigating Brett Favre.

In reality, every state auditor's office in the country drew down a portion of the federal grants we audited. The money was used to pay audit staff, not me. This was how the federal government, through something called the Single Audit Act, had their programs audited without creating an unfunded mandate on the states. Facts didn't get in the way of the Twitter boys, though, as they argued I'd taken home welfare money.

These young men were out of their depth and clearly didn't care to know the first thing about how government works. It was much more fun to lie. I wondered whether they were being paid by Favre through his new attorney. The two Twitter personalities had taken no interest in the case until Favre hired the former White House lawyer to represent him. And their opening salvo against me required deep, obscure knowledge about the case. I doubted they'd discovered an audit fee on their own without the help of an attorney. Trying to ignore the twisted national politics of the welfare scandal became a permanent feature of my life from that day forward.

Several months later, US House Ways and Means staff contacted my office again. Congress wanted to hear the story of what had happened in Mississippi, so I boarded a plane for DC again. Fresh-shaven and fueled by black coffee (I'd been up at 3:55 AM in Mississippi to reach DC in time), I looked the panel in the eye. In that historic building, the smell of aging but fresh-cleaned carpet filled the air. The members sat before me tucked into their pressed suits, looking up behind glasses.

As I leaned in to the pencil-thin microphone and walked through the details of the misspending — welfare dollars spent on a home and iPads and cars — the representatives sat stunned. You could hear a pin drop when I spoke about money going to athletes and celebrities with no work product to show for it. A member from Illinois spoke about the need to reform the program to guarantee that the working poor benefited. A bit defensively, a representative from Wisconsin remarked about how Favre wasn't the only rich person who ended up with some of the cash. The mahogany walls of that room had seen discussions of myriad policy failures over the decades, but this Congress had never heard of TANF abuse like what was presented that day.

"My hope," I told them, "is that the country can learn from Mississippi's experience so that the fraud we saw in Mississippi doesn't happen in other states."

Strong-Arm

The thermometer said fifty-five degrees, but with the wind it felt colder than that on the steps leading to the entrance of Mississippi's capitol building. Flecks of mist dotted Governor Reeves's glasses as he addressed the crowd gathered outside to hear his State of the State address on January 30, 2023.

"Regardless of the crime committed, regardless of who did it, regardless if it happened on the street or in an office building, my administration is and will continue to hold criminals accountable," Reeves said.

Sitting in a white lawn chair behind him, my adrenaline kicked in. Suddenly I felt warm in just my navy blazer.

"That's why my administration remains committed to delivering justice and recouping every dollar possible from those who stole from Mississippians through the theft of TANF dollars," Reeves concluded. The audience clapped their cold hands.

Mississippi's welfare scandal had now fully permeated the collective consciousness of her people. The TANF scandal touched everyone and everything, from our heroes to our politics. Reeves featured it in his State of the State, because he was certain his 2023 gubernatorial opponent, populist Brandon Presley, would try to make hay of the issue.

In his response speech on television, Presley said Reeves had been "caught in the middle of the largest public corruption scandal in our state's history." I cringed at the language, because it hinted there was evidence of wrongdoing on Reeves's part. No evidence of that had been made public. Presley was trying to weaponize the case for his own benefit.

One month after Reeves's speech, Brett Favre sued me for defamation. He also sued former NFL stars Shannon Sharpe and Pat McAfee. I'd told the truth in saying that the funding for Favre was a sham and that Favre knew he was benefiting from taxpayer funds, but those were the very statements that formed the basis of his suit.

Favre's lawsuit was frivolous and had no chance of success, and any lawyer could see that, so I assumed winning was not the real goal. Instead, my sense was that it was a strong-arm tactic to bury me in court costs and shut me up. They made it a point to repeatedly say they were suing me in my "individual capacity." It was an attempt to force me to hire a lawyer out of my own bank account to go toe-to-toe with the well-heeled New York firm Favre hired. My salary as the head of a midsized state agency would quickly be exhausted against Favre's war chest. I suppose they thought they could bleed me dry and change the public narrative while the suit languished.

Eventually, Favre's lawyer let that truth slip. The lawyer was asked by NBC Sports about the case and defendant Pat McAfee's comments. "[The suit] is going to cost Pat McAfee millions of dollars. And if it bankrupts him, then he will have learned his lesson . . ." He wasn't even trying to hide the ball about the desire to make us spend money.

Unfortunately, Favre's lawyers didn't understand that when I was describing an audit or investigation, I was speaking as state auditor. I would be represented by a special assistant attorney general paid for by the state. And it had to be this way. Otherwise, any executive officer — say, an investigator who uncovered a company polluting a river and who told the public about the toxic waters — could be bankrupted for doing her job. No one would take a job like that without the legal protection of the state.

On a Thursday morning when I was at work, a bald, bulky man wearing a black shirt came to my house. My wife was there in her pajama bottoms and an Ole Miss tank top, home with our ten-day-old baby and recovering from a C-section. She heard a knock. When she went to the door, the man was standing with his nose an inch from the windowpane, peering inside. Alarmed, Rina stopped in her tracks five feet from the door, baby in her arms nursing a bottle.

"Who are you?" she asked, brushing her jet-black hair from her face.

"Is Shad here?" he asked.

"Who are you?"

He laughed at her.

"Is Shad here?" he asked.

"I asked who you were," Rina said. "Do I need to call the police?"

"Go ahead. Call them," he taunted.

Rina backed away from the door, angry. "I'm calling the police!" she yelled, moving deeper into our living room. By the time she reached her phone, the man was gone. Rina called me and told me what happened, so I hopped into the truck and raced back to the house but never found the man.

Eventually we identified him: It was one of Brett Favre's lawyers.

A few days after the incident at my door, scuttlebutt started around the Hattiesburg area. Favre's lawyer Bob Sullivan was bragging about coming to my house and scaring my wife. The story made its way to me.

Around that time, I also obtained the security footage from a camera near my neighborhood's entrance. Sure enough, there it was. Bob Sullivan's truck — an expensive white Ford F-250 Raptor with a distinctive Montana tag — awkwardly fought its way into our subdivision. At the front of the subdivision, there was an entrance gate and an exit gate. Bob tried to drive in the exit gate, against the grain of traffic, but nearly had his truck clipped by the black gate arms. He backed up and tried again a few minutes later. A black car drove out, and Bob punched the gas and sped through. The tag on the truck proved it was Bob's.

Sullivan coming to my house was an attempt at pure personal intimidation. I'm sure if Sullivan were ever asked why he appeared at my front door, he would say he was trying to serve me with papers about the case. But that story was empty-headed. If that were his mission, he would have simply identified himself to my wife.

Also, back when we first learned that Favre was suing me, my lawyers told Favre's counsel they could have a process server (a person who serves a defendant with a lawsuit) take the lawsuit and any other papers to my lawyer at the attorney general's office. Team Favre didn't like that idea. Rather than doing that, or trying to serve me at the office (the most logical place I'd be at 10:00 AM on a Thursday), Sullivan opted to trespass and harass my wife.

⚖️

At 5:30 AM in the woods near where I grew up, the sun was still behind the horizon, but its energy had already activated the sky's dark-blue hue. Mornings are peaceful here. The only sounds are crickets chirping and the occasional swoosh of a car passing down a nearby highway. Most days, the smell of the morning dew greets anyone who walks among these pines. On this day, though, another smell overwhelmed the watery sweetness on the grass: oil.

Like my grandfather, my dad was an oil field hand. He managed a series of oil tankers scattered in the Mississippi wilderness. On this particular cool morning, dad's truck creaked to a stop, crunching the gravel road underneath, at one of his tankers. When he stepped out of the truck, his boot met sticky, warm, black sludge — the kind of crude that South Mississippi wells produced. It was all over the ground.

There had been an oil spill.

Oh no, he thought.

Overnight, someone had sneaked onto the property and bashed a valve on one of the two-story oil tanks. Hot black oil poured into the firewall, which is a dirt berm surrounding the tanks. The firewall was there to prevent the oil from spreading into the woods. But the perpetrator was dedicated; he destroyed another valve on a pipe running through the center of the berm. The oil had leaked out into the world, covering the grass and rocks all around.

Within minutes, Dad was on the phone summoning a cleanup crew to help him contain the breach and start cleaning. They would vacuum the sludge and place big white foam pads on the forest floor to absorb what they could. Dad dialed the number for the local sheriff, too. He had an idea of who might have vandalized the place.

In his spare time, Dad served as mayor of the town of seven hundred people where I was raised. It didn't pay much (about $200 a week), but it made plenty of enemies. One thing I admired most about my father was that he always did the right thing no matter who was looking. His moral compass was anchored on true north and didn't budge. If some influential local wanted a pass on their water bills, the answer was no. If a popular resident wanted to dump garbage at a city park, the answer was no. When I was teenager, Dad even told me if I drove my blue Ford Bronco through town too fast and earned a speeding ticket, he would make sure the police made me pay.

In recent weeks, one of Dad's decisions like this had angered a city resident. Dad suspected the resident was taking it out on a tanker Dad managed.

Aside from alerting the police to all this, Dad also called me.

"I'm gonna have to tell the state oil and gas board about the spill," he said over the phone. Any time there was a big incident, the board had to be alerted.

"I know," I said.

There was a pause in our conversation. We both knew what that meant. Dad would be at the regulatory mercy of Jess New, the man who'd pledged to get revenge on those who'd investigated his mother and brother. Despite being the attorney for an organization that defrauded the state, despite being sued by the state for millions, despite declaring in text messages that he would "go after everyone" investigating the welfare scandal, and despite all this being public knowledge, Jess New still retained his spot atop the oil and gas agency.

Some of the oil and gas board members — the people who could hire or fire New — didn't seem to care. One told me they "wouldn't look at anything Jess did outside the office" when assessing Jess's job performance. The board member was an ostrich with his head in the sand. If New had been a serial killer but had decent performance on the job, I would hope they would have at least considered the dead bodies in his closet. But the easier road was to ignore public controversy and the clear signs of unethical behavior by their director. Mississippi was small, after all. Wouldn't want to upset anybody Jess went to church with.

There was no way Dad could prevent someone from sneaking onto private property and laying waste to oil valves, and no reason he should be sanctioned, but I didn't trust New to handle it fairly. I worried about New fining Dad into bankruptcy.

"There's no other option," I said. "You have to report it as normal."

"I know," he said.

"And we'll have to hope he doesn't punish you for my work," I said.

I drove down State Street in Jackson talking on the phone to my chief of staff, Charles. My truck rumbled over the craggy potholes formed over years of infrastructure neglect.

"I can't stop thinking about how we could have prevented this," I said. Was it inevitable that millions of dollars would be set on fire in programs designed to serve the poor? The grants were so large, the oversight was so limited, and the tendency to please the politically connected was so strong here. Maybe the welfare scandal, or something like it, was an ineluctable outcome in Mississippi.

"Or maybe we could have caught it earlier?"

With the benefit of hindsight, Charles and I concluded that technology could have helped, and we brainstormed feasible ways to apply it given our agency's limited resources. In days of old, if an auditor wanted to find fraud, the best she could do was to sample the expenditures of an office. She'd select fifty or a hundred or some other number of random expenses, look at them under a microscope, and determine if there was anything fishy. It was the equivalent of searching for a needle in a haystack — and ignoring hundreds of other haystacks that you'd never have time to explore.

With the advent of machine learning, though, auditors could download every expenditure for an office. An algorithm could run over the expenditures and tell the auditor which were most suspicious. Were two vendors with different names being paid at the same address? Were expenditures too large for the work being performed (say, a plumber billing $100,000)? Was the expenditure just below a threshold that would trigger increased scrutiny (a series of payments of $998 to the same vendor, for instance, when the vendor knew anything above $1,000 would require the review of a manager)? These were the sorts of red flags new software could highlight. The auditor could then focus her time on looking at the documents justifying those dubious purchases.

Though such software was too expensive to procure and fully deploy in my office, we worked with some of the best coders in both the public and private sector to use technology like this in limited cases, especially if the coders would agree to provide their code or services on the cheap.

We tested the effectiveness of one program like this on old data. We wanted to see if it highlighted any expenses from years prior that we'd since determined were fraudulent. So we dumped state spending data from 2017 and 2018 into the machine. Minutes later, it fed us the vendors that looked the most suspicious from that era.

One of the first vendors to hit the screen was New Learning Resources.

"If we'd had this tech when you first started, the largest public fraud in state history might never have happened," Bulldog said when he saw those results.

Of course, technology alone isn't enough. We needed auditors and investigators with the courage to scrutinize even the most connected players.

In my first month on the job, brainy Bo Howard had walked into my office.

"I need to ask an important question," he said.

"Hit me."

There was a slight hesitation. His eyes darted away from mine. "How aggressive do you want to be in investigations? I mean, if you could put it on a scale of one to ten for us, with ten being the most aggressive, what's your guidance?"

As I fixed my mouth to answer, he interjected, "Because there are consequences for saying ten, here. Like I say, ten means we might have to investigate people who are important. Ten means people are going to push back."

I looked back at him and said, "Eleven."

Conclusion

Before the welfare case, Brett Favre was the Gunslinger, a moniker cemented with Jeff Pearlman's biography of him.

Favre was unorthodox, firing the ball sidearm, underhand, and every other way that would make a coach cringe.

He was instinctual, ignoring the finer points of the game. He once claimed he'd never heard of a nickel defense (a pretty common football term) until his second NFL job.

He was illogical at times, shooting first and thinking later by tossing right into double coverage. His interception numbers proved it.

He effectively got himself kicked off his first team, with a lie being the final straw. At the end of his rookie season with the Atlanta Falcons, Favre skipped the team's annual photo shoot. When his coach asked him where he was, Favre said he "got trapped behind a car wreck." It was a falsehood that led the coach to send him packing to Green Bay (along with Favre's subpar play that year).

But Brett Favre was tough. He put his body through hell. He limped off the field too many times to count. He kept getting back up. He set the NFL record for most consecutive games started. He pushed so hard he became addicted to painkillers. All for his team. For the chance to win. For a shot at greatness.

He had *something* we all wanted to see in ourselves. Especially little boys from South Mississippi. If Brett came from nowhere and became a myth, maybe we could, too. This is why people loved him.

So who is Brett Favre now, after DHS?

Pearlman would say he's dumb. After the scandal, Pearlman encouraged people not to buy his own book about Number

Four: "I can say with 100 percent certainty the man [Favre] is an idiot."

Was Favre just an "idiot" jock who stumbled into this dumpster fire? I think it's more complicated than that. When I look at the man's text messages, I see more.

I see someone who was relentless. Like that teenager skipping a night with buddies to stay in his garage and lift weights, Favre wouldn't be deterred from a goal. Over and over he pressed Governor Bryant for the money for the volleyball court, for instance.

Favre to Bryant: "I'm trying to get sponsors, donations etc . . . Maybe you know of someone"

"I'm still trying to save on Vball facility."

"I and we need your help very badly [with the volleyball money] Governor . . ."

"I hope you can pull this off Governor . . . I just am hoping for a first down and not a punt."

"Hey Governor I know your busy but I hope you can take a look at Nancys proposal."

Again, and again, and again. This was for his university, USM — the only university that gave him a shot to chase his dream. I see a man who loved that place.

I see a man who was competitive. He wanted to win. He wanted to win money from the state. He wanted to build the volleyball court. He wanted to get richer with Prevacus. And he would take every opportunity and pull every string to succeed. That was the only way he'd emerged from Hancock North Central to become *the* Brett Favre — by scrapping and fighting for every advantage.

Unfortunately, I also see a man who internalized the benefits of being a rich, famous athlete: Everything could be had at a price. Rules seemed like they were meant to be broken. If you needed to ignore the lawyers saying be careful, or consider paying the guy handing you money, or push for spending to happen faster than the proper process, these were all on the table as ways to get the ball to the goal line. Shoot first. Think later. Sort the details afterward.

Maybe, like most of us, Favre is a walking contradiction — good and bad, admirable and contemptable.

This is a man who would sign autographs for everyone in a bar for cash and then generously give all the proceeds to the bartender. But he was also the worst tipper his friends knew according to Pearlman's work.

On the field, this was the player who threw his body into harm's way without fear. But off the field he was known as the family scaredy-cat by all his relatives and closest friends, said Pearlman.

This was Brett Favre, who grew up humbly and dressed simply even after he made his fortune. But he loved the trappings of a private jet.

And then there was the complexity of his relationship with his father.

Favre's career was almost single-handedly stopped by Irvin Favre. Irv taught Brett to play — and then nearly extinguished any chance of Brett's success thanks to Irv's mulish obstinance.

On the evening of Sunday, December 21, 2003, near the Kiln, Irv Favre crashed his car into a ditch. Police would later say the crash wasn't serious enough to hurt the fifty-eight-year-old. Instead, he'd suffered a massive heart attack. He left behind a shocked and grieving family.

Less than twenty-four hours later, Brett would have to suit up to appear in front of a national audience on *Monday Night Football*. His Packers were on the road against the Raiders. With an 8–6 record, their playoff hopes hung in the balance. John Madden, the game's commentator, said, "How Brett Favre is going to be able to handle this, I have no idea."

Favre looked composed in warm-ups. Another day at the office. He took the field and reeled off nine straight completions. On a tough third and eleven early in the game, he fired a rifle blast downfield more than forty yards to hit receiver Robert Ferguson in stride. A few plays later, Favre tossed his first of four touchdowns in the game. His offensive line ran to him, with two of them picking him up in the air, Favre smiling through his facemask. The Packers never looked back, winning 41–7.

It was one of the finest performances of Favre's career. "I knew that my dad would have wanted me to play," Favre said after the game. He was talking about a man he loved, the man who was so tough on him, and the man who wouldn't let his son play his best game every Friday night of Favre's high school years.

Contradictions.

Just as Mississippi's capital, and sometimes Mississippi, leaves us disappointed in its never-ending cycle of potential and collapse, Favre showed Mississippi something we could admire — one of us who made it — and then tarnished that image in a few short years. There would be many who would never forgive him for taking money he knew should go to people in "shelters," in his words, and then trying to hide that fact from the media and public.

※

In my final months writing this book, I was told I'd be deployed to Iraq. For this assignment, I'd be attached as the JAG to an elite group of Army Special Forces soldiers. This unit was sent to the most dangerous corners of the world; members had been killed in action in previous deployments. The trip would be perilous, too. We were headed to an area that had seen eighty Iranian-backed attacks against US forces since 2021. Just before the departure date, Iran invested more money in IEDs (improvised explosive devices) specifically designed to kill US service members in the area. I had to confront, for the first time in my life, the idea that I might not come back home to my three kids.

As we prepared for deployment, our team conducted various training missions. One night after a mission, when we were all inside the barracks lying in our bunks, I stared up at the underside of the bunk above me and contemplated this.

What happens if you're hit by a drone strike?

Are you killed instantly? That was obviously preferable. *Or are you buried alive?* This was less desirable. *If you're buried, are you knocked unconscious and stay out until you expire? Or are you awake, writhing against the concrete and metal and quietly suffocating?*

I knew other guys thought about it, too. One of the chief warrant officers in the unit — sort of the senior badass in a group of special forces operators — told me that on his last deployment, at night when the air raid siren went off, the only way he could comfort himself was by staring at the ceiling and saying, "Well, if it happens, it happens."

My mind wandered to weird places, too.

If I die, will my family even know which day the garbage truck comes? I wonder if they know the grass needs to be cut occasionally. You know, the worries that occupy the dad-mind.

Then, four days before I was set to deploy, word came down that there was a big fight between Air Force and Army brass. They were at odds over whether the Air Force should send an asset (me) to help the Army. My deployment was canceled. It may seem strange to some, but I was angry and heartbroken to not be going with a group of men I'd grown close to.

All that led me back to this book. I'd been on edge about it for some time. I knew publishing this would reignite all the old anger around this case. The casual Favre fans who were ready for the story to go away, the relatives of the News who wanted to exact revenge, the politicos who feared the full tale coming to light — all would be dismayed to see it hit the shelves. They might find ways to take that frustration out on me.

More than that, the political community in Mississippi is small. Everyone knows everyone. The book would be a hand grenade in the middle of the collegial, let's-keep-this-kind-of-thing-quiet culture.

But the thought of the army unit steeled my resolve. Before most military deployments, you train with your unit at a base in the US long before boarding a plane to go abroad. You learn the newest military technology you might use overseas. You go to the firing range. You learn about where you're going. You work out. My time with the special forces operators — who were real-life heroes, and monster athletes to boot — forced me to ask a question: If these men were willing to leave their families, go into the desert, bash in doors, stand in the way of bullets, and ride roads at the risk of being blown up, what was I willing to do? If they were willing to take these risks in their jobs, what risks was I willing to take in mine as auditor?

The choice was plain. Taxpayers needed to know what happened here. I would publish the book, torpedoes be damned.

One Tuesday morning after Davis's guilty plea, I drove past the building that once housed one of Nancy's useless community outreach centers and a DHS office. My truck lurched to a stop at the next traffic light, the intersection of State and High Streets. This was the heart of Mississippi's government. The Sillers Building, home to the governor's office, towered over me to my right. At my two o'clock was our imposing gray state capitol, a gilded eagle sitting atop it. All around were the buildings of the state bureaucracy, where a thousand tiny decisions about how to spend money were made every day.

At eleven o'clock was a park bench in the shade of an oak tree. On the bench sat a homeless man, shirtless, holding a blue Gatorade. He was hunched over, staring down at worn shoes or into the dirt. The cars at this stop, one of Jackson's busiest intersections, carried lawmakers, lobbyists, CEOs visiting government offices — Mississippi's movers and shakers. All of us hurried to our destinations, scurrying past the homeless man.

Once I reached work, I boarded the creaky Woolfolk elevator alone to ascend to my office. The elevator stopped on the second floor, and an older gentleman joined me in the car. His leathery skin reminded me of my grandfather's but several shades darker. His clothes were plain and too big on his thin frame. I'd never seen him in the building before.

"You're Shad White," he said. Despite the receding hairline and quiet voice, there was an energy in his gaze.

"Uh-oh," I said. "What did I do?"

"Thank you for what you do. You do a good job, is what you do. But I need to talk to you about my community. Can I come see you one day?"

He told me his name, and we set a time for him to come by my office.

Several days later, the gentleman, his pastor — an even older, regal man, who was blind behind his sunshades — and the pastor's young nephew, fresh out of prison, walked in my door. We sat over bottles of water.

"What can I do for you?" I said.

There was no "ask" from my visitors, but they recounted how, for years, they'd watched the typical TANF recipients struggle for lack of services while John Davis ran DHS. Countless neighbors had been turned down for assistance. Programs that were promised never came to fruition. On top of it all, they were surrounded by crime. Bad water. Terrible schools. Gunshots at night.

"And it ain't gotten better," the nephew said. They told me of a single mother in their church who just earned her CDL (commercial driver's license) to drive eighteen-wheelers but couldn't make rent while she waited for a job to pan out. "DHS still won't do nothing."

My heart was breaking in front of them, so I fidgeted with the label on a water bottle, searching their faces. We talked about how DHS now had flush coffers they could deploy, how there were tax credits for working people that would apply to the truck-driving woman (if DHS would begin the program), and about the epidemic of fatherlessness that was plaguing poor families. The tone was somber.

Before we descended too deep into darkness, though, the pastor spoke up. "But listen, Mr. White," he said, sitting up straighter in his chair. Pointing himself right in my direction, he removed his dark sunglasses, revealing glassy eyes. "Now we know something." He paused. "Now we know the money isn't being stolen anymore. That's called hope."

Epilogue

A book about the rich stealing welfare funds in the poorest state in the Union can be depressing. All the people I'd seen in my life who'd borne the yoke of poverty — William, from my elementary school, who ate his breakfast fast and played in the dirt trailer park across the street from my grandparents; Linda Fay Engle-Harris, the Tunica teacher who lived in the house that would never be repaired; Rosita, one of the little girls in the El Salvador orphanage, left there by her father; Drex — rushed to my mind when I thought of the money that had been torched at DHS.

What was equally disconcerting was my sense that schemes like this happened nationwide. The *New York Times* reported in November 2021 that Jack Brown, the head of a nonprofit for housing the homeless, may have flimflammed New York City out of millions of dollars around the same time Nancy and Zach were operating MCEC. Brown's nonprofit won big grants to operate fifteen homeless shelters in the city. When government money started flowing to his nonprofit, Brown allegedly funneled it to his private businesses, like his real estate company. He also hired at least five family members on staff and gave them benefits like cars and gym memberships.

In 2022, the *Washington Post* reported that a Minnesota nonprofit siphoned $250 million in stimulus spending. The grant they stole from was to provide food for needy children during the pandemic. Instead the culprits bought luxury cars and houses.

Where does it end?

When I was feeling down, during the progression of the DHS case, a memory from my time at the US Air Force Officer

Training School would give me hope. On one of the long days of training, where my team (called a flight) had been awake since before the sun was up, with the olive-green undershirts we were wearing beneath our camo ripe with sweat and grime, I could tell unit cohesion was under stress. An uneasy conversation was under way. In the middle of it, one airman stopped and said, "I know not everyone here is a person of faith, but I would like to pray for us. Anyone who likes is free to join me."

The airmen in our flight came from all over, from Alaska to Florida. They were pilots, healthcare professionals, lawyers, intelligence analysts, cyber warriors, and maintainers. Black, White, Latino, and Asian American. Believers and non-believers. Everyone in the room agreed they wanted to pray. We put our heads down, and the first airman led the prayer. When it was done, I looked up. It occurred to me then that every person in the room was taking time away from their families to serve something greater than themselves. Some of us, maybe all, would deploy at some point, risking our own lives and, at a minimum, missing the birthdays and funerals of loved ones. We did it because we all believed this country is great and worth fighting for, even on its worst days.

That's what I thought about my home state, too. And that's what helped me to endure the travails of the DHS case: the idea that Mississippi was worth fighting for. The oath I took as a military officer — to support and defend the Constitution — mirrored the one I took when I became state auditor. As long as good people were willing to take — and keep — such oaths, we would be all right.

Effecting change as state auditor, though, requires more than just dedication to an oath. Mississippi has some of the basic ingredients for fraud. Think back to the Fraud Triangle. First, fraudsters often have a need for cash, whether it's a need of their own making because of their lifestyle (think the News) or financial pressure created by something outside their control, like medical bills. Financial need is common in my state.

Second, fraudsters are often in a position to steal. Mississippi has a small population spread over a relatively large geographic area. We have hundreds of small towns, county governments, and tiny state agencies, not to mention small businesses and nonprofits. Each one presents an opportunity for an insider to commit fraud. According to the Association of Certified Fraud Examiners (ACFE), small organizations are more likely than large organizations to fall victim to fraud. When they do, those small organizations suffer a greater dollar loss per instance of fraud than larger ones.

The third leg of the triangle is for perpetrators to rationalize the theft to themselves.

In a state brimming with these ingredients, it will be difficult to ever cure endemic corruption. The state auditor or FBI is not going to magically increase Mississippi's gross domestic product or centralize Mississippi's government offices. If we, in the state auditor's office, were going to make a dent in a problem that intractable, we'd need a team with the energy, guts, and brains to make it happen.

Putting a dent in it was what we aimed to do, though. And we had two lodestars for reaching our destination. Our first guiding principle was simple: use our cases to create a deterrent. Every time we had a good result, we put the embezzler's mugshot on social media for the public to see. I wanted the world to know there were consequences for stealing.

Some people didn't like our doing this. One veteran politician told me I was just embarrassing the people in the mugshots, along with their families. I disagreed. They'd embarrassed themselves by taking something that didn't belong to them. I was happy to make them famous for it. More important, I wanted anyone else out there who was thinking of stealing or who was already embezzling from the government to know they would be caught soon. In that way, maybe we could prevent criminal activity.

This approach is backed by research. The ACFE has suggested one of the best ways to deter white-collar criminal activity is to increase the perception of detection. Put differently, make the crooks feel like they'll be discovered. Being public about our work was how we achieved that.

The second principle was that we would never let politics stand in the way of an investigation. The story most emblematic of that approach came from my home county.

Not long after I was appointed, we discovered that the president of the county board of supervisors — one of the more popular local politicians — had embezzled funds from a program for public school students. The supervisor also had a county truck scrapped without anyone's knowledge and stole the proceeds. When we concluded the investigation, I took the case down to the DA, Tony Buckley, myself. Tony was a Brit who'd moved to Mississippi and found himself the elected prosecutor for our area. He and I worked well together during his time in office, and he was effective. Oddly, I think his English accent helped in front of rural Mississippi juries.

Tony obtained a guilty plea, making the supervisor a felon and ending his time in elected office forever. At the end of the case, no one had to say the obvious: There would be political consequences for me. The supervisor was known all over the county. He was a guy who'd been in office for decades and was featured in local cookbooks. And in state politics in Mississippi, if you alienated your home — the geographic base of your support — well, good luck winning your next primary election.

In the end, I wagered it was better for me to make pockets of people mad here and there than to fail to do my job. There was an easy way to be state auditor, which was to never do the hard investigations, never hold the popular or powerful to account. I saw countless other politicians do their jobs that way in the hope it would be their ticket to higher office one day.

But I wanted my children to look back one day and be proud of how I performed, even if the way I served made me unelectable to anything else. Making factions of people angry because of a tough audit this year or an investigation of one of their allies next year would hurt over time, because small angry groups tend to be motivated and are able to organize. But it also meant I was protecting the more dispersed, general interests of the taxpayers at large, even if they never noticed. And that was the job.

Part of what motivated me to handle my position in this way was a personal experience I had with fraud. In fact, everyone my age had it. I graduated college in 2008, just a few months before the national economy collapsed around a broken and fraud-riddled mortgage system. Banks had packaged (that is, securitized) mortgages in opaque and complex ways, and they took the entire economy down with them. Credit rating bureaus turned a blind eye to the burgeoning problems. Some of the banks sold securitized versions of their loans to unsuspecting buyers as the prices tumbled. Regulators could not understand what was happening or chose not to act. And yes, some normal people lied to obtain mortgages they couldn't afford or were confused about the interest rates they would pay on the loans.

Everyone else was a victim of this epochal disaster, especially the taxpayers who were forced to bail out the massive banks, insurance companies, and wealthy corporate executives. The whole charade colored my generation's view of the harm that an abuse of influence could cause. Many of my friends couldn't find first jobs out of college as a result. To this day, people my age have a harder time accumulating wealth and financial independence, statistically, in the wake of that recession.

My hope is that one legacy of 2008 will be a cohort of people dedicated to greater transparency and dealing with others in good faith. No one person caused the 2008 collapse, and no one person can prevent another market meltdown. The only way to stop future large-scale failures of important institutions due to fraud is for each person to be an honest broker in their own lives. All of us will fall short, but this should be the goal. For those of us in a position to root out corruption, even in the smallest of sandboxes, we must do so vigilantly.

Ultimately, the DHS case is not just a story about fraud, though. It's about power. It's about how power is accumulated through building networks, through maintaining secrecy, and, most important, through the use of lots of money. It's about how power is leveraged and how it can be used at the expense of the unsuspecting public. It's a story about greed, yes, but it's ultimately a story about how the greedy are empowered by the complacency of those around them.

More optimistically, it's a story about how a group of people, unsatisfied with that complacency, can stop it. They have to be sick of the games and smart enough to sniff out the schemes. They must be willing to be called names and risk their careers in some situations. But it is possible. They fight for the honest everyman — the teacher, the oil field pumper, the retiree, the middle school student, the security guard — who depends on them to ensure he is not fleeced. That must motivate them, along with the courage of their convictions.

In my twenties I'd lost faith that the government could solve even basic problems, much less the intractable poverty I saw in my boyhood. The DHS scandal might've reinforced that belief, adding another datum to the laundry list of government failures. Instead, for me, it showed that a dedicated group of public servants — even if the group was small — could do the right thing and solve problems.

Beyond this, DHS's tale is a story of warning to the rest of the nation. The welfare game in Mississippi — "the Sip," to her natives — was fixed for years, but the lessons learned could put a stop to similar schemes around the country.

If more groups and individuals do not take this stand, the country is in trouble. The honest everyman is losing her patience. Her faith in our institutions is at an all-time low according to the Pew Research Center. She may not know all the exact ways she's being hurt by narrow, powerful groups, but she knows the system is sick. I'd liken it to driving a car. When your car breaks down on the side of the road and is boiling smoke, you may not know which part is faulty. You may not be a mechanic, and therefore do not have the expertise to know what exactly is happening, or you may not be able to see inside the engine at the moment. But you know something isn't right.

Americans know the car is broken. Their government is more powerful than ever, yet Americans have lost faith in government to mind taxpayer resources and make commonsense decisions. Waste is rampant, even if the average taxpayer can't see all the modalities of the waste. Bureaucrats abuse their authority. Some politicians lie and grow rich. Americans know in their bones this isn't how it's supposed to be.

Giant corporations are more powerful than ever, too. They insert themselves into our daily lives — deciding what we're allowed to say on social media, telling us what we're supposed to believe about social issues, tracking where we go and what our eyeballs see — more than ever before. Yet their leadership is not accountable to the people. The use of their power and virtue signaling shrouds their malfeasance, from paying their workers too little to their embrace of repressive regimes abroad for profit. For those reasons, Americans do not trust corporate power, either.

Finally, Americans believe the car is broken because the media, which has traditionally served as a sort of CHECK ENGINE light for our democracy, doesn't work. The media was supposed to tell us when the government became bought off by special interests or when corporate managers sold Americans up the river. But because the media, across the political spectrum, is also captive now to the dictates of an eyeballs-on-the-screen business model, people do not believe they are being told the truth.

Think of Slim Smith, the reporter who ranted about my wife. He posts ideological rants on Twitter one minute and then expects the public to believe he's writing unbiased reports — giving us the straight news — the next. When he types words into Twitter he's an apparatchik. When he types words into the website for his newspaper, he's supposed to be Walter Cronkite. Readers smell the bullshit. They wouldn't trust journalists like him to hold a liberal politician accountable, and they wouldn't trust a journalist like him if he says a conservative has done something wrong. Sadly, it's his type that dominates national media. The public has seen enough to reflexively write off an entire industry.

This is sadder still because our nation's founders viewed the press as a pillar of democracy. Thomas Jefferson famously wrote in 1787 that if he had to choose between a government without newspapers or newspapers without a government, he would "prefer the latter." And yet in 1807, having served four years as vice president and six years as president, he wrote to a friend: "Nothing can now be believed which is seen in a newspaper." Freedom of the press is important for our democracy, but that freedom divorced from a sense of responsibility is corrosive and potentially dangerous.

All these large cornerstone institutions of our society have forsaken the voters, shareholders, workers, and viewers they were supposed to protect. Few people are left to speak for the people. Returning the public's faith in the idea that the entire edifice of American life operates for their general welfare, and not for the powerful forces they see around them, is a twenty-first-century requirement for a healthy republic.

⚖

John Davis pleaded guilty to state and federal fraud-related charges and will likely serve out his prison sentence in a federal penitentiary. He has been sued by the state for millions of diverted TANF dollars.

Nancy and Zach New pleaded guilty to state and federal charges as well. Both have agreed to cooperate with prosecutors by providing information on other potential perpetrators. They have been sued civilly by the state, too.

Jess New is still the head of the state's oil and gas board. He has been sued by the state for his role in orchestrating the misspending of millions in TANF funds. He has never been charged with a crime.

Brett Favre still lives in Hattiesburg. He has been sued by the state for the millions of welfare dollars spent on USM's volleyball court and Prevacus. He has never been charged with a crime.

Jody Owens continues to serve as district attorney of Hinds County.

Attorney General Lynn Fitch is still the attorney general of Mississippi and is rumored to be considering a run for higher office.

Marcus Dupree has never been charged with a crime but has been sued by the state civilly. As of this writing, he continues to own and live on the horse farm purchased in part with welfare money in a suburb of Jackson.

Governor Phil Bryant lives quietly on a small farm south of Jackson.

Mike Hurst left office as US attorney in 2021. He never charged any TANF culprit with a crime. He is currently a white-collar criminal defense partner at a Jackson law firm and is rumored to be eyeing another run for public office.

Richie McCluskey and Bo Howard left the auditor's office in 2021. McCluskey is still in a senior security position at a large bank. Howard is an IRS agent in Mississippi.

Pat Dendy, deputy state auditor, retired from the auditor's office in 2022. He spends his days traveling with his wife and son, who competes on the pro golf circuit.

Stephanie Palmertree was promoted to deputy state auditor, along with **Larry Ware,** to replace Pat Dendy. Stephanie still wears black frequently. She's now a nationally recognized expert on TANF funding and audits of federal funds.

"Bulldog" left the Office of the State Auditor but still works in law enforcement in Mississippi.

Jacob Black was sued by the state for his role in misspending millions of TANF dollars. He is a senior staffer at the state's Medicaid agency.

Anna Wolfe still works as a reporter in Jackson, writing about welfare spending. Her hair stays mostly brown these days.

Christi Webb, the director of FRC, pleaded guilty in federal court to one count of stealing public funds.

Brett DiBiase pleaded guilty to both state and federal fraud-related charges and has been sued civilly by the state.

Anne McGrew pleaded guilty to state charges. Her evidence was critical for bringing down others in the larger scheme.

Jerry Spell and Michael Guynes continue to work at the Office of the State Auditor on white-collar fraud cases.

Bob Anderson is still the director of the Department of Human Services.

Ted DiBiase has never been charged with a crime but has been sued by the state civilly.

Ted DiBiase Jr. (Teddy) has been indicted in federal court for defrauding the taxpayers and using TANF money to buy himself a boat and house, among other things. As of this writing, he maintains his innocence.

Belinda Gartner, the indefatigable front desk secretary, is still the front desk secretary at the Office of the State Auditor. The only change is that, after ESPN wrote a short story about her in 2022, her grandchildren believe that "Granny's famous."

In September 2023, the Chairman of the US House Ways & Means Committee called on the Government Accountability Office to conduct a nationwide "investigation" of TANF spending in every state. "We are concerned that the Mississippi case is emblematic of a systemic problem," he said.

Acknowledgments

"Hey," I said to my wife one evening on the couch. "I think I'm done writing this book."

Her eyes never looked up from whatever tome she was reading at the time. "Thank God," she said.

The biggest helping of gratitude here goes to my wife, Rina, who tolerated me spending late hours yelling at my computer, grumpy mornings when I complained about the writing process, and a pesky husband who kept asking her to read portions of this text to see if they made sense. She is my first and wisest editor. And an amazing mother. And the love of my life. The ultimate trifecta.

She's also a black belt in Tae Kwon Do (I promised her I would work that in at some point).

The book would not have happened without my agents, Margaret Danko and Kim Perel. They looked at a pitch from a no-name auditor in Mississippi who'd never written a book and said, "Yeah, let's take a shot on this guy."

The same is said for my brilliant editor and publisher, Chip Fleischer. He cut through the nonsense I sent him and helped turn this book into what it is. Any shortcomings in the writing are mine. To Margaret, Kim, and Chip, thank you for believing in this project when few others would.

Tons of friends and acquaintances pitched in and helped me navigate the publishing process. Among them were my old boss, Oren Cass; my own personal World War II aircraft expert, Sam Kleiner; Vivek Ramaswamy; Adam Grant; Evan Baehr; David McCloskey; Adam Buckalew; Mary Ann Glendon; a onetime drinking buddy, Wright Thompson; Erin Napier, who was once the better half of a girl-guy acoustic duo with me;

my old racquetball partner, Ben Napier; Sherif Girgis; longtime mentors Catherine and Wayne Reynolds; Erskine Wells; Alexandra Hudson; Andy Mullins; and several others (you know who you are, shy ones).

The advisers and teachers who helped me along the way are legion. The most important are my parents and grandparents, of course. They made me the man and father I am today. And that is far more important than any professional accomplishment.

The thank-yous end where this book started: giving all the credit to the men and women I work with at the Office of the State Auditor. There are too many — from Bill Pope (my Rasputin) to all the individual auditors and investigators who worked the DHS case — to name. They deserved to have their story told.

Notes

Chapter 1

homicide capital of North America: Diana Roy, "Why Has Gang Violence Spiked in El Salvador?" Council on Foreign Relations, May 4, 2022.

Life expectancy for men in some Mississippi counties was actually worse than: Debbie Elliott, "Tackling Obesity Amid Poverty in a Mississippi County," National Public Radio, August 9, 2011.

the average life expectancy in El Salvador: World Bank, "Life Expectancy at Birth — El Salvador," https://data.worldbank.org/indicator/SP.DYN.LE00.IN?loc ations=SV, accessed June 2023.

the most important determinant of people moving up the income ladder was the strength of community institutions like schools and churches. The two-parent family was also critical: Gareth Cook, "The Economist Who Would Fix the American Dream," *Atlantic*, August 2019.

On April 19, law enforcement raced down Memorial Drive about a mile from campus and ended the matter in a shootout in nearby Watertown: "Boston Marathon Terror Ride," *Boston Herald*, March 13, 2015.

most corrupt states: Dick Simpson et al., "Chicago: Still the Capital of Corruption," University of Illinois at Chicago, May 28, 2015.

the corporate executive turned to the topic of the state auditor's position. He told the governor he "needed" to appoint the corporation's favorite — a local state senator — to the spot: Interview with Bryant staff.

shock from professional prognosticators: Geoff Pender, "Gov. Bryant Names New State Auditor to Replace Stacey Pickering," *Clarion-Ledger* (Jackson, MS), July 6, 2018.

Chapter 2

The discussion of why John Davis sent Restore checks to his personal address, the results of his polygraph, and the interview with Richie McCluskey came from interviews with OSA auditors and investigators.

a federal criminal investigator and former Tennessee Auditor's Office employee with few Mississippi connections: Waverly McCarthy, "Gov. Bryant Appoints Christopher Freeze as Executive Director of Mississippi Department of Human Services," WLBT, July 25, 2019.

Temporary Assistance for Needy Families . . . Congressional Research Service: "The Temporary Assistance for Needy Families (TANF) Block Grant: A Legislative

History," Congressional Research Service, May 8, 2023. This citation also provided information on the statutory requirements for TANF later in the chapter.

Black women were equally as likely to be married: Douglas Besharov and Andrew West, "African American Marriage Patterns," Hoover Institution, https://www.hoover.org/sites/default/files/uploads/documents/0817998721_95.pdf, accessed June 2023.

just 24 percent of Black children . . . to 64 percent: George Akerloff and Janet Yellen, "An Analysis of Out-of-Wedlock Births in the United States," Brookings Institution, August 1, 1996.

Ted DiBiase used his fame . . . Clinton, Mississippi: Giacomo Bologna and Luke Ramseth, "Mississippi Gave 'Million Dollar Man' Ted DiBiase's Nonprofit over $2M in Welfare Money," *Clarion-Ledger* (Jackson, MS), February 14, 2020.

The discussion of Brett DiBiase's introduction to Davis and the DiBiase entities was based on interviews with auditors and investigators and a review of the corporate filing documents for Restore, Heart of David Ministries, and Priceless Ventures.

The discussion of Heart of David's activities was based on interviews with auditors and investigators and was recorded in the State of Mississippi's Single Audit for the Year Ending June 30, 2019, published by the Mississippi Office of the State Auditor on April 30, 2020.

personal credit card: Interviews with auditors and investigators.

Trump Hotel: Interviews with auditors and investigators.

"Director of Transformational Change" . . . per year: "Mississippi Gave $2M in Welfare Money to Wrestler's Group," Associated Press, February 14, 2020.

Chapter 3

Mustering a serious look . . . taken thousands from New: "Hood: Reeves Campaign Commercial for Public Education Filmed at a Private School Is 'Fraudulent,'" WJTV, October 15, 2019.

New's biography . . . like her own: Holly Perkins, "A Personal Path with Dyslexia," *Mississippi Christian Living*, October 3, 2016.

The discussion of MCEC is based on their corporate filings with the Mississippi Secretary of State's Office.

Attorney General Hood accused Reeves . . . his own coffers: Courtney Ann Jackson, "Jim Hood Criticizes Tate Reeves' Education Ad," WLBT, October 15, 2019.

At the meeting . . . no next meeting: Discussions with Chris Freeze.

Anne was a heavyset CPA . . . Nancy's school: "Accountant Pleads Guilty in Mississippi Human Services Fraud," Associated Press, October 12, 2021.

The discussion of Anne's interview is based on interviews with auditors and investigators.

Brett had a drug problem . . . enjoy panoramic views of palm trees and the ocean while detoxing: Emily Wagster Pettus, "Mississippi Agency Ex-Leader Pleads Guilty in Welfare Fraud," Associated Press, September 22, 2022.

Description of Rise in Malibu: https://riseinmalibu.com, accessed June 2023.

Davis made trips to see him: Pettus, "Mississippi Agency Ex-Leader Pleads Guilty in Welfare Fraud."

Las Vegas and Washington, DC: Giacomo Bologna, "DHS Embezzlement Scandal: Feds Moving to Seize $1.6M Home of Ted DiBiase Jr. in Madison," *Clarion-Ledger* (Jackson, MS), August 14, 2020.

In some criminal cases . . . calls placed to them by patients: Interviews with auditors and investigators.

While Brett was in Malibu . . . hand over the payments: Interviews with auditors and investigators.

The discussion of the News moving TANF money and Prevacus is based on interviews with auditors and investigators and is recorded in the State of Mississippi's Single Audit for the Year Ending June 30, 2019, published by the Mississippi Office of the State Auditor on April 30, 2020.

For years, Anna wrote . . . the rest was going to something else: Anna Wolfe, "MS Pulse: Agency Rejecting 98.5% of Welfare Applicants to Take Over Medicaid Eligibility," *Clarion-Ledger*, October 27, 2017.

ninety-four people they had helped . . . show for it: Anna Wolfe, "Connecting the Dots: Players in Massive Welfare Embezzlement Case Got Millions from Taxpayers, but Helped Few," *Clarion-Ledger*, February 6, 2020.

The discussion of the Sheffield home, FRC, and the failure to monitor were all based on interviews with auditors and investigators.

Chapter 4

Before I was named state auditor . . . during the wait: "Former MDE Director to Plead Guilty in Kickback Scheme," *Jackson Jambalaya*, May 31, 2023.

The discussion of Dan Schneider was taken from the documentary *The Pharmacist*, directed by Jenner Furst and Julia Willoughby Nason (2020).

Nancy's text messages . . . Hurst says: Anna Wolfe, "'Whipping Child': Nancy New Asked Highest Officials for Help Before Arrests in Welfare Scandal," *Mississippi Today*, June 22, 2022.

Across town . . . we could get him a [F-150] raptor: Anna Wolfe, "Phil Bryant Had His Sights on a Payout as Welfare Funds Flowed to Brett Favre," *Mississippi Today*, April 4, 2022.

could cost north of $100,000: Gary Gastelu, "The $109K Ford F-150 Raptor R Is so Hot It Costs Much More than That," Fox 2 Detroit, March 8, 2023.

Honestly give me your thoughts . . . take home 20 million: Anna Wolfe, "'You Stuck Your Neck Out for Me': Brett Favre Used Fame and Favors to Pull Welfare Dollars," *Mississippi Today*, April 6, 2022.

"I'm going to . . . she's great": Wolfe, "Phil Bryant Had His Sights on a Payout.

The News, per Vanlandingham's request . . . (Nancy's other son): Anna Wolfe, "It's Been a Year Since They Were Arrested for Allegedly Stealing Millions from the Poor. Here's What Happened," *Mississippi Today*, February 5, 2021.

Vanlandingham texted Bryant . . . get on it hard: Wolfe, "Phil Bryant Had His Sights on a Payout."

The texts mentioned in chapter 4 were also corroborated by interviews with investigators and auditors.

Chapter 5

On Elizabeth Holmes: "Elizabeth Holmes Expresses Remorse in Her Criminal Trial," Associated Press, November 23, 2011. See also John Carreyrou, *Bad Blood* (New York: Knopf, 2018).

That deception had its roots . . . in the state: Original grant agreement between DHS and MCEC. MCEC financials are taken from their IRS form 990s.

The News knew they'd received . . . describe all of this: "Audit of DHS Reveals Millions Wasted," Mississippi Office of the State Auditor, May 4, 2020.

Anne could also testify . . . started to look intentional: Interviews with auditors and investigators. Many of these findings are also described in the State of Mississippi's Single Audit for the Year Ending June 30, 2019, published by the Mississippi Office of the State Auditor on April 30, 2020.

In the words of Enron prosecutor . . . big things: *Bad Bets* (Wall Street Journal Podcasts), https://www.wsj.com/podcasts/bad-bets/enron-ep-7-the-trial/708cac07-5524-4d01-8959-32daaaa11299, accessed June 2023.

Brett, to his credit . . . related to the rent: Interviews with auditors and investigators. Many of these findings are also described in the State of Mississippi's Single Audit for the Year Ending June 30, 2019, published by the Mississippi Office of the State Auditor on April 30, 2020.

WorldCom symbolized this . . . to recoup the expenditures: Cynthia Cooper, *Extraordinary Circumstances* (Hoboken, NJ: Wiley, 2007).

And as famed investor Warren Buffett . . . who's been swimming naked: Peter Tchir, "What If Buffett Is the One Swimming Naked?" *Forbes*, May 4, 2020.

Bernie had been swimming . . . understand the financial machinations: Cooper, *Extraordinary Circumstances*.

The proof of Ebbers's knowledge and intent: Ken Belson, "Prosecutors at Ebbers's Trial Turn to Their Tape Players," *New York Times*, February 10, 2005.

Combined with the riches . . . value evaporated overnight: Lisette Voytko, "Bernard Ebbers, Former WorldCom CEO Convicted In $11 Billion Fraud, Dies at 78," *Forbes*, February 3, 2020.

On Cressey: Cheryl Lero Johnson and Gilbert Geis, "Cressey, Donald R.: Embezzlement and White-Collar Crime," in Francis T. Cullen and Pamela Wilcox, eds., *Encyclopedia of Criminological Theory*, volume 1 (Los Angeles: Sage, 2010).

Enron's CFO . . . maintain it: Kurt Eichenwald, *Conspiracy of Fools* (New York: Crown, 2005).

They had access . . . a certain level of luxury: Interviews with auditors and investigators. Many of these findings are also described in the State of Mississippi's Single Audit for the Year Ending June 30, 2019, published by the Mississippi Office of the State Auditor on April 30, 2020.

In fact, Harvard professor Eugene Soltes . . . should not have been punished: Eugene Soltes, *Why They Do It* (New York: Public Affairs, 2016).

Chapter 6

hundred-year flood: Lici Beverage, "Mississippi Flooding: Southern Counties Begin to See Waters Rise Above Flood Stage," *Clarion-Ledger* (Jackson, MS), February 17, 2020.

prison system was in newspapers: "Timeline of Inmate Deaths at Mississippi Prisons 2019–2020," WJTV, January 3, 2020.

When Zach New . . . looking for him: Interviews with auditors and investigators.

Mike Hurst's statement: Geoff Pender and Giacomo Bologna, "Feds: State Auditor Kept Them in the Dark on Mississippi Welfare Embezzlement Bust," *Clarion-Ledger*, February 6, 2019.

Chapter 7

The discussion of the cab case from the Mississippi Justice Institute was based on the court documents in that case, *John Davis and Shad Denson v. City of Jackson, Mississippi* (2017).

Perhaps some of the Framers . . . terrorize others: Alexander Hamilton, James Madison, et al., *The Federalist Papers*, originally published by the New York Packet, 1787.

In their book . . . and other mechanisms: Brink Lindsey and Steven Teles, *The Captured Economy* (New York: Oxford University Press, 2017).

The biggest PBMs bought . . . United States: Denise Myshko et al., "Beyond the Big Three PBMs," *Managed Healthcare Executive*, December 14, 2022.

They gave more than $200,000 . . . and the lieutenant governor: Sharie Nicole, "Company Accused of Overcharging Mississippians a Prominent Donor to State Leaders," WLBT, June 15, 2021. See also Anna Wolfe, "Medicaid Agency Poised to Extend Contract with Centene, Embattled Insurer and Big Campaign Donor," *Mississippi Today*, May 3, 2021; Jerry Mitchell, "State Auditor, AG Investigating Centene on Allegations It Pocketed Millions in Taxpayer Dollars," Mississippi Center for Investigative Reporting, April 14, 2021.

President Joe Biden . . . President Trump: Mitchell, "State Auditor, AG Investigating Centene."

In Mississippi, Centene inked . . . higher per-person fees if they wanted: Interviews with auditors and investigators.

By June 2021 . . . spent money on prescription drugs: Anna Wilde Mathews, "Centene Settles with Ohio and Mississippi Over Pharmacy Benefits Practice," *Wall Street Journal*, June 14, 2021.

Centene paid Mississippi more than $55 million . . . in Mississippi history: Internal records at the Mississippi Office of the State Auditor.

Chapter 8

One of Mike's predecessors . . . in the 2000s: Cynthia Cooper, *Extraordinary Circumstances* (Hoboken, NJ: Wiley, 2007).

The former auditor learned of corruption . . . and won: Paul Hampton, "The Supreme Court Says Sun Herald Got It Right in DMR Public Records Fight," *Sun Herald* (Biloxi, MS), November 16, 2017.

The head of the department was caught in a kickback scandal. The feds prosecuted it: Jimmie Gates, "Chris Epps Sentenced to Almost 20 Years," *Clarion-Ledger* (Jackson, MS), May 24, 2017.

I'd read stories . . . were cheaper at Best Buy: Sarah Butrymowicz and Tara Garcia Mathewson, "Tired of Fighting That Fight: School Districts' Uphill Battle to Get Good Deals on Ed Tech," *Hechinger Report*, March 26, 2018.

Chapter 9

The City of Jackson . . . burning most of Jackson to the ground: The History of
Jackson, http://www.jacksonms.gov/visitors/history, accessed archived version
from January 31, 2010.

Jackson elected its first Black mayor in 1997: Byron Orey, "Framing Race: The
Election of the First African-American Mayor of Jackson, Mississippi,"
University of Nebraska–Lincoln Faculty Publications, December 2005.

The city gobbled . . . lack of water pressure: Charles Marohn, "Financial Fragility Is
to Blame for Jackson's Water Crisis," Strong Towns, September 12, 2022.

Jackson was the per-capita homicide capital: C. J. LeMaster, "Analysis: For Second
Straight Year, Jackson's Homicide Rate Ranks Highest in U.S. Among Major
Cities," WLBT, January 6, 2023.

understaffed by nearly a hundred officers, according to the police chief: Anthony
Warren, "Jackson Police Department Reporting Nearly 100 Vacancies Among
Sworn Officers," WLBT, April 18, 2022.

In March 2020, they gave . . . rent paid in TANF dollars to the News: Giacomo
Bologna and Luke Ramseth, "Mississippi Welfare Money Went to Resort
Hotels, Steakhouses, Lobbyist, Football Stars," *Clarion-Ledger* (Jackson, MS),
March 13, 2020.

"Where did Jack get this?": Call with Anna Wolfe.

By May it was Stephanie . . . two iPads with data for Zach: Interviews with auditors and investigators. Many of these findings are also described in the State
of Mississippi's Single Audit for the Year Ending June 30, 2019, published by
the Mississippi Office of the State Auditor on April 30, 2020.

Nancy's case reminded me . . . The public looked the other way: All the Queen's
Horses, directed by Kelly Richmond Pope (2017).

Stephanie's audit also showed the News . . . how could her wealth be stolen?:
Interviews with auditors and investigators. Many of these findings are also
described in the State of Mississippi's Single Audit for the Year Ending June
30, 2019, published by the Mississippi Office of the State Auditor on April 30,
2020.

In a small way . . . the lives of addicted Americans: Patrick Radden Keefe, *Empire
of Pain* (New York: Doubleday, 2021).

In addition to their donations . . . so few people were helped: Interviews with auditors and investigators. Many of these findings are also described in the State
of Mississippi's Single Audit for the Year Ending June 30, 2019, published by
the Mississippi Office of the State Auditor on April 30, 2020.

Other famous fraudsters . . . Leonardo DiCaprio and Kanye West: Tom Wright and
Bradley Hope, *Billon Dollar Whale* (New York: Hachette, 2018).

Chapter 10

When Brett Lorenzo Favre . . . never turned back: Jeff Pearlman, *Gunslinger*
(Boston, New York: Mariner, 2016).

Here's what we found . . . for a volleyball court: Interviews with auditors and
investigators. Many of these findings are also described in the State of
Mississippi's Single Audit for the Year Ending June 30, 2019, published by the
Mississippi Office of the State Auditor on April 30, 2020.

Nancy I spoke . . . breaking the "brick and mortar" rule: Anna Wolfe, "New Texts

Show USM Had Concerns About Favre's Grant-Funded Volleyball Facility," *Mississippi Today*, October 1, 2022.

Would this . . . one more time a few days later: *Mississippi Department of Human Services v. Mississippi Community Education Center, Inc., et al.*, Plaintiff's Response to Defendant Brett Favre's Motion to Dismiss (filed March 13, 2023). See also exhibits to other filings in the case.

If you were to pay me . . . shrouded in darkness, via Favre: Eric Levenson, "Brett Favre's Texts Included in Lawsuit Over Misspent Mississippi Welfare Funds," CNN.com, September 15, 2022.

And Favre was pleased . . . donate to USM: Anna Wolfe, "Former Gov. Phil Bryant Subpoenaed for USM Volleyball Stadium Documents," *Mississippi Today*, July 27, 2022. See also *Mississippi Department of Human Services v. Mississippi Community Education Center, Inc., et al.*, Plaintiff's Response to Defendant Brett Favre's Motion to Dismiss (filed March 13, 2023) and exhibits.

MCEC eventually found a credulous lawyer . . . Nancy misspelled Culumber's name in the process: Interviews with auditors and investigators. Many of these findings are also described in the State of Mississippi's Single Audit for the Year Ending June 30, 2019, published by the Mississippi Office of the State Auditor on April 30, 2020.

Then Favre went on the radio . . . 100 percent not true: Jason Wilde, "Packers: Favre Denies Allegations of No-Show Payments," *Journal Times* (Racine, WI), May 8, 2020.

Favre lost endorsement deals . . . suspended his radio show: Tzvi Machlin, "Look: NFL World Reacts to Brett Favre Sponsorship News," *The Spun by Sports Illustrated*, September 21, 2022.

SiriusXM and ESPN Milwaukee suspended his radio show: A. J. Perez, "SiriusXM, ESPN Milwaukee, 33rd Team Bench Brett Favre Amid Welfare Scandal," *Front Office Sports*, September 23, 2022.

The other, tragic sports-related part . . . small house back in Philadelphia: *The Best That Never Was*, directed by Jonathan Hock (2009).

Jack Bologna eventually reported . . . called Marcus a "community liaison": Giacomo Bologna and Luke Ramseth, "Mississippi Welfare Money Went to Resort Hotels, Steakhouses, Lobbyist, Football Stars," *Clarion-Ledger* (Jackson, MS), March 13, 2020. See also the State of Mississippi's Single Audit for the Year Ending June 30, 2019, published by the Mississippi Office of the State Auditor on April 30, 2020.

The big money from MCEC . . . "You just don't walk up on my property without getting shot," he said: Anna Wolfe, "Sports Legend's Madison County Horse Ranch Being Paid for by Nonprofit at Center of Welfare Embezzlement Firestorm," *Mississippi Today*, March 18, 2020.

Our audit later revealed . . . someone at MCEC changed the transaction labels to "Contractual Services" in the software: Interviews with auditors and investigators. Many of these findings are also described in the State of Mississippi's Single Audit for the Year Ending June 30, 2019, published by the Mississippi Office of the State Auditor on April 30, 2020.

The texts mentioned in chapter 10 were also corroborated by interviews with auditors and investigators.

Chapter 11

This is like . . . conquer obesity: Michel Martin, "Mississippi Legislature Sheds 1,400 Pounds of Fat," NPR, April 7, 2010.

And worse, in May 2020 . . . paid for with welfare money: Interviews with auditors and investigators. Many of these findings are also described in the State of Mississippi's Single Audit for the Year Ending June 30, 2019, published by the Mississippi Office of the State Auditor on April 30, 2020.

We found that LaCoste's company . . . TANF-eligible: Interviews with auditors and investigators. Many of these findings are also described in the State of Mississippi's Single Audit for the Year Ending June 30, 2019, published by the Mississippi Office of the State Auditor on April 30, 2020.

In 1985, Jesse Jackson came . . . a fancy event venue, and a museum: Chico Harlan, "An Opportunity Gamed Away," *Washington Post*, July 11, 2015.

One of Tunica's casino-fueled . . . Where had all the money gone?: Interviews with auditors and investigators.

One person asking that question . . . given it a death sentence: Harlan, "An Opportunity Gamed Away."

The reason Jones could not fix . . . a demand for more than a million dollars: Interviews with auditors and investigators.

The Brookings Institution has shown . . . but hard to instill: Ron Haskins, "Three Simple Rules Poor Teens Should Follow to Join the Middle Class," Brookings Institution, March 13, 2013.

about half of federal spending went to Medicaid: "Budget Summary 2022 Legislative Session," Legislative Budget Office, https://www.lbo.ms.gov/pdfs/2022_leg_sesn_sum_3.pdf, accessed June 2023.

For the next two years . . . improper Medicaid payments per year: The State of Mississippi's Single Audit for the Year Ending June 30, 2019; the State of Mississippi's Single Audit for the Year Ending June 30, 2020; the State of Mississippi's Single Audit for the Year Ending June 30, 2021; the State of Mississippi's Single Audit for the Year Ending June 30, 2022.

Two of the ineligible . . . forced them to repay $130,000: "Medicaid Recipients Agree to Pay $130,000 to Resolve False Claims Act Allegations of Health Care Benefit Fraud," United States Attorney's Office for the Southern District of Mississippi, September 1, 2022.

Chapter 12

Bob was also inheriting a staff . . . the culture Davis had created: Interview with Chris Freeze.

I'd seen this movie before . . . nine years for the theft: *The Informant!*, directed by Steven Soderbergh (2009). See also Kurt Eichenwald, *The Informant* (New York: Crown, 2001).

That included the cars . . . purchased by the News: The State of Mississippi's Single Audit for the Year Ending June 30, 2019.

The bill passed with one nay vote . . . notwithstanding Bob's opposition: "Senate Bill 2338," Mississippi Legislature 2022 Regular Session, http://billstatus.ls.state.ms.us/2022/pdf/history/SB/SB2338.xml, accessed June 2023.

Chapter 13

Statute defined whistleblower *as the person . . . example of law enforcement*: Mississippi Code § 25-9-171.

Not long after the meeting . . . any higher than what it is: Giacomo Bologna, "Advocates: Lawmakers Target Poor After Top Officials Allegedly Steal $4M of Welfare Money," *Clarion-Ledger* (Jackson, MS), February 25, 2020.

Across town from my office . . . was now the News' lawyer: See also *Serial: Season 2*, hosted by Sarah Koenig (2015–2016); *State of Mississippi v. Nancy Whitten New, et al.*, Petition to Set Aside Injunction (filed February 11, 2020).

Fitch filmed a video around that time . . . enmeshed in the scandal: "A Message for Team Mississippi," Office of Attorney General Lynn Fitch, https://www.youtube.com/watch?v=i_rNZYVkn5g, accessed June 2023.

I saw this scenario play out . . . the change was unconstitutional: Jack Dura, "After Dispute with State Auditor, North Dakota Lawmakers Offer Bills," *Bismark Tribune*, January 12, 2021.

The results stretched forever . . . They forged signatures on documents: Interviews with investigators and auditors. Many of these findings are also described in the State of Mississippi's Single Audit for the Year Ending June 30, 2019, published by the Mississippi Office of the State Auditor on April 30, 2020.

Following our audit . . . to be used by the at-risk community: Anna Wolfe, "Southern Miss Knew Human Services Funds Paid for Volleyball Center Construction, Auditor Found," *Mississippi Today*, May 8, 2020.

Beyond the audit . . . had made it out to be: Discussion with Jack Bologna.

Chapter 14

There were parts of her tale . . . too much money to ask hard questions: Bethany McLean and Peter Elkin, *The Smartest Guys in the Room* (New York: Portfolio Trade, 2004).

They were supposed to be running . . . Costa Rica: Zach New, "From a Son's View," *Mississippi Christian Living*, September 4, 2014.

finance a nice life for Nancy and her children: Interviews with auditors and investigators. Many of these findings are also described in the State of Mississippi's Single Audit for the Year Ending June 30, 2019, published by the Mississippi Office of the State Auditor on April 30, 2020.

Andy Fastow, Enron's CFO . . . Like the Fastow Foundation: Kurt Eichenwald, *Conspiracy of Fools* (New York: Crown, 2005).

Ron Astin, an attorney hired by Enron . . . I represent Enron!: Eichenwald, *Conspiracy of Fools*.

John's heavy hand was on display . . . More awkward laughter. "Amen?": Interviews with auditors and investigators.

The forms that DHS was supposed to submit . . . subject to his occasional demands: Interviews with auditors and investigators. Many of these findings are also described in the State of Mississippi's Single Audit for the Year Ending June 30, 2019, published by the Mississippi Office of the State Auditor on April 30, 2020.

MCEC was audited by . . . the News protested: Anna Wolfe, "Two Court Filings Could Signal Defense Strategies for Nancy New, John Davis in Welfare Fraud Case," *Mississippi Today*, May 28, 2021.

Nonprofits everywhere are walking fraud risks . . . lack of certain internal controls: "Fraud in Nonprofits," Association of Certified Fraud Examiners, https://legacy.acfe.com/report-to-the-nations/2020/docs/infographic-pdfs/Fraud%20in%20Nonprofits.pdf, accessed June 2023.

Charities are not personal piggy banks . . . said Styron: "Hall of Fame QB Brett Favre's Charity Donated to University of Southern Mississippi Athletic Foundation While He Pushed for State Funds," ESPN, September 28, 2022.

This policy states that federal prosecutors . . . something they'd already be punished for: J. S. Allermand, "Petite Policy: An Example of Enlightened Prosecutorial Discretion," *Georgetown Law Journal* 66, no. 4 (1978).

stories about the old days . . . a long-standing culture of corruption: James Crockett, *Operation Pretense* (Jackson: University Press of Mississippi, 2003).

In November 2020, the journalists covering the story . . . welfare funds funneled through MCEC: Anna Wolfe and Giacomo Bologna, "Key Figure in Welfare Scandal Said She Was Told to Make Payments to Florida Drug Company," *Mississippi Today* and *Clarion-Ledger* (Jackson, MS), November 14, 2020.

Later Nancy and her lawyers . . . and my brother Jess: Anna Wolfe, "It's Been a Year Since They Were Arrested for Allegedly Stealing Millions from the Poor. Here's What Happened," *Mississippi Today*, February 5, 2021.

The scheme to pay the News . . . to run from that evidence: Anna Wolfe, "'You Stuck Your Neck Out for Me': Brett Favre Used Fame and Favors to Pull Welfare Dollars," *Mississippi Today*, April 6, 2022.

The Hinds County judge assigned . . . convict herself in public: Anna Wolfe and Giacomo Bologna, "Judge Issues Gag Order in Mississippi Welfare Embezzlement Case," *Mississippi Today* and *Clarion-Ledger*, November 20, 2020.

When the team served the notice . . . he was paid by DHS: Giacomo Bologna, "DHS Embezzlement Scandal: Feds Moving to Seize $1.6M home of Ted DiBiase Jr. in Madison," *Clarion-Ledger*, August 14, 2020. I also relied on interviews with auditors and investigators.

When we found the mayor . . . we worked it jointly with the feds: Lindsey Knowles and Mike Lacey, "Former Moss Point Mayor Sentenced to Federal Prison for Wire Fraud," WLOX, July 22, 2021.

On December 17, 2020 . . . full cooperation with the prosecution: Keisha Rowe, "Brett DiBiase Pleads Guilty in Human Services Embezzlement Scheme," *Clarion-Ledger*, December 17, 2020.

Meanwhile Nancy's school . . . The school didn't reopen: Interviews with auditors and investigators. See also Marcus Hunter, "New Summit School Closing After School Leaders Indicted on Fraud Charges," WAPT, July 29, 2021.

DHS, as an institution, marched forward . . . that was acceptable to all: Discussion with Bob Anderson, auditors, and investigators.

DHS staff didn't know how to pull . . . provide the necessary ledgers: Interviews with auditors and investigators.

The recipients of TANF money . . . with the documents they needed: Interviews with auditors and investigators. See also Wolfe and Bologna, "Key Figure in Welfare Scandal."

Heart of David was required to give us the documents so we could transmit them to the CPA firm: Interviews with auditors and investigators.

On January 19, 2021, Mike Hurst left his position of US attorney: "U.S. Attorney Mike Hurst Announces His Departure from Department of Justice," United States Attorney's Office for the Southern District of Mississippi, January 7, 2021.

The texts mentioned in chapter 14 were also corroborated by interviews with investigators and auditors.

Chapter 15

Jody and his team . . . Anne's deal was not stiff enough: Anna Wolfe, "Judge Rejects Plea Deal for Star Witness in Welfare Embezzlement Case," *Mississippi Today*, February 3, 2021.

Maurice Howard came to mind . . . sat down at counsel's table, and pleaded guilty: Interviews with auditors and investigators. See also "Auditor: Fmr. Aberdeen Mayor Pleads Guilty to Embezzling $3,500," WLBT, February 1, 2021.

He and his assistant prosecutor . . . bureaucrats hadn't made a peep: Justin Vicory, "Nancy, Zachary New Indicted in Federal Court, Accused of Taking Millions from Department of Education," *Clarion-Ledger* (Jackson, MS), March 18, 2021. This section also drew on the federal indictment of the News and interviews with auditors and investigators. See also Anna Wolfe, "Alleged Scam: Nancy New's School Claimed to Treat Hospitalized Kids," *Mississippi Today*, April 8, 2021.

Also that summer, Stephanie's team . . . they were under investigation: State of Mississippi's Single Audit for the Year Ending June 30, 2020, published by the Mississippi Office of the State Auditor.

She managed to talk a bingo hall director . . . patience for Nancy's stratagems was running out: Interviews with auditors and investigators. See also the Mississippi Gaming Commission's investigator report re: Mississippi American Development Foundation.

Her audits of DHS resulted . . . Oscar for accountants: "MC Graduate Stephanie Palmertree Earns National Award," *Mississippi College University News*, August 25, 2020.

Chapter 16

The firm found that the News alone . . . the conclusions looked similar: Interviews with auditors and investigators. See also (CLA) "Mississippi Department of Human Services TANF Forensic Audit: Findings of Possible Fraud, Waste & Abuse," September 21, 2021.

What was worse for the News . . . tragic amount of welfare funds: Interviews with auditors, investigators, and CLA.

The new penny-by-penny audit . . . to justify the payments: CLA, "Mississippi Department of Human Services TANF Forensic Audit."

On October 12, 2021, we served notices . . . repay the millions they'd been given: "Auditor Demands Repayment of Misspent Welfare Money," Mississippi Office of the State Auditor, October 12, 2021.

mafia accountants were brought before . . . better than nearly anyone else: Special Committee on Organized Crime in Interstate Commerce, United States Senate, https://www.senate.gov/about/powers-procedures/investigations/kefauver.htm, accessed June 2023.

Chapter 17

Wolfe drove on a Saturday . . . a three-hour interview: "Inside the Phil Bryant
   Interview Everyone's Talking About," *The Other Side Podcast*, April 25, 2022.
With the microphone hot . . . knew about the Vanlandingham offer before that:
   Anna Wolfe, "Q&A with Former Gov. Phil Bryant About Prevacus, Welfare
   Scandal," *Mississippi Today*, April 4, 2022.
*After the story with the text messages . . . has not yet launched a criminal investiga-
   tion*: Beatrice Peterson, "NAACP Calls on Justice Department to Investigate
   Mississippi Welfare Fraud Case," ABC News, April 18, 2022.
Bulldog recounted . . . moved to seize the Sheffield home: Interviews with auditors
   and investigators.
The News would admit to nearly $8 million . . . less than $2 million in restitution:
   Anna Wolfe, "Nancy and Zach New Plead Guilty to Bribery and Fraud
   in State Welfare Case," *Mississippi Today*, April 22, 2022. See also *State of
   Mississippi v. Nancy New and Zach New*, Petitions to Enter Guilty Plea (filed
   April 22, 2022). This section also relied on interviews with auditors and
   investigators.

Chapter 18

Zach's plea deal went into detail . . . according to Zach: *State of Mississippi v. Zach
   New*, Petitions to Enter Guilty Plea (filed April 22, 2022).
Back then, Favre told Nancy . . . been pretty good this year: Michael Rosenberg,
   "'The Driving Force': How Brett Favre's Demands for Cash Fueled a
   Scandal," *Sports Illustrated*, May 18, 2023.
Zach pleaded guilty . . . they should have a take, too: *State of Mississippi v. Zach
   New*, Petitions to Enter Guilty Plea (filed April 22, 2022).
Nancy pleaded to the same schemes . . . federal instead of state prison: *State of
   Mississippi v. Nancy New*, Petitions to Enter Guilty Plea (filed April 22, 2022).
The texts mentioned in chapter 18 were also corroborated by interviews with
   investigators and auditors.

Chapter 19

Pigott's complaint in the suit . . . total welfare misspending: Sarah Ulmer, "DHS
   Files Civil Suit Against Individuals, Companies That Received Money in
   Welfare Scandal," *Magnolia Tribune*, May 9, 2022.
One of our investigations . . . no intention of seeking repayment: C. J. LeMaster,
   "Audit Requested by MDOC Commissioner Finds Hundreds of Thousands
   in Misspent Funds by Previous Administration," WLBT, December 17, 2020.
   See also "A Review of the Mississippi State Parole Board," PEER Mississippi,
   July 6, 2021. This section also relied on interviews with auditors and investi-
   gators.

Chapter 20

Thank you . . . being that teacher: Anna Wolfe, "Governing by Text: Phil Bryant's
   Hidden Hand Picked Welfare Winners," *Mississippi Today*, April 12, 2022.
Black's proximity to Davis . . . sidestep regulations: Interviews with auditors and

investigators. See also (CLA) "Mississippi Department of Human Services TANF Forensic Audit: Findings of Possible Fraud, Waste & Abuse," September 21, 2021, with appendices released subsequently.

I wondered if a friendship with Black . . . New's document raised these questions: Interviews with auditors and investigators.

The texts mentioned in chapter 20 were also corroborated by interviews with investigators and auditors.

Chapter 21

Byrd, Oklahoma's state auditor . . . despite being outspent: "State Auditor Cindy Byrd Targeted by $1 Million of Dark PAC Money in Race," *Oklahoma City Sentinel*, June 20, 2022. See also Ben Felder, "Oklahoma State Auditor Cindy Byrd Soars to Reelection Despite Dark-Money Political Attacks," *Oklahoman*, June 30, 2022.

Jess New — Nancy's son and attorney . . . both personal and professional: Anna Wolfe, "'Whipping Child': Nancy New Asked Highest Officials for Help Before Arrests in Welfare Scandal," *Mississippi Today*, June 22, 2022.

Jess's mother shared . . . we will go after them all: Wolfe, "'Whipping Child.'"

Favre attempted to push back . . . and received it: Mike Florio, "New Texts Show Former Mississippi Governor Helped Funnel Welfare Funds to Brett Favre for USM Volleyball Stadium," *Yahoo! Sports*, September 13, 2022.

John mentioned 4 million . . . for the volleyball court: William and Ashton Pittman, "Mississippi Welfare Scandal Timeline: Brett Favre and the Volleyball Stadium," *Mississippi Free Press*, September 30, 2022.

Favre showered gratitude . . . Favre texted New: Laura Strickler and Ken Dilanian, "'Santa Came Today': Brett Favre Texts Show His Role in Mississippi Welfare Scandal," NBC News, September 14, 2022.

Favre was insistent on government funds . . . it really is just that simple: Anna Wolfe, "Former Gov. Phil Bryant Moves to Keep Texts Private While Denying He Helped Channel Welfare Funds to Brett Favre's Volleyball Stadium," *Mississippi Today*, September 24, 2022.

Once the public realized . . . he could not legally be paid $1.1 million: Anna Wolfe, "FBI Asked Brett Favre Just One Question, His Attorney Says," *Mississippi Today*, September 8, 2022.

And of course, Favre's claims . . . find out about all this: "Former Mississippi Governor Helped Brett Favre Obtain Welfare Funds for University Volleyball Stadium, Texts Show," ESPN, September 13, 2022.

Bryant pointed out . . . nothing more I can do except follow the law: Wolfe, "Former Gov. Phil Bryant Moves to Keep Texts Private." See also www.bryanttexts.com, accessed June 2023.

And when reporters went too far . . . They quickly apologized: Ashton Pittman, "Mississippi Today CEO Apologizes for Saying Phil Bryant 'Embezzled' Welfare Funds," *Mississippi Free Press*, May 17, 2023.

Governor Reeves even stumbled . . . Republican lawyer to do the work: Anna Wolfe, "Welfare Head Says Surprise Subpoena Led to Attorney's Firing. Emails Show It Wasn't a Surprise," *Mississippi Today*, July 23, 2022.

Rumor had it Zach New was . . . and other millionaires: "Zach Seek OK to Sell (Nearly) Million Dollar Home," *Jackson Jambalaya*, October 21, 2022.

Biden appoints new US Attorney . . . US House Homeland Security Committee: Geoff Pender et al., "Biden Appoints New U.S. Attorney Who Will Inherit Welfare Scandal Investigation," *Mississippi Today*, September 2, 2022.

The texts and evidence mentioned in chapter 21 were also corroborated by interviews with investigators and auditors, along with the Single Audit for the Year Ending June 30, 2019, published by the Mississippi Office of the State Auditor on April 30, 2020.

Chapter 22

ESPN had reported that Prevacus . . . to garner that attention: Mark Fainaru-Wada, "Review Shows Favre-Backed Drug Companies Overstated Benefits, Connections," ESPN, November 8, 2022.

Vanlandingham claimed in marketing documents . . . later denied working with Prevacus: Fainaru-Wada, "Review Shows Favre-Backed Drug Companies Overstated."

And clearly one member of the Prevacus team . . . they were doing: Geoff Pender, "Welfare scandal defendant sues Gov. Tate Reeves, claims he's protecting himself and political allies," *Mississippi Today*, October 11, 2023.

One newspaper even inaccurately called me the prosecutor: "Brett Favre Must Think Mississippians Are Fools," *Natchez Democrat*, February 15, 2023.

Chapter 23

One month after Reeves's speech . . . formed the basis of his suit: Favre v. White, Complaint (filed February 10, 2023).

The lawyer was asked by NBC Sports . . . desire to make us spend money: A. J. Perez, "Brett Favre Settles Lawsuit Against Pat McAfee, Apparently for Free," *Front Office Sports*, May 11, 2023.

Conclusion

Brett Favre was the Gunslinger . . . ignoring the finer points of the game: Jeff Pearlman, *Gunslinger* (Boston, New York: Mariner, 2016).

He once claimed . . . his second NFL job: "Favre Reveals He Didn't Know What Nickel Defense Was," ESPN, https://www.espn.com/video/clip/_/id/27832518, accessed June 2023.

He was illogical . . . For a shot at greatness: Pearlman, *Gunslinger*.

Pearlman would say he's dumb . . . is an idiot: Kevin Harrish, "Brett Favre Biographer Calls Him 'an Idiot,'" *The Comeback*, June 6, 2023.

Favre to Bryant . . . Nancy's proposal: www.bryanttexts.com, accessed June 2023.

This is a man who would sign autographs . . . loved the trappings of a private jet: Pearlman, *Gunslinger*.

On the evening of Sunday . . . Favre's high school years: "Favre's Legendary MNF Game After His Dad Passed Away," NFL.com, https://www.nfl.com/100/originals/100-greatest/games-52#:~:text=On%20December%202022%2C%202003%2C%20the,home%20Oakland%20crowd%20cheered%20Favre, accessed June 2023. See also "Favre's Father Dies at 58," Associated Press, December 20, 2003.

We were headed to an area . . . against US forces since 2021: Bassem Mroue, "Iran-Backed Fighters on Alert in East Syria After US Strikes," Associated Press, March 25, 2003.

Just before we departed . . . US service members in the area: Joby Warrick et al., "Iran Plans to Escalate Attacks Against U.S. Troops in Syria, Documents Show," *Washington Post*, June 1, 2023.

Epilogue

What was equally disconcerting . . . cars and gym memberships: Amy Julia Harris, "N.Y.C. Severs Ties with Housing Boss Who Earned $1 Million a Year," *New York Times*, November 22, 2021.

In 2022, the Washington Post *. . . luxury cars and houses*: Tony Romm, "U.S. Charges 'Brazen' Theft of $250 Million from Pandemic Food Program," *Washington Post*, September 20, 2022.

According to the Association of Certified Fraud Examiners . . . than larger ones: "2020 Report to the Nations," Association of Certified Fraud Examiners, https://legacy.acfe.com/report-to-the-nations/2020/, accessed June 2023.

The ACFE has suggested . . . perception of detection: "2010 Report to the Nations," Association of Certified Fraud Examiners.

Not long after I was appointed . . . was featured in local cookbooks: "Former Jones County Supervisor Convicted of Embezzlement," WDAM, February 24, 2020.

Banks had packaged . . . they would pay on the loans: Michael Lewis, "The Big Short" (New York: Norton, 2011). See also Andrew Ross Sorkin, *Too Big to Fail* (New York: Penguin, 2010.)

To this day, people my age . . . in the wake of that recession: Robert Farrington, "Why Millennials Can't Seem to Get Ahead," *Forbes*, March 3, 2023.

The honest everyman is losing patience . . . according to the Pew Research Center: Brian Kennedy et al., "Americans' Trust in Scientists, Other Groups Declines," Pew Research Center, February 15, 2022.

Thomas Jefferson famously wrote . . . which is seen in a newspaper: "Forbes Quotes: Thomas Jefferson," https://www.forbes.com/quotes/9266/, accessed June 2023. See also Thomas Jefferson, "Thomas Jefferson to John Norvell, June 11, 1807," Library of Congress, https://www.loc.gov/resource/mtj1.038_0592_0594/?sp=2&st=text, accessed June 2023.

Further citations upon request. For all accounts of cases where a guilty plea or conviction has not been obtained, the contents of this book should be considered allegations, not proved in a court of law, though they are allegations backed by extensive documentary evidence and investigative work.